Rails Through Majorca

by

Giles Barnabe

PLATEWAY PRESS

ISBN 1 871980 51 8

ISBN 1 871980 51 8

PLATEWAY PRESS

Taverner House, Harling Road, East Harling, Norfolk NR16 2QR

Printed in England by POSTPRINT
Taverner House, Harling Road, East Harling, Norfolk NR16 2QR

FRONT COVER ILLUSTRATION:
The final days of steam found Number 5 acting as station pilot at Palma.
(D. TREVOR ROWE)

BACK COVER ILLUSTRATIONS:
No. 2 of the Soller Railway approaching Bunyola.
(FELIPE ARANADA – AUTHOR'S COLLECTION)

Palma tramcar No. 107, seen near Establiments, was one of the cars obtained from Barcelona.
(J. WISEMAN)

FRONTISPIECE:
Majorca Railway No. 20 shunting beside the coaling stage at Palma in 1962.
(J. WILLIAMS)

Acknowledgements

In preparing a work of this nature the author has inevitably relied on the knowledge and memory of a great number of people, who so kindly supplied information, excerpts from old magazine articles, timetables, photographs, or spent time digging into various archives. A major tribute is due to a fellow narrow gauge enthusiast, the late David Lloyd, whose enquiry in the pages of Continental Modeller for information on the FC de Soller helped start the whole project.

I should like to thank the Editors of Continental Modeller and Model Trains International for permission to re-use previously published drawings, and also the following for their patience and help:– Celso Calvino Andreu, Michael Andress, John H. Buehler, M. Bunch, Kenneth Dobeson, Martin P. Emberger, Barry Emmott, Anthony Fairclough, Andrew Harris, Andy Hart, Jordi Ibanez, Lawrence Marshall, F. Santiago Marques (Transports de Palma), Ramon Molina de Dios, Pedro de Montaner, Geoff Moore, Jaime Arrom Morla, Matias Mut, Andrew Neale, J. B. Nisbet, Herbert Norman, D. Palmer, Miss J. Patry, K. P. Plant, S. J. Pratt, J. H. Price, F. L. Pugh, Jorge Rabell, Carlos Olmos Riba, D. Trevor Rowe, Toni Sanchis, Don Sibley, F. M. Simpson, Mike Swift, Keith Taylorson, Mike Tebbutt, George Toms, P. K. Widd, John K. Williams, D. W. Winkworth, Gordon Wiseman, Jeremy Wiseman, Conselleria de Treball y Transports (Palma), Babcock & Wilcox Española S. A, Krupp Maschinentecknik GMBh, Orenstein & Koppel, and finally – though not least – members of the AAFB (Palma).

Disclaimer:– Exploring railways, whether they are in use or derelict, can have its dangers and every care should be taken. The description of locations in this book does not imply the right of public access and the writer and publisher can take no responsibility for mishaps, however caused, to readers visiting the Majorcan railways.

Contents

Foreword

Ten years ago when I wrote *The Railways and Tramways of Majorca* the island's lines were much as they had been some 50 years earlier. True, part of the old Ferrocarriles de Mallorca had been closed, and much of it was still rusting quietly away amid the weeds in the centre of the island, far away from the usual tourist haunts. The section still in use had just been converted to metre gauge, although this had not really altered the recent appearance of the line, as the same type of rolling stock was in use. The FC de Soller, still using 3ft gauge, was daily hauling its magnificent vintage trains over the northern sierra to connect with the even older trams which completed the journey down to the harbour at Puerto Soller.

In the intervening years much has happened to change the railway scene in Majorca. While the Soller line continues to cling to its independence, the end of its original concession is almost due, when in theory the line reverts to state control. Meanwhile, as predicted in the earlier book, the Balearic Government has taken control of local transport policy, and the rule of nationalised FEVE on the Palma-Inca section has given way to the SFM:– the **Serveis Ferroviaris de Mallorca.** At last the advantage of a rail system that can take some pressure off the roads has been acknowledged officially, and a policy of reinstatement of the earlier network has begun to be implemented. Already the line to Inca has been modernised, and the renewed section onward to La Puebla (now known as Sa Pobla) is now in service, as is the recently completed line to Manacor. There is even talk of extending from there to Arta, and even including some of the expansion plans from the 1930s in a new master transport plan for the island; perhaps in another ten years…

Since my first visit to Mallorca the emphasis on the use of Castillian Spanish has given way to a resurgence of the local dialect, Mallorquin. This has resulted in changes to some of the local place names. For the purposes of this book I have retained, in the historical sections, the names in use when the railway was built, using as my source the original timetables or the names that are carved on the station walls themselves. I hope that those readers who favour the new spelling will forgive me.

Much of what appears here draws on material used in the earlier book, and the opportunity has been taken to amplify and edit the original text where new facts have come to light. I have also included more accounts from earlier visitors who experienced the island's steam era. The Majorcan railways are very different today to those of earlier times, but no less interesting; long may they continue to serve the island.

Giles Barnabe
London 2003

Part One

The Majorca Railway

Chapter 1

The Birth of the Railway

To set the scene for the dawn of Majorca's "Railway Age" one must forget all tourist pre-conceptions of the island today. In the mid-19th century Majorca was still a poor and rather isolated province of Spain, though some of the earlier trading laws were being eased, leading to a wider contact with the outside world. The threat of piracy had receded during the early years of the century, leading to a maritime trading tradition in the island, which was beginning to become wealthier through foreign trade, mostly with Spanish America. This was aided by the introduction of steam power; however while the number of Majorcan-owned sailing ships far outnumbered the handful of local paddle steamers, a Palma-based steamship company had been set up in the mid 1850s, which among other destinations, traded with Cardiff.

Luckily a contemporary picture of local life has been left by Charles Bidwell, the British Consul who witnessed the inauguration of the Majorca Railway, which he described in his book *"The Balearic Islands"*, published in 1876. At that time the island's economy was predominantly agricultural and primitive, while industry was mostly carried out at home or in small workshops in the Palma area, using cheap labour. As well as rice and olive oil, shoe-making and soap manufacture provided important exports. About a quarter of the inhabitants lived in the capital, while the remainder were spread through the island's towns and villages. Travel depended on animal power and the roads were poor dirt tracks, a round trip of some 20kms being the most that could be accomplished in one day. The Sierra de Alfabia mountains cut off the northern coastline, which was best reached by sea from Palma.

The idea of a Majorcan railway was first mooted as early as 1852 when an Iron Road was proposed to link Palma and Inca, but this scheme never progressed beyond the discussion stage, becoming mired in the political and financial scandals of the time. The revolution of 1854 brought in a more progressive Spanish government, which passed a law the following year, which defined a railway as a public service, to be let out by the State on a 99-year concession to its builders; meanwhile the State was to retain control of the technical specifications, the methods of exploitation and fares. This law led to an explosion of railway schemes, both those that were built and many which remained stillborn, and the total length of Spanish railways grew tenfold from 475 to 4,827kms in the next two years.

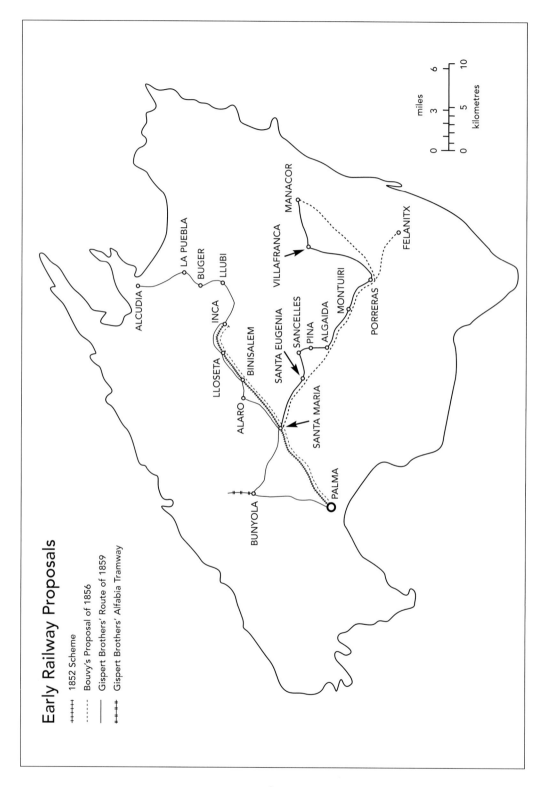

Early Railway Proposals

++++++ 1852 Scheme

------ Bouvy's Proposal of 1856

——— Gispert Brothers' Route of 1859

+#+#+ Gispert Brothers' Alfabia Tramway

No. 6 Palma de Mallorca   Molinar - Environs

Windmills were once a common sight in Majorca, both for grinding corn as well as raising underground water to the surface for irrigation. (COLLECTION – K. TAYLORSON)

One of the schemes planned for Majorca was presented by a Belgian engineer, Paul Bouvy, who proposed a narrow gauge line to link Palma and Inca, with a branch line from Santa Maria to Felanitx, while a second branch would link with Manacor. However at the same time two Catalan engineers from Barcelona, Enrique and Frederic Gispert, proposed a broad gauge line between Palma and Inca, and as this scheme promised a quick return for the investors' capital, almost two-thirds of the required capital of 3,750,000 pesetas was quickly subscribed, roughly evenly divided between Majorcan investors and various banks based in Barcelona (at this time there were no investment banks based on the island). In consequence, Bouvy's scheme appears not to have progressed beyond the prospectus stage. Over the next year disagreements broke out between the Catalan and Majorcan shareholders and the project became stalled. As a result the Gisperts presented another scheme for Government approval in 1859. This time a more ambitious plan was outlined: – the main line was to take a roundabout route northwards from Palma towards Bunyola before heading south-east to serve Santa Maria; it would then run north-east as far as Inca, finally swinging round to the north by way of Llubi and La Puebla to reach Alcudia. From Santa Maria a branch line was to run south-east to Porreras before heading up towards Manacor, via Villafranca. At Palma the station was to be situated just inside the city walls (roughly on the site of the present-day San Miguel market), and there was to be a branch line around the walls to the west, leading to the harbour. Although government funding for these plans was granted in 1862, disagreements over the scheme erupted again, this time between the central government in Madrid and the provincial deputation in Majorca. For a while the Gisperts tried to keep the project going, but in 1865 a cholera epidemic hit the island, killing over 2,000 people, and economic and social life came to a virtual standstill for the latter half of the year. This setback came at a time of general economic crisis, due in part to the too rapid investment in so many railway schemes throughout the peninsular, some of which were of dubious merit, to say the least. Finally a financial crash on the Barcelona money market sounded the death-knell for the Gisperts' plans. Meanwhile there were further political upheavals, ultimately leading to the revolution of 1868, which prevented any further schemes being presented for a while.

The quest for a successful Majorcan railway project was once again taken up when in 1871 another local engineer, Eusebio Estada, produced a study examining the island's commerce and the benefits of linking Palma and Inca by rail; his route was similar to Bouvy's, and like the Belgian's original plan, the line was to be narrow gauge in order to save expense. Later extensions were envisaged which would take the line on from Inca to serve Manacor, with a branch to the port of Alcudia. The following year, in 1872, The Majorca Railway Company was formed to open the line, which was initially to be some 18 miles long. The necessary capital, in total amounting to 8,500,000 Reals (or £88,000 at the contemporary exchange rates) was to be subscribed locally, in order to prevent undue outside influence – the first time this method was used. The sum was raised in shares of 2,000 Reals and the prospectus promised returns of 8.6%, whereas the average at the time was a mere 6%.

By this time several successful narrow gauge lines had been built in Spain, those promoted by British concerns having gauges varying between 3ft 6ins and 4ft, while Spanish-backed narrow gauge lines mostly favoured a gauge of one metre (which, after the passing of the Law of Secondary and Economic Railways of 1904, became the mandatory Spanish narrow gauge for all new lines). Why, then, was the Majorca Railway built to a gauge of 3ft? It has been suggested that a cancelled rolling stock order, intended for a British colony, was diverted to Majorca and thus made the choice for the Majorcan engineer – though this explanation savours somewhat of the tail wagging the dog. Estada considered the question of gauge carefully, convinced that narrow gauge was best suited to the island, but which narrow gauge should be used? Had the suppliers of material for the new line been based in mainland Europe, he would have chosen metre gauge, but by now there were British engineering connections in Majorca, as for some years a British company, the New Majorca Land Co., had been at work draining the marshes between La Puebla and Alcudia. Through the proprietor of this company Estada was introduced to Charles Swinton Spooner, the

Director/Engineer of the Festiniog Railway in Wales, with whom he entered into correspondence concerning many technical aspects of railway construction, though not apparently on the question of gauge. During the autumn of 1872 Estada visited Britain to obtain answers to several technical questions and presumably also to gain first hand experience of narrow gauge lines. On his return he wrote a report recommending the adoption of 3ft gauge, as being the most economical option. However even at this late stage the decision was not final. There were difficulties in finding British locomotive builders who could produce the necessary engines soon enough to suit the company's plans. Ironically metre gauge engines were quoted as being ready five or six months earlier than 3ft gauge examples. Back in Spain, permission was sought to change the gauge of the line to one metre, should this become necessary. Permission was granted, but at this moment Estada found a builder, Nasmyth Wilson, of Patricroft, Manchester, who was able to undertake the work. The following year, in 1873, Estada and a colleague, Antonio Ankerman, visited Britain and placed orders for the equipment needed to open the railway. A link with the British engineering world had been established which was to have far-reaching effects on the island's railways in later years.

Meanwhile, in Majorca, construction of the line to Inca went ahead with few difficulties, as there were no real natural obstacles to overcome. The ruling gradient was 1 in 72 and the sharpest curve was set at 17.4 chains. The original rails were supplied

Palma harbour in the days of sail.   (AUTHOR'S COLLECTION)

in 10 metre lengths and weighed 20kg/metre. They were spiked directly to timber sleepers that had a semi-regular profile, and ballasted with stones, whose sizes varied from one to six inches in length. Construction materials, which were shipped from Britain, included the rails and wires for the telegraph lines connecting the new stations. Tenders for the civil engineering works were let out to local contractors, which accounts for the fact that while almost all the stations are built to the same general pattern, almost every one has some feature that sets it apart from its neighbour. The British influence did not extend as far as the railway's architecture, and station buildings have been likened to the style commonly found in France. The larger ones certainly tend to follow European practice with the railway offices, passenger and parcel facilities downstairs, while the Stationmaster's living quarters occupy the upper floor.

Preparations for opening the new line were almost complete in 1874 when the rolling stock arrived aboard a fleet of ships including one Spanish and seven British steamers. At the time this was the largest collection of British merchant shipping ever seen in Palma. The three steam locomotives, six passenger carriages and twenty-five goods vehicles were soon unloaded and transferred to the terminus at Palma. Majorca was about to enter the railway age.

Maker's photograph of one of the first Majorcan locomotives.   (AUTHOR'S COLLECTION)

Chapter 2

A History of the Majorca Railway

The Railway Opens

The date for the opening of the line was 24th February 1875, and following a period of stormy weather the great day dawned bright and sunny. Outside the railway station at Palma two triumphal arches had been set up near the ruins of the old town walls at the Puerta Pintada (the Painted Gate); one had been provided by the Provincial Deputation, the other by the Ayunamiento (City Council) of Palma. In addition, at the station itself, there was another archway decorated with the coat of arms of each town along the route, while the station buildings were bedecked with flags, flowers and branches of myrtle.

A large crowd had gathered, and at nine o'clock the dignitaries arrived, led by the Captain General of the Province who was followed by the Civil Governor, the Consular Corps, the provincial deputation and members of the Ayunamiento. After this came the railway's Directors and authorities and other distinguished guests. An open-air service was conducted on the platform before the V.I.Ps boarded the train, which then set off for Inca. Crowds had turned out at all the stations but the train did not stop until it reached its destination, taking 64 minutes for the 29km journey.

Inca, like Palma, was in festive attire though here the streets were decorated in a more rustic style. Two local bands met the train and the whole procession moved through the garlanded streets to the town's main church, where a Te Deum was sung. Following this the dignitaries returned to the station for a celebratory luncheon before making the return trip, this time taking the opportunity to inspect each of the stations along the line.

From the start the railway was a great success, no doubt helped by a policy of charging low fares: – 7 Reals for a First Class ticket between Palma and Inca, 4.7 Reals for Second Class (a rough equivalent today would be six pence and four pence). During its first month of operation the railway carried some 40,000 passengers, some days seeing as many as 6,000 travellers. Many of these were carried in special trains that the company ran between the Palma terminus and the first stop, at Pont d'Inca, for those who were not going anywhere in particular, but merely wanted to experience this new form of travel. Among them was the Spanish king, who visited the island in March 1876 and travelled to Inca by train on the 13th of the month. A special saloon coach was prepared for this journey, which went without a hitch, setting the seal of Royal approval on the railway.

Mergers and Expansion

However bright things seemed at first, the balance sheet at the end of 1875 told another story. The cost of equipping and opening the line had been four million pesetas more than the initial capital raised, and despite the Directors adding some personal funding, the interest on the outstanding debt was using the part of the profits that otherwise might be used for the expansion of the system; in particular the company saw the route to Manacor via Inca as its next goal, though there were many shareholders who wanted a line to La Puebla, too. Estada produced a study on these lines, but the Directors were not certain of the profitability of the route, and wondered about reaching Manacor via Lluchmayor and Felanitx. In January 1876 a breakaway group of shareholders formed the Compañia de los Ferrocarriles del Centro y del Sureste (Central & South Eastern Railway Company), backed by the newly formed Banco de Credit Balear (Balearic Credit Bank), which became a major shareholder in the new company. Shares were soon being sold to raise the money needed for the Manacor line, while in late March 1876, at a General Meeting of the Central & South Eastern, the shareholders voted to merge the two companies, and this was confirmed at a joint shareholders' meeting held the following month; in effect the FC de Mallorca was taken over by its new rival, and both companies merged to form the Compañia de los Ferrocarriles de Mallorca (Majorca Railways). Work on the extensions from Inca to Manacor and La Puebla started almost at once, while another more southerly route to Manacor, via Felanitx, was approved the same year.

Following the merger the company also returned to one of its earlier plans, access for its goods trains to the harbour at Palma. Existing buildings barred a direct route, but a street tramway, 2.9kms in length, had been approved in 1875, and work started late the following year. The tramway opened in 1877 and soon helped the company's finances, as inland goods traffic (and in particular agricultural produce) could now be brought directly to the dockside without trans-shipment (for more details *see* Chapter 10).

Meanwhile, in preparation for the new extensions beyond Inca, the company obtained 69,466 sleepers in 1877, costing between 88 cents and 1.25 pesetas each, at a total cost of 82,755 pesetas. Among the suppliers was Pedro Garau, who would later feature as Engineer for both the FC de Soller (Soller Railway) and the Palma electric tramways. In addition to the sleepers the company also purchased 750 telegraph poles and 15,000 fence posts. Earlier sleepers had been hand-sawn, but now a steam-powered saw was imported from Britain and the work speeded up considerably, the saw being run day and night to complete the work. In addition a machine to inject all this cut timber with creosote arrived from Britain on 21st September, and had dealt with 32,000 sleepers, 400 telegraph poles and a small number of fence posts by the end of October.

At the same time track-bed grading had been proceeding across the centre of the island, though not without incident. Two contractors were involved in the work east of Inca, but one of them, Batolomé Oliver, got into difficulties and had to be released from

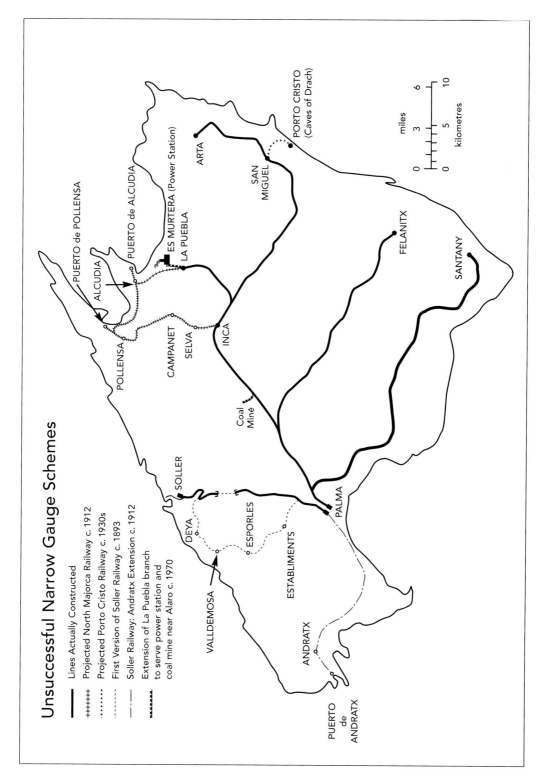

Unsuccessful Narrow Gauge Schemes

Lines Actually Constructed
++++++ Projected North Majorca Railway c. 1912
········ Projected Porto Cristo Railway c. 1930s
------- First Version of Soller Railway c. 1893
—·—·— Soller Railway: Andratx Extension c. 1912
▪▪▪▪▪▪ Extension of La Puebla branch
to serve power station and
coal mine near Alaro c. 1970

PUERTO de POLLENSA

PUERTO de ALCUDIA

ES MURTERA (Power Station)

LA PUEBLA

ALCUDIA

POLLENSA

CAMPANET

SELVA

INCA

Coal
Mine

SOLLER

DEYA

ESPORLES

VALLDEMOSA

ESTABLIMENTS

ANDRATX

PUERTO
de
ANDRATX

PALMA

ARTA

PORTO CRISTO
(Caves of Drach)

SAN
MIGUEL

FELANITX

SANTANY

miles

kilometres

0   3   6

0   5   10

his contract work between kilometre 6.8 and 10, which included an important bridge over the Torrente (river) Son Bordils. After a delay of a couple of months the contract was re-let to Manuel Lete, who was already responsible for the rest of the main line and now finished the whole 14kms from Inca to Sineu, where a loading bank for goods traffic and a temporary station were erected by Pablo Togores. Palma workshops had constructed three turntables, one of which was given a home at Sineu when this opened as a temporary terminus on 17th February 1878. Another may have gone to Empalme, where traces of a turntable pit can still be seen, while the third would have been needed at La Puebla.

The La Puebla branch was constructed by Nicolás Gelabert and Gabriel Llull, who completed the work in time for the inaugural service to be run on 24th October 1878. This new branch was particularly important as it opened up the fertile northern farming region by providing direct access to the port at Palma. Hitherto goods traffic had been relatively unimportant between Palma and Inca, only averaging 30 tons per day in the early months of operation, but following the line's arrival at La Puebla freight tonnage started to increase dramatically, encouraged by the cheap rates of carriage. From a small village, La Puebla grew to become a busy town, due entirely to its situation as the railhead of the surrounding agricultural area.

The increasing freight tonnage soon needed extra motive power, which arrived in the shape of two 0-6-0 tank locomotives, which were provided for goods and shunting duties in 1876, at a cost of £1,650 each. Then, two years later, a further four 4-4-0 tank

No. 4 (formerly MANACOR) at Palma in 1960.   (M. SWIFT)

engines arrived in good time to work the new services beyond Inca. These new arrivals cost £1,530 each, and once again all the new locomotives were obtained from Nasmyth Wilson. At the same time the Palma workshops were extended to include a Carpenters' Shop and a Smithy, complete with two forges and machinery to re-profile the wheels of the rolling stock. The new services required extra vehicles, and during 1877 twenty wagons were added to the fleet, being built locally from parts imported from Britain at a total cost of 8,769 pesetas – a considerable saving over the cost of ready-built vehicles. Ever ready to pick up a bargain, the railway also acquired eight secondhand vehicles for 1,200 pesetas. Neither were passengers neglected, as a further 10 carriages and three brake vans were purchased from various British manufacturers, together with a set of six-wheeled carriages, though these turned out to be indifferent performers, prone to derailments in the early days at least. The railway's extension from Sineu to Manacor was opened in 1879, when the turntable from Sineu was moved to the end of the new section. With the arrival of the line in Manacor the idea of a southerly route linking the town with Felanitx was dropped.

Once again the cost of opening these new lines was more than the company's capital reserves, which showed a deficit of some 400,000 pesetas. By the early 1880s the company's debts amounted to 1,356,900 pesetas, and to tidy up this state of affairs another tranche of shares was issued, which raised 1,600,000 pesetas.

The year of 1879 marked the end of the FC de Mallorca's monopoly of rail traffic when a line was built linking Consell station with the town of Alaró, a short distance away. The concession for this line was operated by the FC de Alaró (Alaró Railway). The larger company had not considered a deviation via the town to be worthwhile, despite the presence of a local coalmine, and looked on the new company as merely a feeder. (For details of the Alaró line, *see* Chapter 10).

Another innovation at about this time was the planned introduction of steam power on the harbour tramway. Hitherto mule haulage had been employed, but in 1879 the Directors sought permission to operate a locomotive on the city section. A four-coupled tram engine was ordered from R. W. Hawthorn (Works No. 1836), and this arrived in 1881. Despite successful tests on the main line, the city authorities failed to be convinced and the locomotive had to remain outside the city walls, being limited to shunting and other light duties, including fetching wagons from the goods yard and handing them over to the mule teams at a spot known as "Four Bells", just outside the Puerta de Jésus.

On the FC de Mallorca passenger traffic fell away slightly after the initial novelty of train travel wore off, although goods traffic continued to increase and, despite the arrival of two more 4-4-0 locomotives in 1881, within a few years it began to outstrip the haulage capacity of the existing locomotive fleet. In contrast to the 5,452 tonnes of goods carried during the first year of operation, between 1882 and 1891 around 72,000 tonnes of goods were being moved annually. Once again the railway company returned to Nasmyth's, whose answer was to supply an enlarged version of the 0-6-0 type with a leading bogie and larger cylinders. Two of these 4-6-0s were ordered at a price of just over £4,350 each, and they arrived in 1887, followed by another pair in 1891.

In that same year a concession was granted to the Sociedad Mallorquina de Tranvias (Majorcan Tramway Company) to construct a line from Palma to Porto Pi. At this point a mystery arises, as the order books of the Brush Electrical Engineering Company of Loughborough, show that four steam tram engines, built to an older Falcon design, were ordered by the Tranvias de Palma – reputedly for the Porto Pi route. However, not only is the company name wrong, but there is no record on the island of steam being used on this route which relied on mule-power. The four locomotives were Works Nos. 198-201, and while at least one of these, number 198, turns up later in Majorcan railway history, there is no trace of the other three. Number 198 was recorded derelict at Palma in the 1930s, having been owned by at least two operators, but its original owner remains unclear.

A few years later the Majorca Railways needed another engine for light duties, and this came in the form of an 0-4-0 tank engine which Nasmyth's supplied in 1889; its Works No. was 389. Although its maker's photograph does not show tramway-style skirts, these were fitted for a time, and the fact that the sanding gear was only fitted to the "rear" wheels below the cab seems to indicate that cab-forward running was envisaged; the lack of a rear sheet to the cab appears to support this theory.

Felanitx, At Last.

The railway's next major extension was the construction of the 43km branch to Felanitx. Although this had been part of the railway's plans at the time of the merger in 1876, there had been differing opinions over which route to choose. Originally the branch was to have followed a slightly different course to that eventually built, and was to have been extended to reach Manacor, while another version included a link between Felanitx and nearby Porto Colom. A study of the proposed route began in 1881 but following representations from several of the shareholders, who objected to the high cost of the project at a time when the island's economy was suffering a recession, the scheme had been temporarily dropped and when reinstated it was without the link to Manacor.

Felanitx had always seemed a natural target for the railway as it had become a major centre for the production of wine, and following the outbreak of phylloxera in France in the 1870s, which had all but destroyed the French wine trade at the time, the town increased its exports and enjoyed a growing prosperity. Now however disaster struck, as the disease arrived in Majorca in May 1891 and wine production fell drastically, leading to great hardship in Felanitx. By coincidence, at almost the same moment a change in the rules governing the concession for the Felanitx line was granted; in effect

COLL No. 24 shunting the harbour exchange sidings in 1953.   (D. TREVOR ROWE)

the branch no longer came under State control and reverted to the company. Following this turn of events the necessary agreements were soon reached, and the Royal Order was passed in 1892. Work started on the line in 1896 and proceeded quickly, the inaugural train running on 7th October 1897. At last, after a delay of some twenty years, the locomotive FELANITX was able to reach its namesake terminus. With the branch under construction more locomotives were needed, and the company once again turned to Nasmyth Wilson who supplied yet another pair of 4-4-0 locomotives, though despite the increased traffic their cylinder capacity remained the same as the earlier members of their class.

Happily the new line led to at least a partial resurgence of trade in Felanitx, but nevertheless for a while no new lines were added to the system, perhaps to allow a few years of dividend payments to be made to the shareholders, though the period was also marked by a general loss of confidence in trade following a decline in the Spanish colonial markets. Then in the early years of the new century more engines were added to the stock books. These were built by Palma Works, one in 1902 the other the following year, and once again they were of the 4-4-0 type, although this time larger cylinders were provided. All the fabrication on these locomotives was carried out locally, only the wheels being imported. The two locomotives were characterized by their flare-topped chimneys, the Nasmyth engines carrying plain stovepipe funnels. Following the successful introduction of these engines, Palma workshops undertook a programme of major conversion work on four of the older locomotives, which were finally out-shopped in 1911. Once again the size of the cylinders was increased to provide more power, and it is possible that from this date the size of the cabs was augmented. Hitherto the cabs had fitted between the tanks and had a very small rear sheet, shaped something like a curvaceous letter Y, with a single central spectacle. Later photographs show that slightly longer, full-width cabs were fitted during the rebuild. New names and running numbers were allocated, the original names falling into disuse. The same year also saw what turned out to be the last locomotives to arrive from Nasmyth Wilson – a final pair of 4-6-0 tanks. By this time the original 90-degree roundhouse at Palma had become inadequate to house the growing locomotive stud, and in 1913 it was rebuilt into a full 180-degree layout.

The same period saw renewed interest in railway expansion through the island, and in 1912 the Ferrocarril del Norte de Mallorca (North Majorca Railway) was granted the concession to build a line from La Puebla to Alcudia and Pollensa, from where a more direct line would link across to Inca, by way of Campanet and Selva. Still later other schemes were floated to build a number of "strategic" lines linking the railway's northern and westerly termini; supposedly useful for moving troops in the island's defence, they would have had little commercial merit. Despite, or perhaps because of, the start of the First World War shortly afterwards, these projects were rendered still-born.

Onwards to Santany

Following the opening of the Felanitx branch, other Majorcan towns had seen the advantages of having a railway connection with the rest of the island, and in 1903 a foreign company had investigated building a power station at Lluchmayor to serve an electrified line linking Palma and Santany, though no more was heard of this interesting project. A few years later the Lluchmayor Town Council signed a contract with an engineering firm from Barcelona to build a line from Palma to Lluchmayor, and thence to Santany, however following the passing of the Law of Strategic Railways of 1908, which included provision for such a line, this contract was allowed to lapse. In December 1908 the Ministry had formally invited the submission of plans for the line, but none had been presented by the closing date for submission on 20th July 1910. Finally in 1913 a scheme drawn up by the railway's Engineer, Eusebio Estada, was submitted for approval. Interestingly, despite the provisions of an earlier law, which stipulated the use of metre gauge, the new line was to be built to the Majorcan gauge of 3ft; sense and practical considerations seem to have prevailed over slavish obedience which would have resulted in bothersome trans-shipment, or the wholesale rebuilding of the entire system (a task which in the event was postponed until the end of the

A comparison in size: a Nasmyth-style 4-40T and a Spanish-built 2-6-0T.   (J. WISEMAN)

An early view of Lluchmayor station.   (A. SANCHIS COLLECTION)

20th century, by which time the railway had shrunk to a much smaller undertaking, more viable for conversion).

To raise sufficient capital for the new line, the company offered 4,000 shares, worth 500 pesetas each. By 5th May this amount had been oversubscribed and 2.7 million pesetas had been offered. Despite this, some difficulties remained – the summer of 1913 saw local disputes among the citizens of Lluchmayor over the size of their proposed station, some maintaining that the site was too small. Work on the track-bed started in 1914 but proceeded slowly, to the fury of those who had subscribed for shares and who felt that they were being cheated. Part of the delay was due to the fact that the route demanded some heavy engineering works, with a high bridge and two viaducts to be built near Arenal. Heavy rains during the winter of 1914/15 delayed matters further, but more importantly the outbreak of war in 1914 had cut the railway's link with its habitual suppliers of rails and rolling stock, and new sources had to be found on the Spanish mainland in something of a hurry. Eventually three 2-6-0 tank locomotives were obtained from La Maquinista Terrestre y Marítima of Barcelona (MTM), with carriages coming from both Carde y Escoriaza and CAF de Beasain. It had been hoped to begin services on the new branch in 1915, but in the end the line opened piecemeal, the 30km section from Palma to Lluchmayor on 6th October 1916; the next 16kms between Lluchmayor and Campos on 28th January 1917, with the final 17.5kms to Santany entering service on 21st July that same year. All was not sweetness and light, however: in August 1917 the Town Councils of Lluchmayor, Campos and

Early days on the Santany branch with a train crossing the Pont des Jueus near Arenal. The seventh and eighth vehicles are some of the Third Class coaches that caused local complaints – the lack of headroom can be appreciated. The open wagon behind the locomotive was common at this time and may be an additional coal supply. (A. SANCHIS COLLECTION)

Santany wrote a joint letter to the company to protest at the state of the Third Class carriages in use on the line, demanding better vehicles and also the provision of Third Class accommodation on all trains. In addition they wanted to improve safety at eight of the level crossings on the line. These teething problems were later resolved and the line soon became part of the daily life of the community.

Steam enters the City of Palma

Apart from the Palma Ayunamiento's prohibition against the use of steam within the city, another obstacle was the Puerta de Jésus whose archway was too small to admit the locomotives. The gate was finally demolished in 1913, and towards the end of the decade permission was finally granted for steam locomotives to enter the streets of the city. When the locomotive used the street tramway a youth was sent ahead ringing a bell to warn passers-by of its approach. Soon after, in 1921, the FC de Mallorca obtained another small locomotive. This was a well tank, built by Orenstein & Koppel, which started to share the dockside work with the other two 0-4-0s, although not long afterwards the Hawthorn tram locomotive was retired.

The Railway's Heyday

The railway entered the 1920s with its traffic potential still increasing, bolstered no doubt by the resumption of world trade following the cessation of hostilities. Once again plans were made to expand the company's empire with extensions from Manacor to Arta, with a branch to Porto Cristo. By the summer of 1921 the line had reached Arta, and this proved to be the last addition to passenger mileage, as the other extension never materialised. To work the Arta services the company obtained six powerful 2-6-0 tank engines from Krupp in 1926, the older locomotives having proved slightly underpowered for the new extension; they also had a rather too small water capacity which was a hazard on the long uphill slog on the final section where, after leaving Manacor, no water was available to top up their tanks until the terminus was reached. For this reason in the early years of the Arta extension train lengths may have had to be limited until the arrival of the larger engines.

In complete contrast, the company also acquired another vehicle in 1926 that was an early indication of the future, and foreshadowed the ultimate end of steam power. In its early form the four-wheeled 40hp petrol driven railcar, built by Berliet, cannot have seemed much of a threat, with its relatively small seating capacity and limited haulage powers. However it proved its worth on the more lightly patronised lines, and in 1930 three De Dion railcars were added to the fleet, becoming the mainstay of the services to Santany and Felanitx. Despite these new arrivals steam had not yet had its final day, and soon afterwards the company added yet more motive power to its books with the

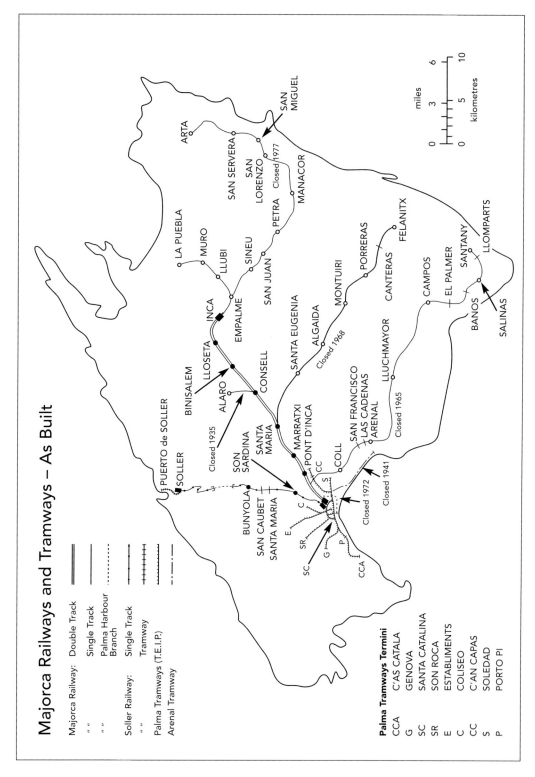

Majorca Railways and Tramways – As Built

Majorca Railway: Double Track

" " Single Track

" " Palma Harbour Branch

Soller Railway: Single Track

" " Tramway

Palma Tramways (T.E.I.P.)

Arenal Tramway

ARTA

SAN MIGUEL

SAN SERVERA

SAN LORENZO

Closed 1977

PETRA

MANACOR

LA PUEBLA

MURO

LLUBI

SINEU

SAN JUAN

PORRERAS

CANTERAS

FELANITX

LLOMPARTS

CAMPOS

EL PALMER

SANTANY

BANOS

SALINAS

INCA

EMPALME

SANTA EUGENIA

ALGAIDA

MONTUIRI

LLUCHMAYOR

Closed 1968

Closed 1965

LLOSETA

CONSELL

ALARO

Closed 1935

BINISALEM

PUERTO de SOLLER

SOLLER

SON SARDINA

SANTA MARIA

MARRATXI

PONT D'INCA

SAN FRANCISCO

LAS CADENAS

ARENAL

COLL

BUNYOLA

SAN CAUBET

SANTA MARIA

Closed 1941

Closed 1972

CC

S

C

E

SR

G

P

SC

CCA

miles

kilometres

Palma Tramways Termini

CCA   C'AS CATALA

G   GENOVA

SC   SANTA CATALINA

SR   SON ROCA

E   ESTABLIMENTS

C   COLISEO

CC   C'AN CAPAS

S   SOLEDAD

P   PORTO PI

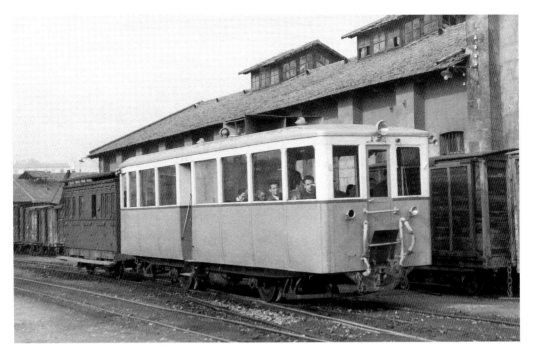

Railcar A-4 leaving Palma en-route for Santany in 1957. Typically it is towing one of the Postal/Second Class coaches. (L. G. MARSHALL)

purchase of some even larger tank engines, this time from Babcock & Wilcox of Bilbao. These 2-6-2Ts went into service in 1930 and had the capability of running between Palma and Manacor without a water stop, unlike the earlier locomotives that needed to top up at Inca and Manacor. Once again the new locomotive purchases called for more shed space at Palma, where a second roundhouse was completed in 1930. To go with the new motive power the company obtained fourteen luxurious bogie carriages from Carde y Escoriaza.

The 1920s had seen an increase in passenger traffic and in 1924 work started to replace the temporary station at Sineu, which had already served for nearly forty-six years. The new building was completed in 1929, and although similar structures were planned for La Puebla and a new station on the foreshore at Palma, this latter pair was never built. With the opening of the Arta extension, the single track between Palma and Inca reached the limit of its capacity, on some days seeing 30 passenger trains and up to 12 goods services. It had become the custom to combine trains to La Puebla and Arta as far as Inca, double heading them to get over the worst gradients between Pont d'Inca and Consell. When this expedient was no longer enough, the decision was taken to double the main line as far as Inca; the new track was laid with heavier rail weighing 30kg/metre and the section was completed in January 1931. At the same time the task of working freight trains through the streets of Palma was abandoned when a new tunnel was opened linking the port with the goods yard at the railway terminus. These services could now be worked by the 4-4-0 tanks, and considering the gradient on the return trip, this may have been a necessity. The tunnel was 1.25kms in length, so working conditions must have been unpleasant, to say the least, and possibly this explains why regular passenger services were never instigated. With the end of street running, the two remaining 0-4-0Ts had little to do, though both lingered on for another twenty years or so, employed on light shunting duties.

By the early 1930s the company's fortunes had reached a peak they were destined never to reach again, although a slight setback came when the Berliet caught fire in 1936 and was almost totally destroyed. Although the railcar had proved useful at first, its engine was by then in a very poor state and so it was never rebuilt. However, other problems were looming on the horizon.

The outbreak of the Civil War in July 1936 brought a couple of days when all rail traffic was suspended, after which things returned to a relative normality, though there were occasional air-raids to contend with. One of these struck the station at Marratxi just as a train was leaving, but luckily the driver managed to stop before reaching the damaged track. Following this, air-raid shelters were built around the terminus at Palma, and entrances to the harbour tunnel were made from the streets above for use as public shelters. The locomotives' lamps were converted to show a blue light and there was a ban on using the whistle, for fear of creating confusion with air-raid warnings. In August 1936 a troop of Republican soldiers landed at Porto Cristo and marched to San Miguel station, where they tore up a short length of track and also blocked the nearby tunnel. Although there was no counter-attack from local forces, the invaders withdrew after a few days and the line was soon reinstated. Other effects of the war were more insidious. There were purges of the railway's staff, of whom 98 were imprisoned or simply disappeared, while almost twice this number suffered other, lesser penalties. The outbreak of the war also caused a temporary shortage of coal and the company was forced to start using wood to fire the locomotives, though by the end of 1936 coal supplies were back to normal. What was more important from the railway's point of view was that a ban was placed on the use of private vehicles and unauthorised public transport, and with this and dwindling petrol supplies, not to mention the requisitioning of private lorries, cars and buses, the railway began, once again, to enjoy the virtual monopoly of public transport of its earliest days.

This period of ephemeral success continued until 1940, by which time the effects of the Second World War were causing concern. Once again there was a coal shortage, with the supply of imported coal ceasing completely during the last three years of the conflict. Wartime shortage of materials for repairs also helped to cause a locomotive famine, and the company turned to its neighbour the FC de Soller, which had been electrified some years previously, and so had five surplus steam engines laid up at Palma. One was the Falcon-designed 0-4-0 tram locomotive used to build the line, while the others were 2-6-0 tanks built by La Maquinista and were similar to those already operating on the FC de Mallorca. All five were purchased although the Falcon and one of the larger engines were almost immediately condemned and scrapped.

By the time the war ended the railway was in poor condition, suffering from years during which maintenance had been deliberately run down or at best neglected. Casualties at this time were the first two Nasmyth engines, MAJORCA and PALMA, which were laid up in 1945 and 1948 respectively, and later scrapped. The Orenstein & Koppel seems to have been taken off the active list about now, as its running number was reallocated to one of the ex-Soller engines, while the little Nasmyth 0-4-0 cannot have been much used by this time. As the older locomotives were withdrawn they were cannibalised for parts to keep the rest of the fleet running and thus the railway struggled on; despite a reputation for being dirty and slow, it still managed to move considerable amounts of passengers and freight. By now separate passenger workings had been suspended in the name of fuel economy, and all steam services were being run "mixed". During this period the use of poor quality locomotive coal, which provided bad steaming and slower running, together with the general lack of money which led to deferred maintenance, all contributed to poor timekeeping which helped to drive potential passengers away. In contrast, road transport was much quicker to recover, and began to be a serious factor as the railway could no longer claim its virtual monopoly over freight traffic.

By the start of the 1950s the company was on the point of collapse, and even had to suspend services to Arta, Santany and Felanitx for a week early in 1951. In that year 379 trains suffered breakdowns, while 149 of these were total locomotive failures, requiring emergency help from another engine to complete their journeys. Following prolonged negotiations with the company, the Ministry of Works took over the lines belonging to the FC de Mallorca from 1st August 1951. The new management operated under the name Explotación de Ferrocarriles por el Estado, shortened to EFE, and was also responsible for running other failed independent railways on the Spanish mainland; thus centralised control came to the island's main railway system, which had previously always enjoyed its independence.

The Nationalisation Era

A survey of the available motive power was not encouraging: of all the locomotives only two, numbers 9 and 55 were in good condition, though a further eight were generally operational (including numbers 8, 22, 24, 31, 33, 53 and 54). The rest were in poor condition, while four (numbers 3, 25, 26 and 28) had been withdrawn from service some time earlier. A programme was quickly put in hand: between 1952 and 1955 Palma Works repaired numbers 12, 15, 21, 25, 32, 34, 50, 51 and 52, while Babcock & Wilcox repaired number 30 and renewed the boilers of numbers 15, 34, 50, 51, 52 and 53. Number 20 was sent back to La Maquinista for attention, while

Sucecoral SA, attended to the two 0-6-0 tanks, 4 and 5. Finally Astiller of Palma rebuilt numbers 10 and 14 and renewed the boiler of number 12.

With the beginnings of the Majorcan tourist boom, one of the weaknesses of the local rail system became apparent: almost nowhere, with the exception of Arenal, did it serve the beaches that were to be so important to the island's expanding economy. Added to this, the railway did not present a very attractive aspect being old, dirty, uncomfortable and slow, although an attempt to improve matters had been made on the Santany branch when some of the old four-wheeled carriages were painted white and blue to act as trailers for the elderly De Dion railcars running between Palma and Arenal. The fact that the railway was built to 3ft gauge meant that new locomotives were more expensive to import than locally produced metre gauge engines, and the gauge difference also made it impossible to transfer secondhand equipment from elsewhere on the Spanish mainland. The danger was that this technical difficulty might be used by the State as an excuse for the total closure of the system.

A fresh policy was obviously needed, as well as considerable capital expenditure. By this time many narrow gauge lines across Spain were having similar problems, and the early 1950s saw many close, though some like the Majorcan system were nationalised. In 1953 the Spanish government introduced a New Plan for the narrow gauge railways under its control, with the injection of some much-needed cash, and various Ministry

Ancient and Modern at Palma in 1956.

(L. G. MARSHALL)

studies were undertaken to look at different modernisation methods. On Majorca, electrification was impossible to justify as traffic levels varied so much between the different routes, and such a scheme would depend on total conversion to allow stock to be used efficiently. However it was obvious that the days of steam power were numbered, and in 1956 the start of a policy of complete dieselisation was implemented with the introduction of four bogie railcars built by Ferrostahl at Esslingen in Germany. Six matching trailers were also supplied.

One of the effects of these arrivals was that there was now a surplus of steam locomotives, and by 1957 the smallest and least powerful were laid aside in various sheds across the system. Lluchmayor was the final resting place of numbers 6, 17 and 25, while Santany played host to number 3. Felanitx shed housed number 26, while the yard at Palma saw numbers 16, 23, 24, 28 and the little Koppel lined up for scrapping. Two years later there were still 22 operational steam locomotives, though the 0-4-0 tanks had been officially retired by this time, as had almost all the 4-4-0 tanks, with the exception of number 27. Still active were four of the Maquinistas (6, 19, 20, 21), the Krupp and Babcock engines, the two 0-6-0Ts and four of the big 4-6-0 goods tanks though two of these had less than a year's life remaining.

In 1959 the dieselisation programme took a step forward when four brand-new diesel hydraulic B-B locomotives were obtained, built by the Sociedad Española de Construccion Naval of Bilbao. On Majorca they were known locally as "The Creusots". With these new arrivals the remaining steam locomotives were confined to goods services and the occasional passenger train to La Puebla and Arta. The Creusot diesels took over the two main daily services to Arta, as well as a daily trip to Inca and Manacor, hauling the Carde coaches. The new policy gathered momentum when two more railcars and four more trailers came into service. They were outwardly identical to the 1956 batch, but had been built by Euskalduna. The new diesels together with the earlier railcars were now able to handle all the passenger services, and steam withdrawals speeded up.

The introduction of the diesels resulted in the reinstatement of some services. Except for the Felanitx branch, which only saw two daily railcars and the occasional goods train, all the other lines were soon back to three daily services, some of these running as mixed trains – these workings perhaps providing the final steam duties. Santany's three trains were all railcars, however. As a whole, the railway was still operating as a "general carrier", and freight tonnage for 1960 totalled 84,100 tonnes, carried in 493 wagons. The passenger fleet comprised 56 carriages, ranging from the earliest Brown Marshall vehicles up to the bogie coaches of the 1930s, plus the railcars. By 1963 the timetable showed all scheduled services being run with railcars, mixed trains having disappeared, and the goods traffic that remained being run separately. At this point there were only three each of the Krupp and Babcock engines still active, along with the two 0-6-0T shunters and the remaining 4-6-0 tanks. Steam power officially ended on 12th December 1964, and starting the following year the lines of derelict locomotives at Palma began to be cut up.

Another Change of Management

In 1965 control of the Majorca Railway (together with the other nationalised narrow gauge lines on the Spanish mainland) was transferred from EFE to a new organisation, FEVE (Ferrocarriles Españoles de Via Estrecha, or Spanish Narrow Gauge Railways).

Despite the economies effected by the introduction of the railcar fleet, the railway continued a slow contraction, although outside factors also played a part. By the mid 1960s the increasing demands of tourism called for the expansion of Palma's airport. Part of the Santany branch stood in the way of this progress and so the line was closed on 4th March 1965, though it is ironic that the growth of tourism should have swept away the only route that might have been of benefit to the increasing numbers of visitors.

By this time too the harbour line was all but derelict, its only recent use having been the export of coal from mines near Lloseta to Alicante; however by 1965 the recorded tonnage was the equivalent of one wagonload, all cargo having been transferred to road transport. Elsewhere, things seemed to be more hopeful, at least for passenger services. Three trains a day had been restored on the other lines and in addition there were four new "short" services on the main line, three terminating at Inca, the other at Manacor. The optimism of these new workings was slightly tarnished on 31st December 1967 when the Felanitx branch closed, though this was partly due to the fact that a section of the line was still laid with 20kg/m rails, which were totally worn out, and there was no money for renewal. This was the reason why, in the later years, only the smaller railcars could use this route. The same date saw goods services abandoned over the entire system, and the official closure of the harbour branch at Palma. Indeed, there was even talk of closing the La Puebla branch and the section between Manacor and Arta, though these decisions were shelved. The cessation of goods services meant that the Creusot diesels were now something of a luxury and two were returned to the mainland, going to the Cantabrian system, while the other pair lingered for a while on the island, before being scrapped.

Even after the take-over by FEVE the future of the railway was uncertain. As the system was still run from Madrid it tended to suffer from the resulting bureaucracy, with decisions having to be ratified at State level rather than locally; this tended to result in stagnation. At the end of the 1960s the service comprised eleven daily trips between Palma and Inca (plus one extra on Sundays); four of these workings continued to Arta and another four to La Puebla. By 1972 timings had been improved and the number of services to and from Inca had increased to sixteen, though after 26th October 1974 one of these was dropped again. However, little maintenance was being carried out and the threat of closure was never far away from the section beyond Manacor, where the number of daily services to Arta was cut from four to three railcars a day from 1st December 1974.

By the early 1970s the railway had a deficit of 38 million pesetas. Passenger figures showed 1,000,200 journeys, of which 950,000 were made between Palma and Inca. In the circumstances FEVE may not have felt much like celebrating the Centenary of the line in 1975. However, the City Council of Palma and the local Tourist Board had other ideas; at first they thought to run a steam service, but it had to be pointed out that all the locomotives had been scrapped some years previously. In the event, a railcar and two trailers ran the official Centenary service, which was also marked by the unveiling of a plaque at Palma station. The President of FEVE attended the occasion, and in the congratulatory speeches grandiose plans were outlined, including electrification of the system and the re-opening of the old tunnel to the harbour. A new underground station would be built to serve the Plaza España with a new waterfront terminal at the Parque del Mar, near the cathedral. All this would render the present terminus redundant, and the site could be sold off to help defray the costs of the scheme. Nonetheless, following the upheavals of the celebrations, the railway returned to more mundane operations, while official pronouncements as to the future of the line returned to their customary vagueness for a while.

The continuing size of the operating deficit meant that new cuts were sought in the following years, and eventually the economics of running the Arta services on minimal maintenance caught up with the line. After a derailment at Petra that needed the help of a crane to recover the railcar from the adjacent field, the section between

Services to Arta were ended in 1977 after this derailment near Petra.   (A. SANCHIS COLLECTION)

Rolling stock awaiting scrapping at Palma, c.1970.   (A. HARRIS)

Empalme and Arta was closed "provisionally" on 20th June 1977, but rather than commit heavy investment into track renewals it was obvious that a FEVE-run bus service provided a more economic answer, and the closure became permanent. By this time it was not only the track that was suffering from a lack of maintenance as the bogie railcars were also in a poor state, often running with only one serviceable motor.

The end of goods services ten years previously and the gradual run-down of services had caused a glut of redundant rolling stock to build up at Palma, where desultory attempts had been made to scrap them. Finally in September 1978 the company decided to burn the survivors, and the remaining ironwork was sold off at 7 pesetas a kilo. Only two passenger vehicles survived the flames, as one of the more modern four-wheeled passenger brake vans was sold off and was later converted into a house, while one of the Carde bogie carriages was preserved, along with a handful of dropside open wagons, a few flat trucks and one brake van, which were retained for use on ballast trains.

Despite the large numbers of tourists visiting Majorca by this time, no effort seems to have been made to encourage them to use the FEVE services. Local information at the stations could be unreliable and likely to be countermanded by chalked announcements on a blackboard, while the published timetables had copious footnotes in Spanish, all of which was liable to deter the casual traveller. Indeed, the writer remembers being told by a tour guide in the 1970s that all the island's railways were closed! Nevertheless, limited numbers of visitors were using the railway, in contrast to the FC de Soller, which was actively promoting its tourist potential. Meanwhile, the FEVE line was left to the local inhabitants though as some competing bus services were faster than the trains, this was perhaps a dangerous policy to pursue.

The 1980s – Worsening Problems and Some Solutions

In 1980 the Spanish Government commissioned a report on Balearic transport, and the sections dealing with Majorca's two railways made bleak reading. On the FEVE line the section between Palma and Inca was in a reasonable state, but beyond here the line to La Puebla was in bad condition, and in particular the section from Inca to Empalme needed complete replacement. The FEVE workshops' equipment, designed for the steam era, was largely obsolete, and only light repairs were possible while major work was being contracted out at a cost of 4 to 8 million pesetas a year. As a result the railcar fleet, despite being within its life expectancy of 25/30 years, had suffered from insufficient maintenance and the continual pounding received from the indifferent permanent way, and a large investment would be needed to rectify matters. The report noted that much of the site of the Palma terminus was under-used, as was the old railway tunnel to the port. Various station buildings were suffering from damp, and required repairs.

A major source of concern was public safety at the 112 level crossings on the Palma-La Puebla line. Of these only fifteen were provided with barriers. (The average distance between level crossings was 2.4kms.) Incidents between trains and road transport were not uncommon, and there had recently been a fatal accident in the outskirts of Palma. It was also noted that the line was run with the trains' movements merely being advised locally from station to station by telephone – a method that lacked a certain sophistication by 1980. In addition the majority of the crossing keepers were not included on the telephone circuit and had to rely on their knowledge of the timetable and the warning whistles of approaching trains. In its favour it has to be said that this system had catered in the past for a much higher traffic density than the present half-hourly service. The report found that the infrequency of services and their general unreliability had led to falling passenger demand over the years, which had not been offset by the railway company's policy of charging lower passenger fares than the competing bus services. In fact the practice had merely helped to speed the slide into deficit.

In conclusion the report made certain suggestions: –

1. Provide more stations in the Palma–Marratxi section, where the new outskirts of the capital were poorly served.
2. Introduce signalling and CTC (Centralised Traffic Control), and improve the railway's telephone system.

3. Improve the state of the permanent way, and provide extra passing loops.

4. Provide automatic crossing barriers to comply with current legislation.

5. Modernise the workshops, possibly on a new site.

6. Modernise the rolling stock. (A two-year plan already existed to spend 16 million pesetas on rebuilding two of the railcars, with a further 6 million going towards upgrading four of the trailers.)

7. Close the section from Inca to La Puebla.

8. Reduce staffing levels in three areas:– by the provision of automatic level crossings, by turning all the intermediate stations into unstaffed halts, and by issuing tickets on the trains.

9. Introduce a gradual fare increase to a level where the costs could be covered, and abolish the concessionary rates offered.

10. Undertake a further study to see whether better use of the Palma terminus site could be achieved. This could involve making a new connection with the FC de Soller beyond the station throat and bringing both lines into a shared station, thus eliminating several urban level crossings on the Soller line.

11. Undertake a study of the benefits of a Metro, using the old goods tunnel (in effect a resurrection of the Centenary scheme).

12. Undertake a study of the possible benefits of introducing a passenger and goods service (coal traffic only) between Palma, Inca and Alcudia.

While the report gave the gauge of the island's railways as 3ft it did not recommend a conversion to metre gauge. However such a change had several potential benefits including the possibility of greater speeds and consequently better utilisation of line capacity. Shorter journey times could help to woo traffic back from road transport, while the ability to transfer metre gauge rolling stock from other FEVE lines on the mainland could help combat the problems posed by a rapidly ageing railcar fleet.

As regards goods services, GESA, the local power company, were planning to build a power station at Es Murtera, between La Puebla and Alcudia, and a scheme was drawn up to supply coal by rail from the mines near Consell, via a 7.5km extension of the line beyond La Puebla and a partial re-opening of the former Alaró branch. It was envisaged that 1,000,000 tonnes of coal could be carried, although the track on the coal-carrying portion of the line would need upgrading from 30 to 40kg/m rail. Meanwhile other experts questioned whether the mines had sufficient reserves to meet this demand. The possibility of extending the line to Es Murtera temporarily revived the earlier plans to include Alcudia and Pollensa on the railway map. The increased speeds possible with new metre gauge track would reduce the journey to La Puebla from 1 1/4 hours to 45 minutes, thus the extra distance might be achieved within the original timetable slot. The existing number of railcars would allow for 18 workings

Railcars at Palma in 1981. Note that each track is numbered and these numbers were also carried on the point levers. The highest number found was 44, on a lever lifted from the old goods yard.   (AUTHOR)

between Palma and Alcudia, and 14 services to Inca were planned. However, ultimately the decision was taken not to proceed with the extension.

By 1981 the balance sheet was still in the red, to the tune of 185.6 million pesetas. Nevertheless the closures of 1977 had helped to bring the figures down from their previous annual total, the sum spent on stations being reduced by 5.6 million pesetas while savings on fixed installations and plant totalled 4.5 million pesetas. It appeared that a combination of cuts and savings was also practiced in the railway workshops where spending fell by 6.3 million pesetas over the same period. However, other costs rose:– Train Operation by almost 6 million pesetas and General Costs by nearly 4 million, though Road Services achieved a small saving. In 1981 passengers carried by rail numbered 931,159 – up from 887,218 the previous year, and earning just over 36.8 million pesetas, to which road transport added a further 5 million.

Despite the deficit some new work was implemented, notably the rebuilding of the railcar fleet to replace the Bussing 100hp motors with Pegaso 150hp engines. Car number 2004 was the first to be fitted, followed by the rest, while the trailers were given a make-over. The following year a further batch of railcars and trailers arrived from lines in northern Spain. They were in poor condition and were laid aside to be worked on at a later date, though in fact this work was never carried out. Some were subsequently destroyed by fire, while the remainder were scrapped in the mid-1990s.

Railcar and trailer leaving Palma for Inca in 1981. Owing to track renewal work, the line ended 50 yards beyond the platform, and services had to shunt off to the left of the picture before departing again via the workshop line. (AUTHOR)

The Batignolles-CAF diesel shunter and all four hopper wagons, at work on metre gauge tracklaying duties – Palma, 1981. (AUTHOR)

More importantly, the metre gauge conversion was implemented between Palma and Inca, although as suggested in the report, the section onward to La Puebla was closed on 31st March 1981. The right-hand running line out of Palma was altered first, trains in 1981 using the old 3ft gauge track alongside for bi-directional travel. For a while, this involved passenger trains running through the workshop lines, as the rest of the station throat had been lifted to install the new metre gauge tracks. The conversion started at both ends of the line and was completed by 1983. At the same time as the gauge conversion, colour light signals were also installed, as well as automatic half-barriers at major level crossings.

The 1990s – The Renaissance Begins

The late 1980s were a difficult time for major investment and while Spain's membership of the European Community might have been thought to be a way of obtaining money for re-development of the FEVE system, the Balearic Islands were low on the EU priority list for grants. Despite this, plans were laid to open a new station to serve a megastore just outside Palma, although the subsequent failure of the necessary investment caused the collapse of this project. Nevertheless, the suburbs of the capital gained three new halts, one at kilometre 3.7 named Verge de Lluch, while further on are Pont d'Inca Nou and Polígon Marratxi, the latter serving a new suburb and its trading estate. The de-staffing of the original stations has brought with it problems of vandalism and graffiti, while the new halts with their concrete slab construction suffer similar problems. To combat this the old station buildings have been leased out, several becoming local cultural centres.

The railway suffered a setback in 1990 when a serious fire destroyed the carriage shed at Palma, together with several railcars and trailers. The resulting shortage of stock brought the arrival of a 2-car multiple unit, built by MAN together with another unit, which FEVE transferred from the Santander-Orviedo line in northern Spain in September 1991. During 1990 and 1991 the original Majorcan railcars had again entered a period of rebuilding with work concentrated on their motors, bogies and transmission, however the arrival of these new units caused the cancellation of the planned renovation of railcar 2019. Another MAN 2-car unit arrived in 1992 and a fourth the following year. Once the MAN units entered service the older railcars were retired, with the exception of 2004, which was used for p.w. duties. Although by this time the Ferrostahl railcars were in poor shape, they had managed to keep the railway operating for 40 years, when otherwise it would certainly have closed. Meanwhile the site of the old carriage shed was paved over, and a small single storey café/bar built. The remains of the approach tracks to the shed were still just long enough to provide three sidings, each just capable of taking a 2-car unit. By this time plans were also in hand to develop the derelict goods yard at Palma to provide car parking facilities and a new bus station.

By the early 1990s a new policy was in force for the FEVE lines everywhere, which were gradually being handed over to be run by the autonomous regional governments. Negotiations regarding the underwriting of costs delayed this initially from happening in Majorca, while negotiations were further complicated by the possibility of a merger between FEVE and RENFE, the nationalised broad gauge system. For a while progress was delayed, but matters were resolved in 1994, when control of the former FEVE section on the island passed to the Serveis Ferroviaris de Mallorca (SFM), the Majorcan Railway Service. During the run-up to the handover period plans to re-open the line to La Puebla (now known as Sa Pobla) were dusted off again, with the added possibility of rebuilding the Empalme–Manacor section later. In addition the railway also suggested that it might be able to handle the island's domestic refuse, transporting it to a proposed central incinerator, thus bringing about a reduction of many thousands of road journeys each year. The traffic would be handled at night when it would not conflict with the needs of passenger movement and eventually, as further former sections of the line were re-opened it might be possible to serve the whole island. Once again objections were raised, pointing out the inadvisability of burning household waste and the danger of causing even more pollution than was being prevented, and the scheme appears to have been shelved.

Railcar 2358 and trailer 5017 in the final FEVE livery – Palma, 1994.   (AUTHOR'S COLLECTION)

The SFM Takes Over

The Serveis Ferroviaris de Mallorca was incorporated on 1st January 1994 and took over the running of the railway on 1st April the same year. An early sign of the new management's control came the following April, with the delivery of four 2-car diesel units built by CAF to a very modern design. These new arrivals were numbered 61-01 to 61-08, and entered service on 22nd June 1995, at first sharing the timetable with the MAN units. However, in 1997 there were more new arrivals: – power cars 61-09 to 61-12, and four centre trailer cars (numbers 62-01 to 62-04). These CAF motor-cars weigh 31.63 tonnes, while the trailers weigh 31.5 tonnes. The power units have NTA 855A motors developing 310kw, and maximum speed is 100km/hr. A dual hydrodynamic and air braking system is fitted, plus pneumatic suspension. The carriages are also fitted with air-conditioning. Seating capacity is 48 in the power cars and 96 in the trailers, while 78 and 156 standing passengers can be accommodated; there is also provision for wheel-chair passengers. All these combined units make up two 2-car trains and four 3-car sets. With their arrival the ex-FEVE railcars and trailers were finally rendered redundant, and following their withdrawal all of them were sold to the Servicios Ferroviarios Chaqueños of Argentina, for 108 million pesetas. The Ferrostahl units left Majorca in March 1997, while the rest were retained for a few

Palma in 1997, after the demolition of the carriage shed. From L to R:- 2364, 2348, 2314 and 2365 (corridor end) – all MAN units, carrying the new SFM livery. 2002, 5017 and 2019 still carry FEVE liveries.

(M. BUNCH)

months longer, until the arrival of the final new units from CAF. The last working formed of MAN units was a special train organised by the Friends of the Balearic Railways (AAFB) on 27th October 1997, which ran from Palma to Inca and back, and the following month the last units of ex-FEVE stock were shipped to their new home in South America.

When the MAN 2-car units had first arrived the original rail-height platforms sprouted humps the length of the new trains. Now even higher platforms were required, and these have transformed the look of the system from a traditional narrow gauge appearance and given it a "main line" look. When this work was carried out at Inca, an elegantly curved wooden roof was also provided, covering the platforms of both running lines, which are now laid out as Up and Down tracks, as befits the station's renewed through status. There is still a siding facing towards Palma, near the overbridge at the outer end of the station, though the trailing sidings have been partially covered by the new platform and some track has been lifted.

By 1997 the Balearic Government announced the intention to re-open the section of line between Inca and Sa Pobla as the first phase of an eventual extension to serve Alcudia. Work started in November 1998, with a target date of 2000 for completion as far as Sa Pobla.

The year 2000 also marked the 125th anniversary of Majorcan railways, and SFM organised a special exhibition at Palma station to celebrate the event, lasting from 22nd December 2000 to 25th February 2001. This coincided with the re-opening of the Inca-Sa Pobla section. The exhibition was divided into three sections, housed in

"Salvem S'Estacio" - pro-train graffiti at Manacor, 2000.   (AUTHOR)

CAF multiple-units 61-07/08 approaching Palma in 1997. Loco 1207 just visible beyond.   (M. BUNCH)

marquees erected along the platform. The first section comprised the Ferrotrade diesel from the FC de Soller, together with the surviving Carde bogie coach. There were also cases of historical documents relating to the railway, a selection of ex-FC de Mallorca train lamps, a model railway provided by the AAFB, and a bar. Next came a history of the railway in photographs, and finally a section displaying present and future plans for the system.

Shortly afterwards these plans began to be implemented, and have radically altered the look of the Palma terminus where a new station has been built on the site of the former carriage shed. This has involved demolishing part of the old workshop complex (with the exception of the boiler house, where the original workshop's power plant, an Alexander steam engine of 1875, has been preserved), and slewing the approach tracks across this area, south of the overbridge at the station throat. The running lines divide either side of a central berthing road, which faces the platforms and access to either one is provided by a scissors cross-over. The single island platform is taller than before, matching the height of the floors of the new rolling stock. At first the platform was unprotected, but later a sloping roof was provided supported by slanting girders. The new passenger approach to the platforms is via the courtyard (and former car park) that existed between the old station and the Hostal Terminus. This area, too, has been given an overall roof, and for a time there was a small kiosk selling rail tickets, while the old ticket hall was being refurbished. This has now re-opened and the kiosk removed. Meanwhile the former track-bed into the old station has been landscaped and has become a small park, with a footbridge crossing the lines a little way beyond the platform ends. The site of the former workshops has been used to create a new bus station, which opened on 5th June 2001. This new facility had a slightly chequered

The new station at Palma. Beyond the canopy is the park created on the old station site.   (AUTHOR)

introduction, as on the first day of operation it appears that bus passengers had not been informed, and many continued to queue at their habitual bus stops, presumably wondering about the lack of services.

On 26th August 2001 the Balearic Government announced plans to reconstruct the line from Santa Maria to Felanitx, and ordered the Ministry of Public Works to look into the viability of such a project. This link was to form part of the master plan for transport that was in the process of being drawn up. The experts pointed out that the only drawback to this idea was that the old right-of-way had been sold, and that in places buildings had been constructed across the track-bed, thus to complete the plan a certain amount of new alignment would be required plus some expropriation of land. They felt that a more profitable (and technically more viable) idea would be to run direct from Palma, rather than via Santa Maria. In effect this would partially recreate the Santany branch, duly diverted round the airport and a nearby supermarket, both of which have covered all traces of the former line in this section. The benefits would be the ability to put the towns around the Bay of Palma back onto the railway map, among them Lluchmayor and Arenal – the latter with its potential for tourist traffic. From here a cross-country link would be needed to join the course of the Felanitx branch with a

CAF units in the countryside, en-route for Inca in 2001. (A. SANCHIS)

further new section, 14kms in length, taking the line on to Manacor. With the added reinstatement of the section between Empalme and Manacor, this would give the SFM a triangular axis based on Palma, Manacor and Felanitx. However the funding for such a scheme will have to involve Madrid, and so far little interest has been forthcoming from central government, which nonetheless appears to want to keep some control over local transport.

A few months later, in October 2001, the first part of this grand plan was implemented when the reinstatement of the Empalme-Manacor section was put up for tender, the work being subsequently given to COMSA, the contractor that had been responsible for the renovation of the Sa Pobla branch. The renewal of the line was given a budget of 32 million pesetas to provide a single-track link 30.2kms long, following the old route across the centre of the island. Proposed journey times of 58 minutes between Palma and Manacor were announced, and work started almost immediately to lift the surviving 3ft gauge track and to regrade the old formation, working away from the junction at Empalme. While special materials were specified for tracklaying in order to reduce noise on the urban sections, this did not satisfy a number of the residents of Petra, many of whom vetoed the initial proposal. A complication on this section of line is that the track has been cut by recent road improvements, and a section near the station has become an unofficial roadway. Petra's mayor, Joan Font, stated in 2002 that two options were being studied:– taking the rails around the town, or going underground for some 400 metres to avoid obstructions. However, a local faction, probably supported by those whose land was likely to be expropriated, contended that a station on the outskirts of the town would be less convenient, and thus less used than the former station, leading to a potential drop in passenger numbers. This argument had a good basis; the rebuilt end of the Sa Pobla branch stops at the edge of the town, 500 metres short of the old terminus, with the result that many passengers, particularly the elderly, prefer to take the bus which serves the centre of town. In consequence the number of rail passengers at Sa Pobla has not been as high as was hoped.

To provide better access for the inhabitants of villages where the nearest railway station is some distance away, a system of feeder buses has been implemented, which has resulted in the number of passengers increasing dramatically. A service linking Consell station and Alaró started in the Autumn of 2001 with 3,914 passengers being carried in the first quarter of operation; a year later this had risen to 18,468 passengers a quarter. More recently a bus linking Santa Maria with the outlying villages of Sencelles, Biniali, Ses Alqueries and Santa Eugenia has been inaugurated, with another route linking Inca with Costix and Sencelles, while the inhabitants of Muro and Llubi should also be included soon.

To mark the start of restoration work on the Manacor route, a ceremony was held there in January 2002, attended by various local politicians, when a short length of ballasted track was laid at the station. Once the accompanying speeches had been given and the gathering had dispersed, the rails were removed again within a short while. Meanwhile, work started to restore the station building, ready for the resumption of rail services.

During 2002 work proceeded swiftly on the Empalme–Sineu section and new metre gauge trackwork began to be laid in place. However, further along the route, the various factions around Petra continued to delay work in this sector, with several sit-down protests to stop the deployment of earth-moving equipment, which resulted in the Guardia Civil being called out. Despite a vote having been taken locally that ratified the plan to by-pass the town, those who were likely to suffer loss of land still tried to overthrow the decision in favour of the original route. Ultimately the work proceeded on the detour, 3 kms of which will be in a deep cutting, but the legacy of the new station will no doubt be years of simmering resentment in some quarters.

Meanwhile, early in 2002 SFM suffered a serious accident. On 12th February the morning train to Sa Pobla was approaching the terminus in foggy conditions, but the driver was unaware that he had almost reached the end of the line until the platform appeared through the mist. Despite performing an emergency brake application, the train was still travelling at 40km/hr when it hit the buffer stop, rolling it over, and ending up with the leading coach, number 61-06, balanced on top of the concrete block with its back broken. Despite the train being full of commuters, many of whom were shaken, only five passengers as well as the driver suffered minor injuries, though all were later released from hospital. However the ticket collector, David Tirado, who had been riding in the cab with the driver was more seriously injured. Efforts to remove the stricken train continued all day and with the help of a large crane it was eventually removed by road during the following night. The railway set up a special investigations board, headed by the SFM chairman and the railway's lawyer, with the brief to study all possible causes of the accident, human, technical, meteorological, etc. The buffer stop was said to have functioned correctly, as it had absorbed the impact of the train and prevented a complete derailment. For a while the damaged unit remained on the ground at Son Rullan works, wrapped in blue plastic sheeting, until the decision was taken towards the end of the year to write it off the books. The two other coaches, 61-05 and 62-03 were repaired in the workshops.

Another notable event in 2002 was the integration of the SFM's trains with the local bus services, under a new body, Transports de les Illes Balear (TIB). This merger has resulted in yet another change of livery.

By the turn of the year the finished trackwork on the line to Manacor had reached Sineu, and on 5th January 2003 an unofficial First Train was run to the town, where it was greeted by Ministers of the Balearic Government and local government officers, as well as local inhabitants dressed as the Three Kings, whose festival falls on the following day and is the cause of much celebration in Spain. Public services were not due to start until April or May 2003, but the date for the celebration may have been chosen as an exercise in good publicity. The renewed line eventually re-opened to Manacor on 11th May, 2003.

Schemes for the New Millennium

With the advent of the SFM several former railway schemes have been integrated into the future transport policy of the island. The north-east of Majorca has become a popular tourist zone, and the importance of a rail link with Palma has been recognised as a means of diminishing road traffic in the area. The expansion of Sa Pobla means that the original route towards Alcudia is no longer available, and the new extension will be diverted around the town and a new station provided. Meanwhile a Spanish company has expressed an interest in developing a tramway system to link Alcudia and Pollensa, though no further details have yet been published.

With work on the reconstruction back to Manacor already under way, thoughts turned to the reinstatement of the complete route to Arta, with a further extension to Cala Ratjada, which has been given a provisional completion date of 2006. This section of the old line has a substantial band of supporters who have organised an annual railway walk along part of this route for several years to draw attention to this unused resource; it seems that their patience will soon be rewarded. Another possibility is that the proposed line to Cala Ratjada might run via Porto Cristo and the coastal resorts, rather than inland via Arta. A Canadian company has proposed that it might run its own trains in parallel with SFM services on this route, specifically to cater for the tourist trade. This suggestion has been favourably received by the SFM's management.

New and Proposed Lines (2003)

——————— Existing lines, including Inca-Manacor Section (2003)

+++++++ SFM Alcudia extension (2006)

— ·· — ·· — SFM Arta extension (2006)

××××××× SFM alternative route with Cala Ratjada extension (2006)

— — — — SFM Palma-Manacor, proposed southerly route

┤—┤—┤ Proposed Alcudia-Pollensa tramway

✶✶✶✶✶✶✶ Proposed University tramway (2005)

·············· Proposed "Bay of Palma" tramway/light rail

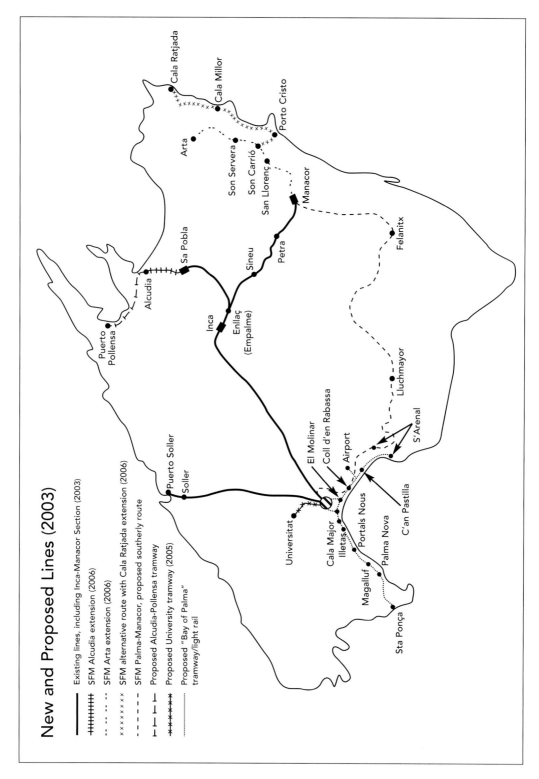

(A. SANCHIS)

MAN units in the suburbs of Palma in the 1990s – 50 years before this was all fields.

Finally there is the project to link Manacor with Palma via a southerly route, possibly reactivating part of the former routes to Santany and Felanitx, in effect a return to some of the first proposals put forward in the nineteenth century by Bouvy and the Gispert brothers. It has to be said that this route would involve some heavy engineering work as it would run partially across the grain of the landscape, and at present no further details are available.

Meanwhile in Palma, the Balearic Government wants to create a link between the city centre and the university campus (UIB), situated to the north-west of the capital near Son Sardina. At one time it was suggested that the FC de Soller might be diverted to serve the campus, but this idea has been overtaken by the more radical plan to link the UIB, the Plaça España, and the airport to the east of the city with a new tramway. The initial route will be 8.69kms in length, with stations at Plaça España, Jacint Verdaguer, Son Hugo and Son Pardo, which will all be underground, while Son Castelló, Son Sardina and Universitat will be on the surface. The projected journey time will be 15 minutes, and it is thought that some 5,400 passengers a day will use the line. A budget of 27,050,000 Euros has been allocated, and a target date of 2005 set for completion.

Another projected tram route might link the towns along the Bay of Palma from Santa Ponça in the west to S'Arenal in the east. This line would link with the intermodal terminus at the Plaça España. This ambitious scheme will need financial help from central government in Madrid, and so may be some time in coming to fruition, however such is the local enthusiasm for the project that the first stage was officially announced in January 2003. This was for the section linking the centre of Palma and running via the main avenues circling the old city centre, then proceeding via es Molinets and Coll d'En Rabassa to S'Arenal. Five years has been allocated for its construction, giving a 2008 completion date. It is anticipated that the new line will need to attract 10 million passengers a year to be viable; at present the comparable bus routes carry 8.5 million passengers annually.

Finally in response to residents of the Palma suburbs living between the present terminus and Son Rullan, who have complained that the line creates a diversion through their neighbourhoods exacerbated by the lack of former level crossings and the prohibition on creating new ones, there is a scheme that may see this section of the line covered over with a false tunnel. As if all this was not enough, there have also been discussions with a number of companies with a view to establishing a local railway museum, although no definite proposals have yet emerged.

Majorca is thus still an island with a vibrant rail system, and though in some aspects the planning wheel seems to be turning in a rather slow 130-year cycle, there are plenty of developments planned for the future which should continue to make the island a suitable destination for narrow gauge enthusiasts for the foreseeable future.

Chapter 3

Locomotives and Other Motive Power

The 4-4-0 Tanks (series 1, 16 and 25)

In the early days the Majorca Railway patronised British firms for both rolling stock and motive power, the latter being supplied by Nasmyth Wilson of Patricroft, Manchester, who continued to do so until their connection with the island was severed by the First World War, although by that time Palma works had proved they were quite capable of turning out new locomotives themselves. With the relatively short distances involved the company never employed tender engines, but as the system spread and loads became heavier, the later locomotives were larger and more powerful. Despite the universal use of tank engines, turntables were provided and locomotives always travelled chimney first.

The first three locomotives to be supplied for the opening of the line were 4-4-0 tank engines. They had a rather short boiler and firebox, while the frames were raised above the front bogie to support the smokebox, with the cylinders bolted onto this upward

ARTA, No. 27, on station pilot duties, Palma, 1957.   (L. G. MARSHALL)

Nasmyth Wilson picture of ALGAIDA, No. 20, one of the more powerful goods locomotives required by the increasing traffic in the late 19th century. The small coal bunker was later enlarged on some of these engines. (AUTHOR'S COLLECTION)

extension at an inclined angle. The bogie wheels were of a solid pattern with raised spokes; above them the locomotive's frames extended forwards from below the smokebox to carry a wooden buffer beam and a cow-catcher. The original cabs were little more than a pair of weatherboards supporting the roof. Names and numbers were allocated to this trio, which became MAJORCA, PALMA, and INCA. Given running numbers 1-3, they were also known as series 1 locomotives.

In 1878 four generally similar Nasmyth locomotives were obtained, although these had an increased wheelbase and enlarged cylinders. They formed series 25 and were named SINEU, LA PUEBLA, SANTA MARIA and BINISALEM. Running numbers 6-9 were allocated. The next arrivals in 1881 were named MURO and PETRA (numbers 10-11); they had still larger cylinders reflecting the increased traffic of the times, and formed a new series, 16. Another significant alteration that became standard from now on was the enlargement of the boiler, while the firebox size was also increased. Finally in 1897 another pair of 4-4-0s named PORRERAS and MONTUIRI (series 16, running numbers 16-17) were brought into service. These locomotives were also of the larger type and weighed 16.3 tonnes.

Quite why the series numbering appears to be random is hard to explain. In very general terms, the running number of the first engine in a series provided the series number for its fellows, and this was certainly true of later days in the case of the Krupp and Babcock engines. However it does not work for series 16 – first running number 10, and series 10 with a first running number of 12. Series 25 dating from 1878 originally started with a locomotive numbered 6, which was later re-numbered 25.

The 20th century saw the first engines emerge from the workshops at Palma. Once again they weighed 16.3 tonnes and with a burst of patriotism, no doubt to celebrate the Spanish King's sixteenth birthday, they were named ALFONSO XIII (number 18, built 1902) and ESPAÑA (number 19, built 1903). Both belonged to series 16. Both engines were once again back in the workshops in 1911 for a rebuild, which resulted in their weight being increased by another half a tonne. The same year also saw the four series 25 locomotives, as well as MURO, undergoing similar rebuilding which resulted in a weight increase to 16.8 tonnes. This rebuilding may have been an increase in boiler size or larger cylinders to match later locomotives. Another change that started towards the end of the decade was the extension of the locomotives' cabs. As noted, the first engines had very rudimentary protection, which did not extend the full width of the tanks and whose back-sheet was attached to the front of the coal bunker. By the time of the First World War locomotives were appearing with narrow cabs reaching back to the rear of the coal bunker and by the mid-1920s, full width cabs had begun to be fitted. With this final modification the former round spectacle glasses were replaced with oval ones.

Meanwhile the opening of new lines caused the re-allocation of some locomotives to cover the new services, and names and numbers were changed to reflect these new duties. When the Santany line opened in 1916, MURO was thus renamed COLL and given the number 24. Similarly ALFONSO XIII and ESPAÑA were renumbered 22 and 23 respectively, though their patriotic names were left unchanged. However, with the deposition of the Spanish monarchy and the advent of the Republic in 1931, ALFONSO XIII became the less controversial SALINAS. Other name changes resulted from the opening of the Arta extension, when locomotives 6-9 lost their original names and numbers and became 25 – SAN MIGUEL, 26 – SAN LORENZO, 27 – ARTA and 28 – SON SERVERA.

During the 1920s the 4-4-0s remained an active part of the locomotive stud, though no doubt they were rostered on lighter duties with the advent of more powerful machines. For instance the original three locomotives were only allocated to work the slower trains to Santany and Felanitx, while on the Arta line they were confined to mixed trains or goods services. The first withdrawals came soon after the end of the Second World War when MAJORCA, PALMA, INCA, SAN MIGUEL, SAN LORENZO and SON SERVERA were laid aside and while the first two were scrapped soon after, the others remained, though possibly cannibalised for parts, until they were finally cut up for scrap in the 1960s. Other casualties occurred during the mid-1950s when PORRERAS, MONTUIRI and ESPAÑA were withdrawn. The remainder seem to have survived until about 1957, when the final withdrawals started, and by the end only one 4-4-0T is recorded as being active. The honour of being the last-known working survivor seems to have gone to ARTA retired c.1959/62, although COLL was recorded shunting the harbour branch in 1957 (and withdrawn that same year) while

SALINAS, too, was known to be on the active list shortly before this date, though it was withdrawn in 1958, as was PETRA.

The 0-6-0 Tanks (series 4)

Shortly after the line's opening the need for more engines became apparent, resulting in the arrival of two 0-6-0T locomotives from Nasmyth Wilson in 1876. To give extra power the size of the cylinders was increased to 330mm by 455mm. These new locomotives weighed 16.2 tonnes and proved to be ideally suited to their function of shunting and goods haulage. They were originally going to be known as SANTA MARIA and BINISALEM but in a public relations exercise, possibly as a gesture to the shareholders of the newly merged Central & SE Railway, they were given the names MANACOR (number 4) and FELANITX (number 5), in honour of the towns about to be given new rail connections. While nameplates were carried in the early days they had been removed by the time the engines were withdrawn during the final years of steam.

The 4-6-0 Tanks (series 10)

The extensions of the late 1880s, and the increased tonnage of trains, began to demand a heavier class of locomotive; Nasmyth's answer was a 4-6-0 design that was virtually a larger version of the series 4 engines, with the addition of a leading bogie and bigger cylinders. The extra length was used to advantage as the tanks were extended and for the first time a continuous footplate was provided. Nevertheless they were thirsty beasts and had to make frequent stops for water, one reason they were not often pressed into passenger service, though they did get used on troop trains in the 1940s and 1950s. The bogie wheels were unlike the earlier engines as they were of the disc variety pierced by six holes. At first the engines were given very small coal bunkers and usually travelled with extra coal piled on the footplate. However, the need to operate on inferior coal later brought about a minor alteration on some locomotives to give a greater fuel capacity.

Two engines of this class, SAN JUAN and LLOSETA (numbers 12 and 13) were put into service in 1887, with two more, MARRATXI and ALARO (14 and 15) being added in 1891. Finally in 1911 another pair named ALGAIDA and SANTA EUGENIA (numbers 20 and 21) were obtained. As a class they lasted until the end of the steam era, being employed in later years on freight workings and troop trains. In 1957 all were still active, though LLOSETA was to go that same year followed by ALGAIDA, which appears to have been dumped at Felanitx shed by 1958; by 1960 it had been partially dismantled. ALARO and SAN JUAN were still working in 1960, though MARRATXI and SANTA EUGENIA were reported as "derelict" in June that year. By the end of steam three of the class were still in use, the third perhaps being SANTA EUGENIA, which had undergone a major refit as recently as 1958.

The Maquinista 2-6-0 Tanks (series 19)

With the contemplated opening of the Santany branch yet more engines were needed, and the selection process started in the early days of the First World War. The protectionist trade policy of the time decreed that a Spanish supplier should be used, and the company therefore turned to La Maquinista Terrestre y Marítima of Barcelona (MTM) who had supplied the most recent locomotives to the neighbouring FC de Soller. The offered engines were too expensive for the FC de Mallorca's budget, beside which they did not meet the technical specifications that had been laid down, and the company opened the tendering process to foreign companies; an offer was received from Nasmyth Wilson as well as a new bid from La Maquinista. The company chose Nasmyth's bid in 1915 but by then the conduct of the war meant that the company were unable to fulfil the contract, which was awarded by default to MTM. The three

LLUCHMAYOR, No. 19, was one of the engines obtained to work the Santany line. Seen here at Palma, in 1957, about to run round its train. (L. G. MARSHALL)

new locomotives which went into service in 1917 were similar to those built for the neighbouring FC de Soller, and were a standard design that MTM supplied to other Spanish lines. On the Majorcan system they were the largest locomotives in use, although they did not enjoy this distinction for long. As usual the new arrivals were given local names, becoming LLUCHMAYOR, CAMPOS and SANTANY; they were given numbers 19 to 21, which had become free owing to the re-numbering of three 4-4-0Ts. Later, in 1944, when another World War had caused a locomotive famine on the island, the FC de Mallorca obtained their neighbour's remaining Maquinista-built engines and the line's original little tram locomotive, all of which had been lying derelict at Palma ever since the Soller's electrification in 1929. The tram and one of the larger engines were unfit for further use and were immediately scrapped, but the three survivors put in another 15 years' service, taking the spare numbers 7, 8 and 9. For some reason the names that vanished in the 1916 era re-numbering were not re-used and the new purchases never received names, a practice which died out after the First World War, possibly because the stock of available towns had almost died out, though in theory Llubi, Arenal, and Pont d'Inca (plus a scattering of halts on the Santany branch) were still available. In general, however, locomotives assigned to work a particular line received names reflecting this allocation, thus in 1916 MURO was renamed COLL, in time for the opening of the Santany branch, the new MTM locomotives not having arrived in time to inaugurate the service, while in 1921 four of the series 25 locomotives were re-christened with names reflecting the opening of the extension to Arta.

All the Maquinista engines lasted well into the final days of steam, being often employed on services to La Puebla in the 1950s, though numbers 7 and 8 were reportedly withdrawn by 1958, with number 9 out of use a couple of years later. No. 19 LLUCHMAYOR seems to have been a particular favourite, working on a variety of services. By June 1960 she was stored at Palma, while number 21 SANTANY was still active. Because of their origins in Barcelona, the local railwaymen called them "The Catalans".

The German 2-6-0 Tanks (series 30)

To cope with the gradients of the Arta section, together with its long stretches between water supplies, the company again felt the need for some more powerful locomotives, and in 1926 they purchased six engines with a 2-6-0 wheel arrangement from Krupp of Essen. These newcomers were numbered 30 to 35 and appeared towards the end of August, the honour of being the first in service falling to number 34 on the 21st of the month. The new class was superheated and had slightly larger driving wheels and cylinders than the Maquinista locomotives. As a class they brought a belated 20th century look to the motive power department with an electric headlamp,

Krupp-built 2-6-0T No. 34 passes a line of partly dismantled wagons in Palma yard, 1960.   (M. SWIFT)

which also displayed the running number on an illuminated panel on each side. Another innovation was the provision of a conventional hook and screw-up coupling set below the narrow gauge "chopper". Number 32 was the first to go, in 1958, while the others survived for a few more years, though by now employed on goods trains. Once again the class acquired a local nickname, being known as "The Germans".

The 2-6-2 Tanks (series 50)

The final development of steam power on the Majorcan railway system took the form of a set of six 2-6-2 tank engines numbered 50-55, built by Babcock & Wilcox of Bilbao in 1930. Four of these went into service during the last three months of that year, though possibly there were teething troubles as the final two emerged after slight modification the following year, number 52 on 28th February and number 55 on 6th March. The new engines, which were also superheated, displayed several new features including water feed heaters, and were capable of running from Palma to Manacor without a water stop. Some of the class were fitted with vacuum hoses on the front buffer beam, so this could have been part of the modifications that delayed the introduction of the last two members of this type. This equipment appears only in pictures of number 55 as running in 1953, and had been removed by 1957. The class lasted until the end of steam; when the railcars took over the last of the passenger services, they and the Carde coaches were finally redundant, though both probably had some life left in them. However the State was in the process of closing down loss-making metre gauge lines, and introducing diesel power on the survivors, and with the difference in gauge, there was little hope that they could be used elsewhere, and they were scrapped at Palma during the mid-1960s.

The 0-4-0 Tanks

Three small locomotives existed which were primarily used to haul goods trains destined for the docks, and for shunting duties. After about 1920 they were allowed to use the tramway in the city centre, but some ten years later the harbour tunnel was built, robbing them of their primary task. They appear to have been allocated to a separate list at first and may only have become part of the FC de Mallorca's stock around the time of the First World War.

Little is known about the first, a totally enclosed tram locomotive bought from R. W. Hawthorn in 1881, which was built with the Brown system of cylinder linkage.

Nasmyth Wilson photograph of the tramway 0-4-0T, known on Majorca as "La Inglesita".

(AUTHOR'S COLLECTION)

The Koppel, seen at Palma in 1958, by which time it had been withdrawn from service.

(J. WISEMAN)

This locomotive was still active as late as 1926, but was definitely laid aside by 1928. The local engine crews called it "The Brown".

The next oldest tram locomotive, built in 1889, was from Nasmyth Wilson – an 0-4-0T weighing 12.5 tonnes. Originally it spent much of its time working between the railway goods yard and the city gateway, a few hundred metres distant. The maker's photograph shows that a conventional hook coupling and traditional buffing gear was fitted at first, together with a tall capped chimney. Later Palma Works fitted a stovepipe chimney and also "chopper" couplings and side chains; for some of its life tram-style side skirts were fitted. It became number 6 on the company's books (a number vacated in the 1911 rebuilding programme), but was nicknamed "La Inglesita" (Little English Girl). Retired in 1951 and latterly derelict, number 6 does not seem to have been broken up until 1960.

The other four-coupled locomotive was an Orenstein & Koppel, built in 1921, which became number 7 on the railway company's books. This number was re-allocated in 1944 and the Orenstein & Koppel worked on, un-numbered, until the early 1950s by which time its shunting duties had been taken over by the two 0-6-0Ts. After this the "Koppel", as it was nicknamed, lingered in a line of derelict locomotives at Palma, until it was broken up in 1960.

Steam Locomotive Livery

FC de Mallorca steam engine livery was green, perhaps originally lined out round the edges of the tanks and bunker with a thick black band. An ex-works picture of ESPAÑA suggestes that the green was a very dark shade, showing little variation to the black parts, and so may perhaps have been holly green. This style of paintwork certainly survived on one of the 0-6-0 shunters during the later years, when water spilling down the tanks of number 5 showed the remains of a faded green livery as late as 1957; other contemporary Nasmyth engines show no hint of any lining. For a while after the original opening of the line, the cylinder covers were polished brass, but from about the start of the 20th century this reverted to a painted front, with only the outside ring on the cylinder cover being polished. Fifty years later eye-witnesses speak of the locomotives being an indeterminate colour combining a lack of fresh paintwork with a patina of coal dust. It is possible that only the Nasmyth engines were painted green, and that the Spanish and German locomotives were black.

The Early Railcars

During the 1920s the FC de Mallorca turned to internal combustion as a way of saving money on lightly patronised services. The first railcar was built by Bereliet in March 1926 (Works No. 9); on arrival in Majorca it was given the number A-1. The four-wheeled vehicle had a doorway towards the rear of the body on each side, and 30 seated passengers could be carried. Although there was no luggage space provided, the 40hp engine was capable of hauling a couple of smaller carriages when necessary, so this was not an insuperable problem. The drive was by means of mechanical transmission to one axle, however the vehicle was dogged by a succession of mechanical breakdowns in the early days, no doubt due to the operating staff's lack of experience with internal combustion engines.

Faced with these early difficulties the company tried to interest the FC de Alaró in purchasing the railcar, which made a couple of trial trips between Consell and Alaró in 1927. However, it was not really suited to this route; despite being faster than the existing Alaró motive power it used far more petrol and would have required the installation of turntables at either end of the line. Besides this the Alaró company simply did not have the money for such an acquisition.

From its early days A-1 does not seem to have been popular with its crews, who described its engine as "lousy", and it may have already been out of use in 1936 when it caught fire at Inca. After this the remains were stored at Manacor for a number of years. Unlike the later railcars, A-1 was a single-ended vehicle with a radiator at the front of the body, but this would have been no particular operating disadvantage given the number of available turntables throughout the system.

Despite the teething problems experienced with A-1, the financial advantages of railcar use were undeniable and led to another three vehicles being brought into service in 1931. These had bodies constructed by Werkspoor NV of Amsterdam, while their running gear and the 85hp diesel engines, whose four cylinders measures 125 by 150mm, were supplied by the Société des Automobiles De Dion-Bouton of Puteux, France, although they were erected at the Carde y Escoriaza workshops at Saragossa. Their top speed was 55km/hr. Like A-1 they were four-wheeled vehicles with a long rigid wheelbase which must have made them rough riders. The seating capacity was 40 passengers, and a toilet compartment was provided. Driving controls were fitted at both ends and the radiators were mounted centrally on the roof with large air scoops facing in either direction. Livery at first was light blue below the waist, with white above, the two colours being separated by a narrow band of scarlet beading. The running number was displayed over the central end window. As well as passenger duties they were also useful on light p.w. tasks when their ability to carry a work crew and haul a wagon or two was used to full advantage.

During the 1950s, in an effort to present a smarter image to any potential tourist traffic, some of the old four-wheeled compartment coaches were painted to match the railcars. They were used on the Arenal and Santany services, whereas the regular trailer on the Felanitx line was an old Postal/2nd class composite coach – one of the vehicles obtained for the opening of the Santany branch – which retained its brown livery. This rake was strengthened, when required, by the addition of one of the Brown Marshall compartment coaches. After 1951, under State ownership, the railcar livery was changed to dark green below the waist and very pale grey-green above. There was a horizontal band of this paler colour just below the top of the darker green panelling.

In 1952 A-3 caught fire and was burnt out, making a complete rebuild necessary, the work being completed in 1954. This may be the reason why the original motors in the other units were replaced with Berliet engines between 1954 and 1956. A-4 was retired in 1964, while numbers A-2 and A-3 continued in daily service until the closure of the Felanitx branch in 1969. Despite this the last two survivors were still in existence in the Palma roundhouse in August 1979, possibly retained for p.w. duties. The reason for their longevity was the fact that the Felanitx branch contained stretches of original 20kg/m. rail up to the date of closure, and the De Dions were the only railcars light enough to be used on the branch.

The Bogie Railcars and Trailers

Following nationalisation, EFE undertook a wholesale programme of dieselisation on all its lines during the late 1950s. Twenty-five bogie railcars were obtained from Ferrostahl, some apparently coming from the Esslingen factory while others were manufactured under license by Euskalduna of Bilbao. These were given running numbers 2001–2006 and 2011–2029, although not all of these appeared in Majorca.

The original Majorcan allocation were railcars 2001 to 2004 which arrived in 1956, entering service the following year. The original order was for five vehicles, but it seems that news of Majorca's unusual gauge failed to reach the maker, and the first unit to be delivered was metre gauge. Urgent telegrams to the factory resulted in the others having the correct wheels fitted. The Majorcan batch had been built at Esslingen (Works Nos. 23782‑56 to 23785‑56). Each was capable of carrying a total of 95 passengers (54 seated, 41 standing) and the principle dimensions were:– Overall length 15 metres; Overall width 2.45 metres; Height (above rail) 3.4 metres. Bogie centres were 10 metres apart and the bogie wheelbase was 1.6 metres. The driving controls included foot pedals for the throttle and whistle, with a manually operated gear lever and brake handle. The motors were by Bussing, capable of speeds up to 75km/hr, which had an immediately beneficial effect on the timetable.

Another railcar, number 2005, arrived in 1956, to be joined by 2006 four years later. Once on the island they had to be converted to 3ft gauge, which delayed their introduction by anything up to a year. Eventually the total rose to nine units, as 2019 arrived in 1966 with 2026 and 2027 being added in 1969. By 1979 the number had been reduced to six, three vehicles having suffered fires, and the railcars then in service were 2002, 2004‑2006, 2019 and 2027. The problem of overheating was finally cured by replacing the original 150hp. motors with 250hp Pegaso engines.

To go with the new bogie railcars five matching trailers were provided in 1956. These were distinguishable by having no headlamp above the central door in the car end, and by being numbered 5001‑5005. Originally they all had toilets and a mail section, but 5001 and 5003‑4 were rebuilt soon after their arrival to give a total passenger accommodation of 100. Additional trailers were provided as new railcars arrived – 5017 in 1966 and 5018 in 1969. For a time 5002 retained its postal compartment at one end, which was designated by the exterior end panels being painted yellow below the waist, but it was also rebuilt to match the others at the end of the 1980s, by which time all the trailers had lost their toilet compartments. Trailer 5018 was of a different design, as it had no luggage compartment, making it 2.5 metres shorter than the others. In 1982 FEVE transferred five more trailers that had become redundant on the lines in northern Spain; they were numbers 5011, 5013, 5015, 5016 and 5019. As they were all metre gauge they were laid aside for eventual conversion to Majorcan gauge, but were in fact never used, being scrapped in 1995. Although the second generation of railcars were arranged to be coupled in multiple units when necessary, the trailers had no driving controls. It was thus necessary for railcars to run round their trailers after each journey.

These units maintained the service, until several were lost when the Palma carriage shed burned down in 1990. As a result of this fire damage, two 2-car units were transferred to Majorca in August that year, having come from northern Spain where they had been displaced by electrification. They were part of a series of single railcars, originally built by MAN (and later also by Euskalduna) between 1966 and 1973.

MAN 2-car diesel unit displaying the final FEVE livery. Palma, 1992.   (AUTHOR)

Between 1983 and 1985 they were rebuilt into 2-car units and given 300hp. Pegaso motors in place of the original 150hp MAN engines, but they had the same general body style of the earlier Majorcan units, the difference being that each car had a single driving cab, with a passenger door at the other end giving access to the second car. The first arrivals were followed by a similar unit in 1992 and another the following year. Running numbers were in the 2300 series. On arrival they carried the white and yellow FEVE livery, but this was soon to give way to the all white livery with stripes of blue and green below the windows, the new colour scheme of the SFM. Following the arrival of the CAF units the MAN railcars and their surviving predecessors became redundant, and they were sold to Los Servicios Chaqeños, a rail company in Argentina.

The CAF Railcars

Not content with repainting its secondhand vehicles, the SFM soon ordered some railcars of its own. These were built by CAF and the first four new trains arrived in 1995, with two more units being added in 1997. All have a very modern appearance, with squared-off driving ends that are almost entirely glazed with dark anti-impact glass, to give maximum driver visibility as well as protection in the event of a collision. Each car is 16 metres long overall and 2.550 metres wide. Height is 3.754 externally, 2.050 internally. The bogies are set at 10.300 metre centres, the bogie wheelbase is

2.200 metres and the wheel diameter is 860mm. A dual braking system is fitted as well as pneumatic suspension. The passenger compartments are fitted with sliding doors and the interiors are air-conditioned, though this has suffered minor problems from time to time. Seating capacity is 48 in the power cars, with 78 standing, and 96 plus 156 in the trailer cars, although there are extra folding seats inside the doorways. The motors are type NTA 855 A, supplying 310kw, giving a maximum speed of 100 km/hr.

In all six trains have been provided, the first two being formed as 2-car units (61-01/61-02 and 61-03/61-04) while the rest, with the addition of a central trailer car, numbered in the 62-00 series, make up 3-car trains (61-05+62-03+61-06; 61-07+62-01+61-08; 61-09+62-02+61-10 and 61-11+62-04+61-12). The centre trailers were added for the reinstated services to Sa Pobla. In January 2002 car 61-06 was written off in an accident at Sa Pobla station, although the two other cars in the train received only minor damage and are currently in store at Son Rullan works. Meanwhile, a programme of upgrading the units was initiated, and for major rebuilding work units are sent to the CAF factory at Irun. The latest units to be returned to Palma are 61-01 and 61-02 which have received new underframes and replacement central windows. They have also been painted in the new TIB livery. In exchange, units 61-07 and 61-08 were sent to Irun at the end of February 2003.

3-car CAF unit at Son Rullan in 2003.   (AUTHOR)

Railcar Liveries

The earliest railcars on the system carried a pale blue and white livery during the railway's independent days. This may have continued to be carried after Nationalisation (evidence from contemporary colour photographs is difficult to interpret). Railcars supplied to the line by EFE and FEVE have carried five different liveries over the years. At first they were painted two-tone green with ESTADO in metal lettering on the side panels. This paint scheme was recorded on 2001 in 1960, and on 2004 and 2019 as late as 1974. However, by this latter date most of the fleet had been repainted following the change of control from EFE to FEVE, which resulted in a new livery of medium light blue with thick and thin horizontal silver stripes below window level and another thick stripe above. The roof was also silver. This scheme was certainly carried by 2004, 2005 and 2019 during the 1970s, and also by trailers 5003, 5005 and 5018.

Another version of the FEVE livery was introduced around 1980. Midnight blue lower bodywork was set off by "spilt milk" above the waist. The FEVE logo of a double-track crossover within a circle, and all the lettering and numbers were white. The final FEVE colour scheme, outshopped from 1989, was white bodywork with a simple style of lettering. Roofs were yellow. Once again there was an overlap of liveries, as a visit in December 1991 turned up one railcar still in blue and cream, while several other vehicles were still in the all blue colour scheme although these appeared to be derelict.

The change of control to SFM brought about yet another change, as some MAN units as well as the new CAF trains were turned out with white bodies with thin blue and green stripes below the windows. This also has turned out to be a short-lived colour scheme, as following the integration of all the island's publicly-owned transport under one organisation, the Transports de les Illes Balear (TIB), both buses and trains now share a similar livery. In the case of the trains this consists of a white upper body, with red and yellow panels taking up the space below the side windows. The car ends are divided vertically into a yellow area and a smaller red one. A small SFM logo appears on some windows, while the logo of the TIB is carried on the side panels behind the driver's door, and on the front end yellow panels. This colour scheme first appeared in 2002, and by early 2003 only 61-03, 61-09 and 61-10 were still in the earlier colours, being due for a repaint on their next overhaul later in the year.

The Diesel Locomotives

During the final years of steam operation up to the final withdrawal of freight services there were four 675hp B-B type diesels at work on the system. They formed part of a series of 20 locomotives originally ordered by the Spanish Ministry of Public Works from the Sociedad Española de Construccion Naval and built under license

An unidentified Creusot diesel, en-route for Arta, pauses at Inca. (M. SWIFT)

from Le Creusot, of which half (numbers 1101-1110) were diesel hydraulic, while the rest were diesel electric (1151-1160). The Majorcan locomotives were of the first type and were numbers 1101-1104. They carried the EFE green livery and the first three went into service in 1959, joined by 1104 the following year. They were locally known as "The Creusots". Their maximum speed was 70 km/hr and they were fitted with a dual brake system – air brakes on the locomotive and vacuum brakes for the train. Despite these advantages they weighed 52 tonnes, with an axle load of 13 tonnes compared with 9.5 tonnes on the largest steam locomotives. This turned out to be too heavy for the Majorcan tracks, some of which had to be strengthened for them; in fact they were banned from certain areas altogether. Besides being prone to damaging the track and the occasional derailment they were also heavy on fuel. At first they were employed on passenger services, hauling the Carde bogie coaches, but as their shortcomings became apparent they were down-graded to goods services after 1964, having become unpopular with the public (!). Two engines (1102 and 1104) were returned to the mainland in 1965, where they went to the Cantabrian system, while the other two stayed to eke out their days on freight workings, but when these ended in 1967 they no longer had an effective role and were laid aside – one can imagine with a prayer of thanks from the operating staff. They were still to be seen in store at Palma as late as 1974, though they had been scrapped by the end of the decade.

In 1981 another diesel was introduced. It was a metre gauge six-coupled Batignolles locomotive, built by CAF in 1960, being capable of 70 km/hr in passenger service and 40 km/hr on goods trains. It was a member of another FEVE "standard" class, and similar locomotives have worked on the Alicante-Denia line, among others. The Majorcan example is numbered 1207 and still carries the light blue FEVE livery of the

Batignolles-CAF shunter, No. 1207, pauses between shunting moves at Palma in 1981. As usual it is lacking its side panels. (AUTHOR)

1970s, although it was usually to be seen running without its bonnet side-panels. Its first duties were working on early track re-gauging p.w trains, though later one of the Esslingen-style railcars took over some of these duties. Originally it had also been intended for the proposed coal trains to serve the power station at Es Murtera, but as these never materialised it has seen little use since the gauge conversion was completed, and is at present undergoing prolonged rebuilding work in the Son Rullan workshops.

The latest acquisition is a small four-wheeled diesel shunter, built by CAF under license from General Electric. Built in 1971, its number/maker's plate reads: – Fabricada por CAF Beasain/No. 14 1971/Bajo Contracto Asistencia Tecnica GE USA.

Other Motive Power

Various other items have been employed from time to time on the system, especially in connection with the conversion of the railway to metre gauge. At different times since 1981 a Matissa ballast tamper, a Plasser track tester, a rail profiler and an unidentified self-propelled rail-lorry have been sighted, all painted in Vias y Obras (permanent way department) yellow livery, although they were operated by the contractor, COMSA, and when the initial gauge conversion was complete they appear to have been transferred elsewhere. The reconstruction of the Sa Pobla section made use of a small four-wheeled diesel, also owned by COMSA, of unknown manufacture.

In earlier times the V y O department owned a selection of powered trolleys that do not appear to have survived the change of gauge. Two were built at Palma in the 1950s with Isso motors hung beneath the chassis and bench seating for the track gang on an

Matisa ballast tamper at work at Consell y Alaró in 1981. Note the operator's appropriate safety clothing!
(AUTHOR)

Contractor's diesel resting at Inca in 2000, during the rebuilding of the Sa Pobla branch.   (AUTHOR)

The new GE diesel at Son Rullan, 2003.   (AUTHOR)

open platform. They were based at Llubi and Santa Maria. Another pair of draisines were bought from Eyher and were kept at Lluchmayor and Manacor. These were of a different pattern, and had a small bonnet enclosing the 2-speed motor at the front of the chassis, with a transverse seat for the driver and a low-sided open body behind containing more seating. Finally, there was another vehicle formerly in use on the railway, this being a Renault inspection car similar to one in use on the FC de Soller. The FC de Mallorca's manager was so impressed with the original conversion that he asked for another for himself. It was built in the Soller's workshops in 1945 and used by the manager to travel between Palma and his estate at Arta. Painted in carriage brown, it was known as "The Climent", after its builder, Climent Hernàndez. Though by now derelict it was still in evidence inside the Palma roundhouse in the late 1970s.

Road Vehicles

In addition to their railway stock, the company also owned a small collection of road vehicles. In the 1920s two 18hp Fordson tractors were acquired and used to position wagons on the Palma dockside sidings. They were fitted with heavy beams across the front of the radiator to assist with these duties. The company also owned a couple of elderly lorries dating back to the 1930s, which were used for parcel deliveries around Palma. All were still garaged in the roundhouse at Palma in the 1970s, though by this time they were out of use.

Chapter 4

The Rolling Stock of the FC de Mallorca

Passenger Vehicles

The first coaches obtained for the opening of the line came from Brown Marshall of Birmingham. They were four-wheeled compartment vehicles offering Preferente (First Class) and General (Second Class) accommodation. A total of ten of these were supplied for the opening, together with five Second Class coaches, which arrived shortly afterwards. In 1876 a further ten vehicles entered service, seemingly including a saloon coach which was used by the King on his visit to the island that same year. For the opening of the La Puebla line 1878 the company ordered twenty more carriages, comprising two First Class, four Composites and fourteen Second Class vehicles, and these came from the Swansea Wagon Co. The initial order had omitted any brake vans, but now some were provided. While almost all had roof-top birdcage look-outs, an early batch received from Brown Marshall had duckets in the guard's compartment,

Three Brown Marshall coaches and a Spanish-built brake van. Palma, 1957.   (L. G. MARSHALL)

Coach No. 3, the "Royal" saloon, in 1960. The vacuum pipes and end doors (presumably a later addition) seem to indicate that it may have been in use as a trailer with one of the De Dion railcars.　(M. SWIFT)

and one can be discerned in a photograph of a train at La Puebla in the 1950s. At least one of the signed Brown Marshall designs shows buttoned, upholstered seating in Second Class and bare boards in Third. Evidence seems to suggest that this accommodation was re-classified as First and Second Class, and while Third Class carriages also feature in Brown Marshall's designs they appear not to have been built, in the early days at least. It was not until the concession for the Santany line was granted that the company was obliged to cater for this class. Another design was a Second/Third Class coach with a roof-top shelter for a brakeman at one end. Despite the Directors' signatures on this plan it is possible that the design was modified before production and the roof-top seat deleted, possibly to save money; however, a carriage with similar window spacing appears to have survived to the 1950s. The earliest carriages were all four-wheeled and had wooden underframes. As designed they had fully panelled sides, though later batches may have been supplied with matchboard lower panels (possibly a less costly option) in which condition the survivors were photographed in the 1950s. A second roof was fitted to protect the occupants from the sun's heat. Livery was brown.

By 1878 more carriages were needed, and at first the company planned to buy the parts for 10 four-wheelers from the Swansea Wagon Co. However, Palma experienced supply difficulties in obtaining the timber to finish these vehicles locally, and instead the order was changed to six complete six-wheeled carriages, which went into service the following year. Despite their Cleminson wheel arrangement there were problems with these vehicles, which were prone to minor derailments, and they became little used. They appear to have been scrapped or modified at an indeterminate date and by 1951 only one was still showing on the stock list; it, too, had gone by 1960. Two others may have been rebuilt as "special wagons" as two such six-wheelers were recorded in a wagon census in the 1940s. The final order from England was the ironwork for a batch of 10 carriages, which arrived in 1904.

Although there was no official Third Class when the railway opened, there were times when the company wished to cater for low-fare passengers at prices below its Second Class tariffs. The first instance of this was following the opening of the Inca line, when there was a massive demand for seats, to which the company responded by converting several high-sided open wagons into toast-rack vehicles. These lasted from 1875 until 1877 when they were returned to goods service. Similar temporary conversions were again carried out in the early years, and also in connection with the state visit to the island by King Alfonso XIII in 1904, though this may have been the last time this "Fourth Class" accommodation was provide, as by now some enclosed Third Class carriages had begun to arrive from England. Later, when the company tried to lure the last passengers away from the road diligences, four vehicles known as "passenger wagons" were provided, which were said to be only really suitable for shorter journeys on the line. They must have been basic indeed, looking more like goods vans than coaches, having heavy external bracing with diagonal stays on the lower panels. There was a central doorway flanked by small windows, with solid upper panelling at the corners. Inside there were six longitudinal benches and the maximum height was less than 6ft internally. In 1903 some "official" Third Class coaches were provided and by 1908 there were 14 of them in service, though this total may have included the passenger wagons, which were later withdrawn. The new Thirds' dimensions were still restricted, and when they were used for the opening of the Santany line, owing to the delayed arrival of newer carriages, the local Lluchmayor paper commented that one could not stand upright inside them, and sitting was hardly less uncomfortable, particularly when crowded. Pressure on the company mounted and the earliest Third Class vehicles were taken out of service in the 1920s, leaving only the five latecomers.

Eventually there were sixty coaches in use on the main line as well as the branches to La Puebla and Felanitx. These comprised four First Class saloons and seven other First Class coaches as well as sixteen First/Second Composites, three of which also had guard's accommodation. There were twenty-eight Second Class coaches, including three with brake compartments and eight others with postal facilities, plus the surviving though temperamental six-wheeled vehicles. The Postal/2nd Class coaches became favourites for use as railcar trailers on the Felanitx branch in later times. The

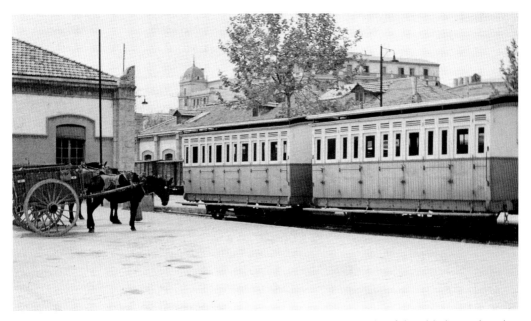

A study in patience, as two mules wait for their next load beside a couple of the elderly coaches that were spruced up in the 1950s to act as tourist carriers between Palma and Arenal.　(P. K. WIDD)

five remaining Third Class coaches had been retired by 1933, although two of them found a final existence on the Alaró Tramway. Lighting in earlier times was by acetylene lamps – one per compartment in First Class, two to a coach in Second and Third Class. Later, after 1913, electric light was provided with the power coming from a battery in the Guard's van. Continuous brakes were only fitted to the original coaches in the 1930s, and there is some pictorial evidence to suggest that it was later out of use though the carriages were still in service.

Because of the outbreak of war, the company had to approach Spanish suppliers to stock the new line to Santany in 1916. Carde y Escoriaza of Saragossa built two First Class and two composite First/Second coaches, while CAF, Beasain, produced three more Seconds (one of them with a postal compartment) and seven Brake/Third Class coaches, one of which was also equipped to carry mail in a separate compartment at the opposite end to the guard's van. All these had steel underframes and were longer than the British-built vehicles. The Brake/3rds were Spartan vehicles as their passenger compartments only had windows in the compartment doors. The main line coaches merely carried numbers, but the Santany line's coaches were numbered in a separate series with a letter prefix denoting the type of vehicles. These were A – First Class, B – First/Second composites, C – Second Class, and D – Third Class. By 1960 of all the four-wheeled passenger stock there remained twenty-nine main line and six Santany coaches still in service, but these were all retired when the Creusot diesels took over passenger services.

During the 1930s fourteen luxurious bogie carriages were provided by Carde y Escoriaza. These had vestibule ends with wrought iron balconies as well as central doors, and came in two varieties – First/Second Composite and all Second Class. The last survivor, number 107, is a composite and shows that the three First Class compartments, whose well-padded seats are upholstered in moquette, had a tiny side corridor giving access to a toilet next to the centre door. At the other end of the coach the Second Class compartment was a saloon fitted with comfortable armchairs, though others of this type had two seats on either side of a central walkway. This accommodation was far superior to the normal Seconds and a supplementary fare was payable for its use. The Composites were numbered 101-108, while the Seconds were numbers 109-114. The new coaches weighed around 20 tonnes, but carried fewer passengers than the FC de Soller's coaches which weighed 5 tons less. This lack of capacity caused the re-allocation of the Second Class seating in the 1950s to give eight more places in the Composites and eighteen extra seats in the other vehicles.

The bogie coaches remained in use until the Creusot diesels were withdrawn, when they were abandoned in the goods yard at Palma. In 1978 almost all were scrapped with the exception of 107, which is preserved at Son Rullan workshops.

Brake Vans

In the railway's earliest days there were no brake vans, although six of the line's eight vans were converted to act as brakes for the first couple of years. The first purpose-built vehicles arrived from the Swansea Carriage & Wagon Co. in 1877, followed by further lots of four from other manufacturers in each of the two following years. After this, further examples were constructed at Palma until there were eventually thirty brake vans which were used on both passenger and freight services, though their construction was more akin to goods vehicles, with horizontal planking and vertical metal angle strapping. There were several batches with minor design differences, one being the change from wooden underframes to steel in later examples. All had a birdcage look-out, and a central pair of sliding doors giving access to the goods section, which had a capacity of 3 tons. The raised floor beneath the Guard's look-out was used to provide a dog-box, which had small barred doors on the exterior of the vehicle. Numbering was in the F-series (Furgón = Brake Van), though the seven brakes built at Palma in 1916/17 for the Santany line were numbered in the S-series. Later in the 1930s three of the Santany line's Third Class coaches were rebuilt as brake vans, with vertical matchboard bodies, and these were given E-series numbers. They had postal compartments and toilets, and the end doors had fall-plates to allow access between the vehicles when used with the new bogie coaches. After withdrawal one of the vans was removed to Cala S'Almonia and converted into a house.

The last surviving Carde coach, AB107, on display at Palma in 1997. Trailers 5003 and 5001 beyond.

(M. BUNCH)

Brake van E2, one of 3 vans that were rebuilt from Santany-line coaches, for use with the Carde bogie carriages.

(M. ANDRESS)

Goods Stock

The railway was abundantly provided with wagons, which numbered 576 in the 1930s. Although this appears to be a generous total, it had to encompass traffic moving over the various lines and also the wagons being loaded and unloaded at stations throughout the system, and on private sidings, not forgetting the vehicles working on the Soller and Alaró lines. The initial order from Brown Marshall was for 35 vehicles, which were quickly followed by 20 more, supplied in kit form, which were erected at Palma. Following this another batch were obtained secondhand. For the La Puebla and Felanitx lines the company used Swansea Wagon Co. and the Lancaster Wagon Co. as well as other unspecified British firms. It is also likely that Palma Works was also building wagons during the 1880s. The final British wagons to arrive on the island were a batch of 50, which were supplied by Pickering in 1913, after which CAF and other Spanish firms were patronised. Meanwhile, Palma Workshops were responsible for another 70 wagons built during the 1920s. With few exceptions the company's wagons were four-wheeled vehicles that carried a payload of 7 tonnes. During the early years wagons were provided with wooden underframes, but steel was used for later vehicles.

To augment the lack of brake vans in the early days many of the original wagons had been fitted with vertical brake standards and seats for the brakemen (84 opens and 56 vans), which must have been uncomfortable, if not actually dangerous, in adverse weather conditions. To ease this situation it was proposed in later years to add brake cabins to 103 of the wagons, but this was never officially approved. Nevertheless a couple of wagons did get experimental cabins in 1933 (open A173 and van C161). The rest of the wagons had traditional brake levers.

By 1930 the railway owned 139 high-sided open wagons, 173 low drop-side wagons, 184 vans, 22 cattle trucks, six bolsters, and two bogie and 49 four-wheeled flat trucks. This list was augmented by a hearse wagon and two breakdown vans fitted out to deal with minor accidents. The late 1950s saw the number drop sharply, almost 100 wagons being scrapped over a period of six years. By 1968 all that were left were seven vans, 13 high-sided opens, 30 lowsides and 23 flat trucks. After goods traffic ceased almost all were scrapped except for a handful of lowsides and flats, which were retained for p.w. work, though not all of these were converted to metre gauge and lingered on in the derelict 3ft gauge sidings in Palma works for some time after gauge conversion.

Series A. Open wagons (1-98, 150-174, 201-216)

These were originally a Brown Marshall design having bow ends, diagonal planking and outside wooden bracing. Cupboard-style doors were fitted. Another variant had sides of five horizontal planks with metal angle bracing. Of the total, 42 had screw brakes, the remainder having brake levers. The axle boxes were joined with a tie-bar and had small W-irons; the wheelbase was 2.133m, External body length was 3,963m. and the sides were 0.915m. high. The bow ends were 3.963m high and 1.980m wide. The spoked wheels were a nominal 600mm in diameter. The A-series was mainly used for coal traffic but they could sometimes be seen loaded with firewood.

Series B. Drop-side Wagons (1-140, 301-333)

These two-plank drop-side wagons were used for the carriage of general goods. Pictures show them loaded with manure, bundles of timber (possibly firewood), stone building blocks, and in the case of B41 a cylindrical tank for weed killer.

Originally the series started as a Brown Marshall design with the same length and width as the A-series vehicles (including numbers B27 and B30). Later examples built by CAF retained the vertical brake at first but lengthened the chassis to 5.180m with a wheelbase measuring 2.490m. A total of 127 were fitted with brake levers acting on one wheel on one side of the wagon only; the remainder had screw brakes.

In 2002, four had survived and were stored out of use at Son Rullan. Most of them had had two vertical posts, made of old rail, welded to the metal buffer beams. These had presumably been added to aid their final work in transporting sleepers during the track re-gauging work during the 1980s.

Palma goods yard, 1960. The Tangye crane and assorted goods wagons, including van C158, with a high-level brakeman's seat built into the bodywork. (M. SWIFT)

Series C. Goods Vans. (1-132, 150-174, 201-227)

In the railway's earliest years no brake vans were provided and the goods vans performed this function, only two of them being recorded as general freight carriers in the Annual Report of 1877. The original design was for a 12-plank vehicle with external wooden bracing and a sliding door on each side. A sample number of this original style is C86. The body was unusual in being as wide as it was high – these were low vehicles so as to give sufficient headroom for the brakeman seated on the roof. Another variation was a low-bodied van with a brake lever, as typified by vans C57, C80 and C97.

Yet another style of van is typified by C5, C9 and C158, all of which were high-bodied vans of 19 planks whose brakeman's seat was let into the bodywork so that the brake handle only just cleared the peak of the roof. In addition there was also a ventilation hatch covered by a vertically sliding metal plate at the opposite end to the brake equipment. Yet another type had a high body together with a solebar brake lever. At least one of this group had no hatch (C27), while another had a narrow hatch with two bars and no metal cover plate. Fifty-six of these vans had screw brakes, while the rest had brake levers at solebar level.

Series D. Cattle Wagons. (1-22)

These vans had a semi-open body with 15 horizontal slats approximately 75mm wide separated by gaps measuring 50mm. The earlier examples had wooden underframes, and wooden bracing for the body which had diagonal bracing bars below waist height. These wagons were 4.270 metres long (over solebars). A later batch had metal underframes that were 4.420 metres long. These had metal body strapping, but without the diagonal bracing. All were fitted with brake levers at solebar level.

Series G. Workshop Auxiliary Wagons (1-2)

In addition to the regular goods vans, two similar vehicles were fitted out with emergency equipment for use in case of derailments. They lasted until the 1960s, when they were withdrawn and a Third Class coach from the Santany line (D2) was converted to act as the breakdown wagon; this lasted until the end of the 1970s.

Series P, R and T. Flat Wagons (P1-6, 11-12; R 1-2; T1-49)

These three classes were all flat wagons, though the Ps had a single swivelling bolster at one time, later removed. Early examples had the short chassis (P6 was a late survivor), while P1, 3, 5 and 11 were the long wheelbase variety. During the 1950s wagon P3 was fitted out as a weed-killing spray wagon with a 3 cubic metre tank and a

The weed-killing tank wagon, P.3 and a trio of brake vans. Palma, 1960.   (M. ANDRESS)

pump mechanism, and survived in this form until at least the mid-1980s. One of the dropside opens, B41, also gained a tank and was used to supplement the capacity of the spray wagon.

The two R-series vehicles were unique to the island as they were the only bogie goods wagons owned by the FC de Mallorca. Their main dimensions were:– body length 7.60m., bogie centres 4.60m., bogie wheelbase 1.220m, wheel diameter 0.760m. The wagons were 2 metres wide. A brake lever was fitted to each bogie, the lever projecting towards the centre of the wagon with the pivot crank working the brake shoes being on the outer end of the bogie frame. A line of four ringbolts along the side frame enabled the load to be roped down for transit. These details are based on R2, which was measured at Palma in 1984; at this time it still had 3ft gauge wheels fitted. Since then it appears to have been scrapped.

Miscellaneous Rolling Stock of the FC de Mallorca

Mobile Crane. A small crane, built by Tangye of Birmingham, was mounted on a very short flat wagon and used around the yard at Palma to unload goods and stores. No couplings were fitted.

Hearse Wagon. This seems to have been converted from a goods van. It was painted black and was lined with fringed black velvet inside, with four large candlesticks at the corners of the bier. When needed, it was run in a special train along with a carriage for the mourners and a brake van. No fare was charged for its use.

Metre Gauge Rolling Stock Imported From Other FEVE Lines.

Hopper Wagons. In about 1981 four metre gauge hopper wagons were brought to Majorca from the FC Sierra Menera, for use in ballasting the renewed metre gauge track. One subsequently suffered a broken axle and was laid aside, while the others have been given a coat of yellow paint since their arrival in Palma. Since the mid-1980s their number has been reduced again, and the two survivors now form part of the SFM's equipment roster, although they are currently stored off the rails in the yard at Son Rullan. These hoppers appear to have last been used by the contractors for the reinstatement of the Sa Pobla line, where they were joined by at least two bogie hoppers, the property of COMSA, who removed them when the contract was completed.

Tool Coach. Also belonging to the Brigada de Vias y Obras (p.w. dept.) is a clerestory bogie coach, which originally had formed part of an electrical multiple unit dating from 1927, latterly running on the Valencia suburban system, although it had its origins on a Portuguese line. In 1981, newly arrived on the island, it still retained its original dark though somewhat faded green livery with a yellow stripe below the windows, but by 1984 it too had received a coat of yellow paint with black warning chevrons at each end, together with steel plates or heavy metal mesh protecting the side windows. The inside has been gutted to make a mobile tool store. Since the 1980s it has suffered badly at the hands of graffiti artists.

The two surviving hoppers; originally they worked on the FC Sierra Menera, hauling ore.   (AUTHOR)

In 1981 the p.w. coach still carried its original green livery. Next to it is the unique "tall" open wagon, No. M10.   (AUTHOR)

Open Wagon. Finally there was an odd open wagon, numbered M10, seen at Palma in 1981, which carried no other identifying marks. It had no brakes at all, and the body sat much higher than any of the other wagons. On arrival the couplings were lowered to match the rest of the Majorcan stock. It does not appear to have survived the FEVE era.

A Note on Couplings

The FC de Mallorca always used "chopper" style couplings whose centre line was set at 0.670m above rail height. On most vehicles the top of the hook was swept back into a loop that provided a convenient grip when coupling up. In addition there was originally a light chain about 30cms in length, with a small ball-shaped weight at the end, hanging from the shank of each coupling – possibly this was to wrap around the coupled choppers to stop them being jolted apart. Side chains were also provided for increased safety. The MTM locomotives were additionally provided with a coupling hook and screw coupling set below the chopper and this became standard for later locomotives. The bogie coaches certainly had similar dual couplings and the Santany coaches may have been similarly fitted. There was no incentive to add this sophistication to the wagon fleet, which in a mixed train would bring up the rear of the train. However, at least one van was fitted out with a screw coupling and was pictured in the FC de Soller's yard at Palma in the 1950s. Presumably this was to facilitate through running between the two systems, as FC de Mallorca vehicles regularly ran through to Soller.

KEY TO STATION LAYOUT PLANS

A	Staff Accommodation	**P**	Pointsman's Hut	**Palma Workshops**	
C	Coaling Stage	**PTA**	Prefabricated Track Assembly Area	**1**	Power House
CL	Coal Wharf			**2**	Wheel Shop
CP	Cattle Pens	**R**	Railcar Shed	**3**	Forge
CS	Carriage Shed	**S**	Shed/store	**4**	Mechanical Workshop
D	Dwelling	**SB**	Station Building		
E	Engine Shed	**T**	Toilets	**5**	Boiler Shop
F	Forge	**TS**	Tram Shed	**6**	Wagon Workshop
G	Goods Shed	**V**	Permanent Way Department	**7**	Carpenters' Workshop
H	Hotel				
Ind	Industrial Buildings	**W**	Water Tank/column	**8**	Coach Workshop
K	Kiosk	**WR**	Railcar Washer		
L	Loading Platform	**Wks**	Workshops		
O	Offices	**X**	Crossing Keeper's Hut		

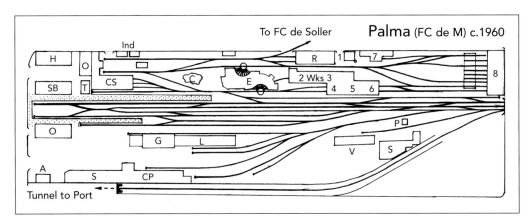

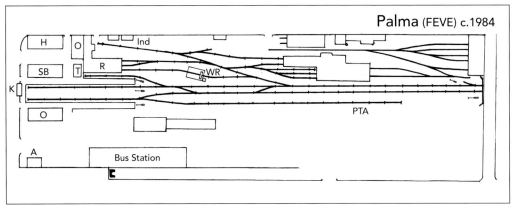

Chapter 5

The Route Described

Author's note

For just over the first 100 years of its life the FC de Mallorca remained much the same, after which a period of major changes to the infrastructure began, culminating in the wholesale rebuilding of the Palma terminus at the start of the 21st century. For this reason it is hard to provide a complete description of some areas without appearing muddled, and where there are appreciable differences in the following descriptions they have been divided into different eras. Despite the re-development of the currently closed sections of line, hopefully what follows will remain recognisable for some time to come.

In the following descriptions the use of the words Right, Left, Down, Facing, Trailing all apply to trains travelling from Palma toward the outer terminus.

Palma station 1875/c.1999

The original station of Palma was built just outside the northern extremity of the city. This was at the insistence of the War Ministry who stipulated a distance of 150 metres between the old town walls, then in ruins, and the new railway installations.

The original station building on via 2 at Palma. (AUTHOR)

At the same time, the station buildings were limited to a single storey to avoid providing a vantage point or shelter for enemy marksmen. Eventually with more peaceful times this area in front of the town became a large square, the Plaza España, and it is here that the stations of the island's two railways can still be found. The FC de Mallorca station had two platforms, serving four tracks, which were shaded by plane trees. Both platforms were flanked at their inner end by station buildings, that on the right-hand platform (via 1) housing the offices of the various operating departments. The opposite platform (via 2) had a short bay alongside it (via 3). The building on this side of the station included the General Waiting Room, Booking Office and the office of the Jefe de Estación (Stationmaster). Both structures were given hipped roofs with Grecian-style acanthus leaf decorative plaques at the corners. The walls were whitewashed and the woodwork of the doorways and window shutters was painted green. In addition on the western platform there was a toilet block, beside which was the carriage shed which spanned three roads flanking the bay platform. In former times each of the longer platforms had an engine release line, which met to form two linked tracks in the centre of the station. These lines were often left full of goods wagons and partly made up trains during the less busy times of the day, when mule carts were driven across the tracks to unload directly from the newly arrived goods wagons.

The western side of the station yard was once almost wholly taken up with the facilities for servicing and maintaining the line's motive power and rolling stock. At one

Palma roundhouse: Winter 1955. Nasmyth Wilson 4-6-0T ALGAIDA and a Palma-built 4-4-0T await the next call of duty.   (AUTHOR'S COLLECTION)

time there was a double roundhouse served by a pair of turntables but after the demise of steam power this was replaced by a single-ended running shed for the railcar fleet, behind which a single line threaded its way through the workshop area. At one time there was a gateway in the perimeter wall with a connecting line giving access to the FC de Soller, whose tracks run down the street outside. Until the cessation of goods traffic, the goods yard filled the eastern side of the station layout, though latterly the only reminder of this traffic was the capacious goods shed, by now devoid of tracks, which remained in place until almost the end of the 20th century.

At the outer end of the yard four tracks originally left the station. The centre two were the main line, and it should be noted that the railway has always run right-handed – that is trains departing to Inca or beyond take the right hand line (Ascendente), while trains arriving from the outer destinations (Descendente) come in on the left-hand line. The exception was the connection to Santany, which was used by traffic in both directions and was in effect a single track branch which started at the outer end of the goods yard, where it also acted as a headshunt clear of any main line trains. Just beyond the road bridge which marks the outer end of the station, a fourth line turned off from the Descendente line to serve several private sidings, among them a wine warehouse and an industrial zone, whose name "La Fertilizadora" hints at its main product. After about 0.5km this siding turned through about 90 degrees to the left and split to run on either side of a large building; on one side there was a run-round loop and a short dead end siding was also provided, on the other merely two long sidings. Another private industry was tucked into a corner of the station yard between the carriage shed and the perimeter wall:– this was a mason's yard where stone was sawn into building blocks, though by the early 1980s it had become a depot selling general building supplies.

At the outermost end of the goods yard a trailing connection off the Santany branch led to a single line which swung off at an angle across the top of the goods yard, but once parallel to the nearby road, began a steep descent to vanish into a tunnel that eventually brought the tracks to the dockside a short distance east of the cathedral. Today the seaward end of this tunnel is closed by locked gates, however a nice touch is provided above the tunnel mouth by a relief carving showing one of the Nasmyth Wilson 4-4-0 engines hauling a train of vans. This medallion is garlanded with fruit and a plaque shows the construction date, 1932. The spoil from the tunnel, which is 1.25kms in length, was used to reclaim part of the foreshore where a marshalling yard of five parallel loop tracks was laid out. At one time a passenger station was planned here, but this never materialised, falling a victim to changing plans following the Civil War. Beyond the loops the line split to serve the southern and eastern wharves of the main harbour, and a triangle of lines was provided to turn the larger engines that could now reach the harbour.

Such was the steam-era layout of the capital's terminus. The advent of diesel railcars together with the end of goods traffic brought about various subtle changes in the

Palma yard in the winter of 1957, with a Nasmyth locomotive shunting in the middle-distance. The wagons on the right are awaiting attention from the fitters in the workshops.　　(AUTHOR'S COLLECTION)

The same view as above, but taken 31 years later with the new metre gauge main line in place. To the left is the area where the track was pre-constructed, before being shipped to the railhead. On the right, the works yard is still laid to 3ft gauge.　　(AUTHOR)

3ft gauge as certain tracks became disused and vanished under the ballast which over the years had become a mixture of stone, earth and coal dust covering the sleepers to rail-top height. The engine release lines between the platforms were simplified and eventually most of the goods yard was lost beneath a concrete apron that was laid down for a new bus station.

Yet more radical changes came with the change to metre gauge, which caused a wholesale sweeping away of all traces of the former layout and the demolition of the old steam roundhouse, which photographs taken in 1979 show had fallen into a rather ruinous state. Work started in 1980 and by the following year the basics of the new formation were nearing completion, although services were still being worked by 3ft gauge stock. The site of the goods yard was covered with a huge heap of old rails lifted from around the yard and out along the main line to Inca, and where the goods yard headshunt had been there remained only a short length of unconnected 3ft gauge track providing a resting place for the last surviving F-series brake van.

Three years later the metre gauge was well established, and the station layout almost complete apart from the line through the workshops, which was still laid in 3ft gauge track. During this interim period, if a railcar needed heavy maintenance it had to be jacked up and have its bogies replaced to allow it into the works. A carriage washer had been built on via 6, one of the approach roads to the old carriage shed, while a kick-back siding from via 1 now served a construction area, complete with tower crane and large stocks of new rails, for pre-fabricated trackwork. The self-propelled track testing vehicles and rail lorries seen in 1981 were still in evidence. By now all trains were running on the metre gauge, which was double track for about half the distance to Inca. Trains could use both tracks as far as Santa Maria although beyond this only one line was operational. Trains were crossing at Santa Maria, and though loops were also provided at Consell y Alaró and Lloseta these did not seem to be in use.

For the first time in the railway's history comprehensive signalling had been introduced with 3-aspect electric signals. Control of the station's turnouts remained as ground throw levers beside the lines, though a new pattern of lever was in use, somewhat similar to those on the FC de Soller.

One final change to the station's infrastructure came about accidentally. Following a fire, which destroyed the carriage shed, the lines leading to it were shortened to provide berthing sidings for the 2-car trains that had by then started operating. The spare area was paved over and a small cafe-bar installed. As things turned out this was not destined to last long.

Palma, 2000 onwards

The station currently used by the SFM's trains is a product of the 21st century. A new plan to integrate the local transport links has resulted in a bus station being built

Two CAF trains ready to leave Palma, in 2001.   (AUTHOR)

The re-aligned approach to the new station at Palma has meant the demolition of some of the old running sheds and workshop buildings.   (AUTHOR)

on the site of the old carriage repair yard in the workshop area, which has retained the old carriage workshop building. Almost all the other workshops and running sheds have been swept away, and the running lines have been slewed over to serve a new station built on the site of the former stonemason's yard and the steam engine coaling roads. There is an island platform, which at first was open to the sky, but which has now been provided with a sloping roof supported on inclined girders. The pedestrian approach to this is by way of the courtyard of the Hostal Terminus. Approaching the station, the two running lines split apart a short distance before the platform and there is a berthing siding between them, with connections to both lines that lead directly into a scissors cross-over at the end of the platforms. The former station yard has been landscaped with hillocks and trees to form Station Park and there is a sloping walkway and footbridge connecting the park with the street beyond the station. The two original station buildings have been left in place and by 2002 what the local paper described as a "pergola" had been erected in the space between them, covering the former platform area.

PALMA TO INCA

The present journey between Palma and Inca, while being of some interest to the narrow gauge fan, had only limited appeal for the railway historian. The gauge conversion coming on top of over fifteen years of operation by diesel railcars has wiped away many of the original features of the line; however, echoes of the past can still be picked up here and there.

Son Rullan workshops, 2003.   (AUTHOR)

Sa Pobla-bound CAF unit arriving at Verge de Lluch station, 2003.   (AUTHOR)

The initial run out of Palma is arrow-straight through the industrialised suburbs of the capital. Just before Pont D'Inca (4kms) the Santany branch turned away to the right on a south-easterly course which can still clearly be seen on a map of the city where a road curves away from the main line towards a new motorway over-pass. The station building at Pont D'Inca is a large one, with a two-storey central section and two wings which run back from the line of the platform. Provision of freight sidings was fairly minimal, although there was formerly a goods shed on the right-hand side and a kick-back siding serving the large Farinera Mallorquina flour mill.

Shortly afterwards the line curves round to the right and the new workshops and running sheds of Son Rullan have been built on land that was formerly a military hospital. There are access lines at both ends of the works yard, but the main sidings face towards Palma, while the workshop tracks are reached by a reversing move. A fuelling point is located near the main line, which is separated from the yard by a wall. Beyond Son Rullan the railway runs through an area of apartment buildings and there is a steep underpass that must once have been a level crossing, followed immediately by a new halt, Verge del Lluch. Within sight of this halt is a level crossing with automatic barriers and another halt, Pont D'Inca Nou, which was opened in 2002, while yet another new halt has been opened a short distance further on. Known at first as Fira de Fang, it has been renamed Polígon Marratxi, and serves the local trading estate and an area of new housing. After this there is a more curving section of line before the train arrives at Marratxi (9kms). From here a gentle, but none-the-less steady climb starts until the summit of 158 metres is reached just beyond Consell y Alaró. Beyond Marratxi a stopping place known as La Bomba came into use in 1877. It was situated at a level crossing and served the hamlet of Marratxinet, however, traffic must have been disappointing as the halt was closed in 1879.

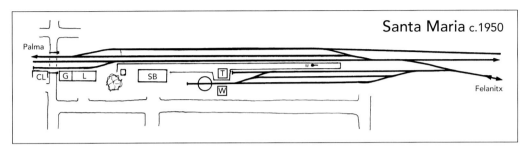

Santa Maria (14kms) was the most important stop in this section, as it was the junction for the line to Felanitx. In steam days there were three tracks through the station; the centre one was linked to both of the running lines by trailing connections, being mainly used by goods trains during shunting moves to allow following passenger trains to overtake. The branch line connection came just after the platform and there were trailing lines running into a bay platform for the Felanitx services, which in early days terminated here. A turntable and coal and watering facilities were provided, but

La Bomba, seen here in later days with Palma-bound MAN units passing, was a halt for a short while in the 1870s.

(A. SANCHIS COLLECTION)

Automatic barriers at Santa Maria in 1988. Not as romantic as the old hand-powered ones, but less work.
(AUTHOR)

there were only limited goods facilities comprising a short siding serving the goods shed and a domestic coal wharf. Today the two running lines pass straight through, although there are cross-overs at each end of the station.

The next station, originally Consell and now known as Consell y Alaró (19kms), was once the junction for the line serving Alaró, which closed in 1935. The first metre gauge layout included a loop serving a new island platform on the Ascendente side, the Descendente line passing straight through, but today the loop turnout at the Palma end of the station has been removed to leave a dead-end siding. In steam days the goods yard consisted of a single siding running off the main line behind the station building where it became part of the Alaró line. At first goods facilities never amounted to more than an open platform alongside this connecting line, but later a small goods shed and loading bank appeared, together with a couple of dead-end sidings.

On leaving Consell the summit of the original section is passed, and the line starts to fall slightly towards the next stop Binisalem (22kms). Today there is little more than the platform and the refurbished station building, but formerly there were trailing sidings on both sides of the line, that on the station side leading back to a coal wharf situated just before the buffers, and with two kick back roads running behind the platform serving the goods shed and loading bank. For most of the journey so far the railway and the road have kept relatively close company. Now they separate, the railway running through an area of fruit trees to reach the town of Lloseta (26kms), which has

Binisalem station, newly restored in 1981. This building is identical to the one at Santa Maria. (AUTHOR)

the usual two-storey station building and a loop similar to the one at Consell. Once again, this was a more important station in the past, being the railhead for a local colliery which used a long coal wharf situated on a siding facing Palma. At the Inca end of the station, a private siding served a cement works. On the other side of the main line were two long sidings for general goods traffic, with the usual goods shed being provided.

INCA 1875/c.1999

The railway enters Inca (29kms) on a right hand curve from the west. At the Palma end of the yard is a level crossing, and in steam days shortly after this on the right was the turntable and a long siding ending in a locomotive shed. On old plans there was also a large building marked as a carriage shed, though the track arrangement shown in the plan is conjecture, as the old plans do not show any access for coaches. Opposite this shed was an island platform, with beyond it the Descendente line and a longer platform serving the large station building. At the Palma end of this platform was a small water tank, originally set on a hexagonal stone base. Later this was replaced with another small tank that was fed from a larger stone tank, which formed the roof of the office at the end of the adjacent goods shed. Behind the platform was a rather bare looking two-storey building that provided staff accommodation. The station building was also a large two-storey affair with roof-corner decorations to match those at Palma. At one time there was a bar at the Palma end of the building, which appeared to have been added during the 1960s. The original goods yard comprised three sidings running off the Descendente line; the middle one served the goods shed and shared access to a coal wharf with the outer track. At the outer end of the station, both tracks singled up and the main line crossed the main street below on a masonry bridge. After the cessation of freight services the goods shed remained *in situ*, but the yard tracks were removed as the area became used as a car park and bus yard. The same rationalisation of tracks probably saw the removal of the turntable and engine and carriage sheds.

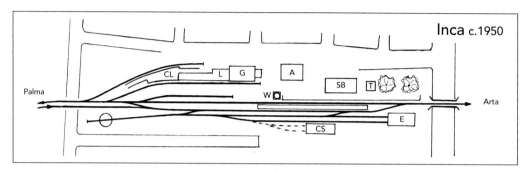

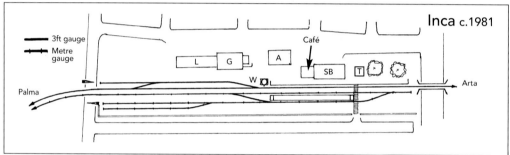

Babcock-built No. 55 engages in some desultory shunting at Inca, while the passengers for Arta wait for their journey to re-commence. 1957.

(D. TREVOR ROWE)

FEVE railcars await their next departure from Inca in 1977.   (K. TAYLORSON)

Majorca Railways Inca Goods Shed

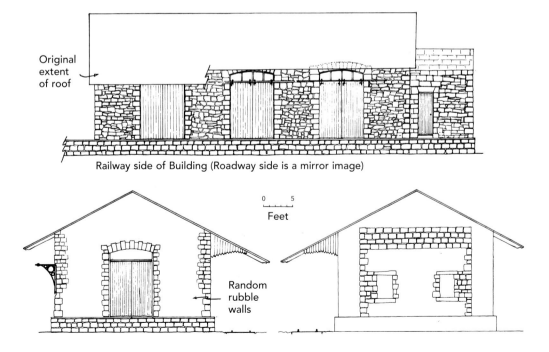

Original extent of roof

Railway side of Building (Roadway side is a mirror image)

0   5
Feet

Random rubble walls

87

A general view of Inca staion in 1994, showing the station bar and the staff quarters behind it; beyond is the goods shed.   (AUTHOR'S COLLECTION)

By the time that the gauge conversion was under way in the early 1980s the Descendente line at first remained to 3ft gauge, being provided with a loop and a short siding at the Palma end of the platform. The Ascendente line, converted to metre gauge, was provided with loop embracing a new island platform, with a couple of sidings trailing back towards Palma. This line ended on the embankment above the street, and was not connected to the old main line. Later with the conversion of the Descendente line crossovers were provided, but at the outer end of the platform the metre gauge track tapered down to link up with the old 3ft line.

INCA, 2000 onwards

The arrival of the latest rolling stock and the re-opening to Sa Pobla (formerly La Puebla) has transformed the appearance of the station. The platform height has been raised, the old trailing sidings have fallen out of use and their connection with the running lines have been removed. The Ascendente line now ends in a short facing siding beyond the platform, while the running line negotiates a new facing cross-over to join its neighbour. The station bar has been demolished, while the most obvious change is the new curving timber canopy that spans both running lines and platforms. Other alterations have seen the demolition of the former staff quarters, the renovation

Inca in 2003, with a new overall roof and a different track layout. Still no footbridge, though!   (AUTHOR)

of the goods shed – though without the roof overhang that once shaded the neighbouring siding – and the provision of a bus station on the site of the former goods sidings.

EMPALME

After leaving Inca the main line continues in a south-easterly direction and crosses the town's by-pass on a modern girder bridge. The town is soon left behind and the tracks are once again running through open farmland. After about a kilometre there was formerly a level crossing over the road linking Inca and Sineu, but this has been replaced by a road overpass. Another change is the closure of a large number of

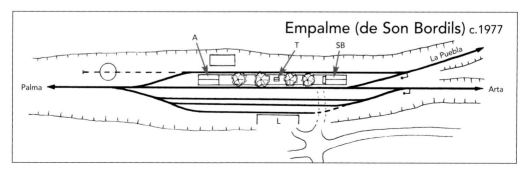

Empalme slumbers on as winter storm clouds gather in 1988. Conversion is still 12 years away.

(AUTHOR)

occupation crossings, whose dirt roads were once protected by American-style cross-bucks carrying the warning 'Ojo al Tren'. After a short while the station at Empalme (34kms) is reached; while the name conjures up a mental picture of an oasis, the word Empalme merely means Junction. The earliest timetables give the name as Empalme de Son Bordils, naming it after the local farm, whose owner donated the land to the railway. Uniquely this station was only provided for railway interchange, and had no road access for the general public, although there was a goods loading bank possibly for the private use of the Son Bordils estate. The dirt road that led to the loading bank ran through the nearby farmyard with its single tall palm-tree and eventually reached the road beyond.

Approaching the station the running line split into five tracks, the two on the left running on either side of an island platform, which had a rather narrow building at either end. That at the Inca end was staff living-quarters, while the Stationmaster had the other building, beyond which was a tiny garden, sandwiched between the tracks and a well. It is assumed that passengers did not have access to this building, but there was a toilet block for their use and the platform was shaded by a number of plane trees planted along its centre. Beyond the platform the left-hand track swung away towards La Puebla, while the main line entered a shallow rocky cutting beyond which the line started a long descent into more open farmland. In the days when the branch lines were worked as separate entities, the engines of trains arriving from La Puebla could run straight ahead from the platform onto a siding leading to a turntable; there was a run

Track clearance on the way to Manacor. Empalme station in the distance, 2003. (AUTHOR)

round loop from here which connected back to the La Puebla line beyond the end of the platform though this was removed after the withdrawal of steam power.

In the mid-1980s it was still possible to see the old track layout, half lost in weeds and saplings, but the re-opening to Sa Pobla has resulted in a general tidying of the site, and a single track now runs through to the right of the old platform. The re-instatement of the line to Manacor should see that station re-open as a transfer platform between Sa Pobla and Manacor services. The timetable for 2003 shows the new line as projected and gives the new name of Empalme as Enllaç. Access to the station will be possible via a new unmetalled roadway, provided for farmers' access, which by-passes the Son Bordils estate.

THE OLD MAIN LINE (closed 1977. Re-opened to Manacor, 2003)

Leaving Empalme the main line runs along an embankment, flanked by mature trees, which may be removed as part of the modernisation scheme. The line here is on a falling gradient, and a short way beyond is the bridge over the Torrente Son Bordils, whose construction had caused such problems for the original contractor. Nearby there was a very short-lived halt provided for the inhabitants of Costix; this only remained open between February and October 1978.

SINEU (pre-2002)

After Empalme the main line enters an area of low rolling hills, which force the railway to change direction a number of times before it reaches the outskirts of Sineu. Here two roads are crossed in quick succession, the places formerly protected by crossing keepers who were provided with small wooden shelters, now vanished. The station (43kms) consisted of three loops and there was formerly a facing siding (later lifted) serving several cattle pens, and the goods shed which still stands next to the station. On the far side of the line there was a shorter loop that had once served a coal wharf. As with many other stations there was a very narrow platform between the two running loops, opposite the station building that dates from the 1920s.

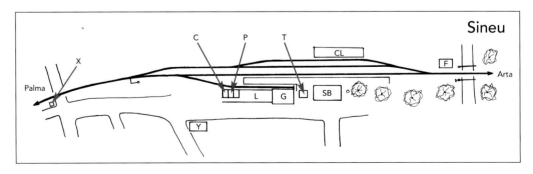

Sineu station in 1984 when it was still derelict. It later became used as an Art Centre. Now the trains have returned.

(AUTHOR)

P. W. Dept Hut (Sineu)

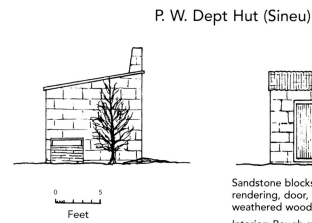

0   5

Feet

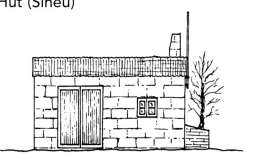

Sandstone blocks with remains of thin cement rendering, door, window frames and coal bin, weathered wood.

Interior: Rough stone block floor. Hearth for blacksmith work in rear corner, rusty tools.

93

When the line to Manacor was being opened Sineu acted as a temporary terminus and was provided with a turntable, water tank and a wooden locomotive shed capable of housing a single locomotive. All signs of these vanished long ago. Since the line's closure in the 1970s the station building has passed into private hands and has been an Art Centre for some years; the owners established a garden, or at least a lawn, that spread across the track. The lines through the station were re-laid in 2002 in preparation for the renewed services to Manacor.

Beyond the platforms the former loops combined to form a single line that continues on towards Manacor. At the end of the station is a level crossing whose barriers were once worked by a winch situated beside the station house. Just before the crossing on the left of the line stands a small smithy built of sandstone blocks. Leaving the town the line runs into a shallow, wooded cutting and shortly after the road linking Sineu with Petra passes over the line.

SAN JUAN

The station at San Juan (45kms) does not appear on the present maps of the island (although many of these continued to show the railway in its pre-1977 state for a number of years later). The reason is, like Sineu, that the building is now in private hands and is used as a dwelling; access is therefore impossible. The line at this point is on a steadily falling gradient but there was a loop at the station with a facing siding running into the goods shed behind the platform. The loop was later lifted, probably after the cessation of goods traffic. The modest station building has no upper floor. Passing on, the line swings round to run east once more, as the countryside becomes more mountainous and wooded. Eventually the land flattens out and fields once again border the line.

PETRA (pre-2002)

Approaching Petra the line passed a couple of level crossings. During the 1990s part of the nearby track was removed for modern road construction as the town expanded. This perhaps helps to explain why the 21st century plans to reinstate train services on

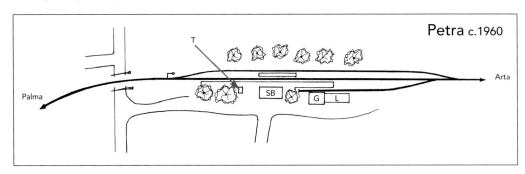

Petra c.1960

The controversial station at Petra, seen here in 1984 when the rails were still visible. Now the line goes round the edge of the town.   (AUTHOR)

this section have had a less than enthusiastic reception locally, and this has resulted in a new length of line, much of it in a cutting, which by-passes the town; in consequence the new station is on the town's outskirts.

The old station at Petra (54kms) was within the built-up area, its position formerly marked by the tall poles of the adjacent level crossing, now no longer standing. Perhaps because of the distance to the operating windlass on the platform, there was once a spindly gantry made of old rails next to the crossing, which supported extra counterweights to aid in the operation of the barriers. The station buildings at Petra are finished in a rougher more rural style than at Sineu, but there are the normal three doorways leading off the platform, the station name being carried on a plaque over the centre door. The stonework, like Sineu, is randomly shaped, with only the corner blocks and lintels being squared off. However, where Sineu is built of roughly similar hexagonal blocks, here the stones are much more random, giving the walls the appearance of an old Chinese vase whose surface glaze is covered with minute cracks. At the Palma end of the platform a row of magnificent plane trees once provided shade for any waiting passengers. Latterly the layout at Petra merely consists of a long loop of track opposite the platform, though since the 1980s earth has covered most of the layout, which has become used as a parking area. However, the presence of the goods shed just beyond shows that there was a siding here too, and that unusually it faced away from Palma.

After Petra the countryside becomes rockier as the railway breaks through a line of hills in its path. Beyond them the road and railway are within sight of each other

The goods shed at Petra. The window looked out over the weighbridge, and there was a small crane attached to the far end of the building to assist unloading. (AUTHOR)

separated by small fields, until the line meets the main Manacor road at a level crossing once protected by lifting barriers which have now been removed. The cottage for the crossing attendant remains however, and was still inhabited in 2002, although road resurfacing had covered the rails with asphalt. Given that even quite minor roads have recently been provided with bridges, it seems likely that this important road crossing will become a bridge when the line to Manacor re-opens; the resulting works may well sweep away the nearby cottage.

MANACOR (pre-2002)

Approaching from the west the line opens up into a long loop at what was once the edge of the town, and there is a stone-built shelter, now in ruins, for the pointsman on duty here. On the right-hand side is the large Can Reus factory once provided with a

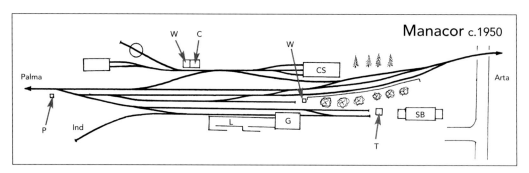

Majorca Railways Crossing Keeper's Cottage (Near Manacor)

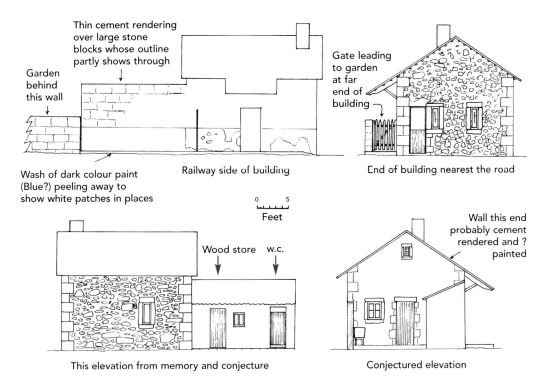

Thin cement rendering over large stone blocks whose outline partly shows through

Garden behind this wall

Gate leading to garden at far end of building

Wash of dark colour paint (Blue?) peeling away to show white patches in places

Railway side of building

End of building nearest the road

0   5
Feet

Wood store   w.c.

Wall this end probably cement rendered and ? painted

This elevation from memory and conjecture

Conjectured elevation

trailing siding, beyond which formerly stood the goods shed which had an extra long loading bank, now replaced by modern housing. After this comes the station platform, which originally ran parallel to the station building; however, the later extension to Arta needed a slight re-alignment away from the building, so that the tracks could thread their way along existing alleyways in the town. In consequence the buildings are some way away from the line.

At the Palma end of the station was the two-track engine shed, itself a roofless ruin by the 1980s and also the water tank and coaling stage, which had similarly suffered with the passage of time since the end of steam. Facing the engine shed there was once a three-road carriage shed, which became the last resting place of the Berliet railcar. After about 1970 the track layout was gradually lost as sidings were lifted and new buildings appeared on the perimeter of the original yard. These have gradually encroached further and caused the final demolition of the ruined locomotive facilities and most of the former carriage shed. At the Arta end of the station there was once an old two-aspect colour light signal (looking more like a traffic light than anything else) and a tiny stone hut for the attendant responsible for the level crossing over one of the major roads through the town. On the far side the line used to run between a couple of old houses before traversing another intersection of minor roads and curving to the

Manacor in 1984, pre-restoration. Originally the line terminated in front of the building, but the later alignment was to the left of the photographer. (AUTHOR)

right along an unmade street, eventually to traverse yet another level crossing at the far end of the town. Local road developments in the early 1990s have covered this section almost entirely with a dual carriageway.

Although derelict for many years, the station site was used for a while as a horse training ground, although later this use ceased. Nevertheless, a local groundswell of opinion maintained that the line should be saved, and graffiti reading Salvem S'Estacio, with a drawing of a couple of railcars, was discovered on a nearby wall in the late 1980s.

SAN LORENZO

By the time the line reaches San Lorenzo (78kms) it is some 20 metres above the level of the town and the station is situated on a shelf cut out of the hillside. Normally the station building was provided on the side of the line nearest the town, but here the

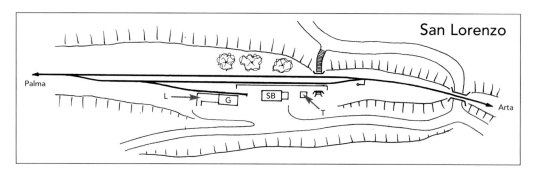

San Lorenzo station displays the Art Deco style of the Arta extension.   (AUTHOR)

The goods shed at San Lorenzo.   (AUTHOR)

terrain was unfavourable; although a rough track passes under the line and eventually arrives in the station yard, passenger access for pedestrians was via a long flight of steps that led through a subway beneath the platform loop. A short facing siding served the goods shed, and the less intensive service on this section is reflected by the lack of an extra platform between the two sides of the loop.

Majorca Railways San Lorenzo Goods Shed

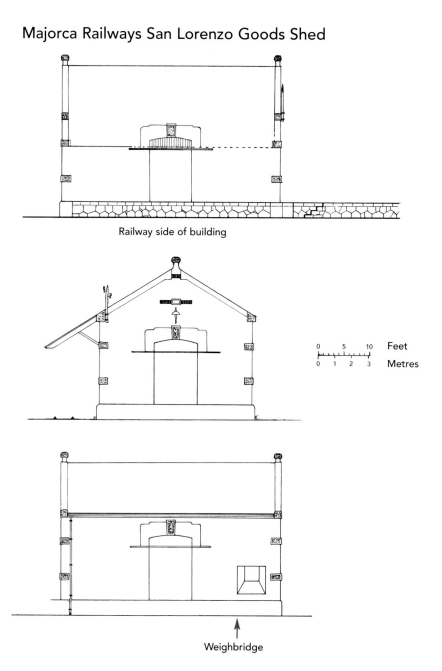

Railway side of building

| 0 | 5 | 10 | Feet |

| 0 | 1 | 2 | 3 | Metres |

Weighbridge

SAN MIGUEL

After San Lorenzo the countryside is more wooded and there is a short tunnel to negotiate on this stretch. The railway changes direction yet again to reach the small town of San Miguel (77kms), from where there was once a plan to build a branch to serve nearby Porto Cristo and the Caves of Drach. The station buildings have a pleasant rural style characterised by rather lumpy stone plinths at the end of the roof ridges, which are a typical feature of the Arta extension. The design is somewhat redeemed by the attractive red and white tile decoration applied to the gable ends. The track layout was always very simple and consisted of a goods loop opposite the platform with no freight facilities apart from an open loading bank. On the opposite side of the line there was a facing siding just beyond the platform.

A short way further on there was a halt, known as Na Penyal, which was provided for troops manning a wartime gun battery on the nearby cliffs. The battery was dismantled in the 1960s but the halt remained until the line closed.

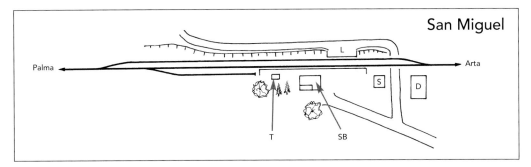

A general view of San Miguel. (AUTHOR)

A typical bridge on the Majorcan system.

(AUTHOR)

Majorca Railways – San Miguel Station

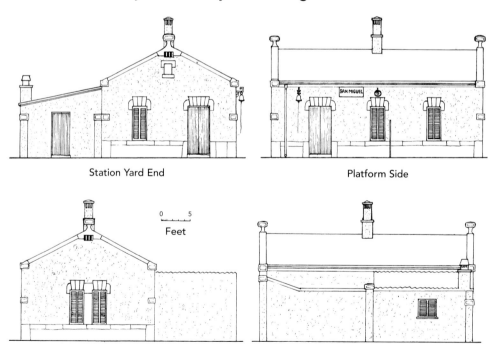

Station Yard End

Platform Side

0   5
Feet

Stippled Area: Gritty pebbledash – probably painted a faded yellow-ochre colour.
Stonework: Very pale grey. Red/white striped tiles at gable ends.
Doors and Window Trim: Very pale green (eau-de-nil).

SON SERVERA

Beyond San Miguel the line is carried on an embankment above the fields for some distance, and the line turns northwards again to reach Son Servera (84kms), where the station is situated in a cutting below the town. As usual there is a loop line opposite the platform and a facing siding on the left of the line that serves a loading bank and goods shed, the latter shaded by a luxuriant palm tree.

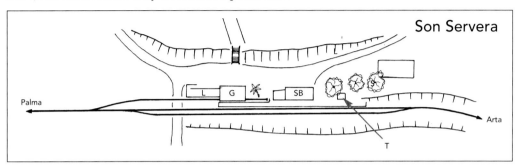

At the edge of the town a minor road is crossed, and the farmland soon gives way to hilly woodland with rocky outcrops. Some 2kms further on there is a rather sudden level crossing, which must have needed a full-time attendant, as there is a wooden hut nearby. The line continues through the woods and re-appears to cross the road once more. This section also includes another short tunnel and a bridge over a dried up riverbed.

ARTA

Nearing journey's end and still climbing, the railway approaches Arta, swinging round so as to arrive from the west. A warning of the nearby town is provided by the local cemetery, whose access road provides yet another level crossing. Ahead the town now comes into view. A final level crossing carries the line over a side street just beyond the running sheds. On the right of the line trailing turnouts (now lifted) gave access to the two-road carriage shed, while opposite is the double-track engine shed, now also devoid of rails, and recently used as a stonemason's workshop. The bricked up doorways at the inner end of the building once led to the turntable.

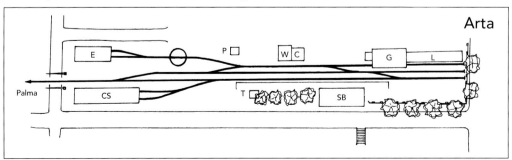

The former locomotive shed at Arta was being used as a stonemason's works in 1988. The door at this end has been added since the station closed. (AUTHOR)

Arta station – 11 years after the departure of the last train, and nature has taken over the site.

(AUTHOR)

Opposite the platform two loops open up on the left. The outermost one serves the combined coal store and water tower, and here there is an ash pit between the rails. The turntable and engine shed were reached by setting back from here, although these rails have been lifted or obscured by new buildings that have invaded the site. Beyond the water tank a facing cross-over allows access to the headshunt at the inner end of the yard, while the single track continues as the goods shed siding. The passenger platform is shaded by pine trees whose cones litter the ground, while the station house is a tall building much embellished with coping stones which project from its rendered walls. Behind the station the roadway rises up parallel to the line, which ends at a sheer stone wall a short distance beyond the platform, 94kms from Palma.

THE LA PUEBLA BRANCH (closed 1981/2000)

LLUBI

Llubi is today the first stop on the branch after Empalme, although between the 1950s and 1981 there was a stopping place at Tirasset, which never seems to have attained true halt status or a timetable entry. Like all the intermediate stopping places on the branch it was some distance from the population it purported to serve, the result of the company deciding on taking the easiest, rather than the more convenient but costlier route between the main line and La Puebla. At one time both Llubi and Muro enjoyed a road service to link them to their stations, and this service seems likely to be reinstated now the line is once again open; the inhabitants of the area around Tirasset, where the halt has not been reinstated, have not been so lucky. Llubi (39kms) formerly had a simple layout comprising a loop and a single siding facing towards the junction. At a later stage, possibly during the EFE era, it was downgraded to halt status and the loop was removed. By the 1980s there was only a single platform and a single-storey station building, devoid of any architectural frills. The platform was shaded by a row of cypresses and the stationmaster's garden had a pleasant arbour of vines. The siding merely had an open loading bank, but this was the scene of much activity, judging by the Freight Consignment book for 1939/1941 discovered abandoned in a nearby store.

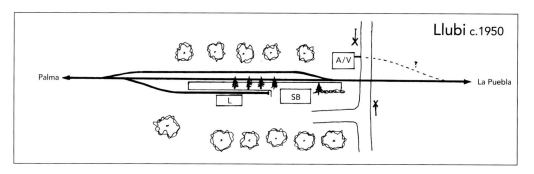

Llubi, three months after closure in 1981. (AUTHOR)

Llubi, just before re-opening. The car park needs finishing as do the fences, and the platform still lacks a canopy. The old station house still survives, but the view is taken from the bridge that has replaced the former level crossing. (AUTHOR)

Having been weighed, the freight was loaded (and sometimes stored) in wagons or vans awaiting dispatch. Two or three wagonloads a day seems to have been the average plus several small consignments that probably travelled in the brake van.

Where the narrow road from the village crossed the line road users were protected from the trains by lengths of chain that could be slung between red and white painted posts beside the tracks. Beside the level crossing was a large stone building with a set of rails protruding from the doors leading to the road. From the shape of the adjoining field it is possible that this may have been part of a trailing siding, and in 1981 the lower floor was the home of a platelayer's trolley and some tools, though these had gone a couple of years later. The upper floor had once provided staff living quarters, while at one time the lower floor could have been used to garage the station bus.

With the rebuilding of the Sa Pobla branch the station loop has been reinstated and an island platform set between the two tracks. The station building still exists, unused, although the stationmaster's little garden has vanished to provide a car park. In the interests of safety the level crossing has been replaced with an overbridge.

MURO

Like Llubi, the village of Muro is some 2kms away from the railway, though here the traffic must have been greater as the facilities in steam days were more generous. Approaching from the junction trains emerge onto an area of open ground, shortly before the station, and there was an ungated crossing of a minor road, formerly marked by the usual X-shaped sign. From here the railway runs across a slight embankment towards a rocky hillock, which it penetrates by means of a cutting. Meanwhile the nearby road climbs the hillock to cross the line by a stone arched bridge, before skirting the station and then turning off towards the town.

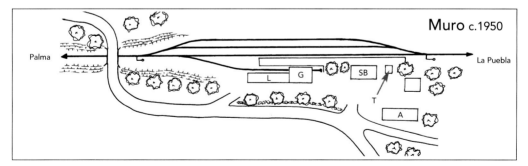

As the tracks emerged from the cutting under the road two loops were thrown off the left, the point levers at each end fitted with indicator discs to warn approaching drivers which way the road was set. By 1981 the second loop had vanished beneath dumped earth and ballast, but on the other side of the line a siding still ran behind the platform and underneath the goods shed canopy, although the turnout leading to the through

A general view of Muro in 1981. Note the kilometre marker post in the foreground, once typical of the system.

(AUTHOR)

Work on the new station at Muro nears completion. The old station appears to have shrunk, as the new ballast is now level with the top of the old platform.

(AUTHOR)

line had been lifted. Opposite the platform was a marker post showing the distance to Palma 42.4kms. The present layout is merely a through line with a new higher platform replacing the old rail-height structure. The station building and goods shed have been left in place, though unused.

Between Muro and La Puebla the countryside becomes richer and more intensively farmed. The fields are generally rather small, with the soil raked into parallel ridges to aid irrigation from the storage tanks, which are dotted about the countryside. These are made of stone blocks rendered with cement, and feed water channels resembling walls with a grooved top. These lead to the various fields where temporary earth channels water the peppers, maize, alfalfa and olives, although all kinds of fruit and vegetables can be found growing in the area. The more prosperous farms, which tend to have larger fields, nowadays employ automatic water sprinklers.

LA PUEBLA (1878/1981)

Having traversed the fields from Muro the railway entered La Puebla at a wide road junction. Once the line was protected by the usual chains, but after closure road resurfacing covered the tracks with asphalt. In former times this was open ground with scattered trees, but the enlargement of the town resulted in the line from here onwards threading its way between the backs of houses and light industrial buildings to reach the terminus. In steam days this was generously laid out, although there was only one loop serving the station, which had a bay platform, from which a siding set back to the turntable and engine shed. A long single-storey station was provided on opening, and still survives, although there were abortive plans to replace it with a structure similar to Sineu station in 1929. The station was framed with pine trees that shaded the small courtyard on the street side of the building, which was surrounded by a high stone wall with a gateway leading out into the Plaça del Tren. At the far end of the building was a small private garden whose fence was covered in a trailing creeper bearing large purple flowers. On the opposite side of the yard were three sidings, two

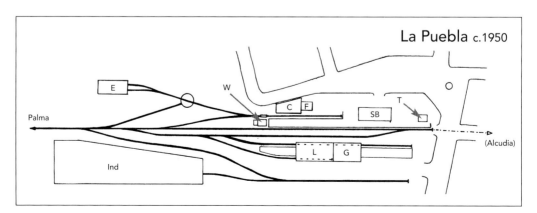

La Puebla c.1950

of which served a large goods shed and a very long loading bank, which after 1941 was partially covered with a tiled canopy, added at one end of the goods shed. From the third siding a line struck off to enter the warehouse belonging to the local agricultural co-operative. The tracks ended without a buffer stop at a gap in the boundary wall, opposite an alleyway (Carrer Passatje d'es Tren) leading towards the nearby farm produce market, and a map shows that the tracks may once have continued to the far

The water tank at La Puebla, seen in 1981, shortly after closure. The station can be seen in the background.   (AUTHOR)

La Puebla Water Tank

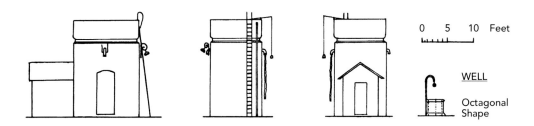

0   5   10   Feet

WELL

Octagonal Shape

end of the town. This would have been the start of the extension to Alcudia and beyond, had it ever been built, but in the event La Puebla remained as the terminus.

The gradual diminution of goods traffic resulted in the co-operative's siding being lifted in 1958, while the locomotive service area probably followed not long after. With the demise of steam it would have been redundant and occupied valuable building land. Similarly after 1977 the goods yard vanished beneath new housing developments, leaving just the loop line and the bay platform by the time of the 1981 closure. As well as the station building, the toilet block and the attractive water tank survived, though gradually becoming more decrepit with the passing years. In 1981 the station's walls were painted a brownish maroon, which had weathered to a pinkish shade. Around the base of the walls was a strip some 800mm high painted a yellow-ochre colour, while the doors and windows were an eau-de-nil green. Following the inevitable vandalism of any unused structure, all openings in these buildings were closed with cement breeze blocks by the early 1990s. However, a new life awaited the site, and today the station has been restored and is in use as a Business Promotion Centre. A plate on the wall reads: – "For a hundred years passengers, freight, and mail arrived and departed from here. [ ]" Over the years since closure the track has been covered with tarmac to become a car park and the old water tank, which had become too ramshackle for preservation, was eventually demolished though part of the pump mechanism and some blocks of masonry have been used as a sculpture on its site.

Outside the old station the road leading towards the sea provides a bit of local history. It is named Carrer Enginyer Mister Green and recalls the man in charge of draining the nearby swamp, La Albufera, during the mid-19th century. Bidwell, the British Consul on the island during the 1860s, mentions making a detour to view the works. The trip nearly had a tragic ending when his coachman accidentally strayed off the road across the marshland during a torrential storm, and the carriage became bogged down in the mud, almost threatening to sink into the marsh. Luckily the party managed to extricate themselves from their predicament, but the story throws an interesting light on the hazards of island travel before the days of the railway.

SA POBLA (opened 2000)

• For safety reasons the former level crossing at the edge of the town has not been re-instated, and the line now ends about half a kilometre short of its old destination. Facilities today are simple in the extreme, and comprise a platform capable of holding a 5-car train, plus a simple booking office/toilet block. There is also a facing siding long

The new station at Sa Pobla in 2003, with a CAF train waiting to return to Palma. (AUTHOR)

The old station at Sa Pobla, now restored to a new life. (AUTHOR)

enough for a 2-car diesel railcar set. Beyond the old station the projected alignment has now been blocked by new buildings, so it appears that the Alcudia extension will have to start with a detour further from the town centre. It is then possible that a completely new station would have to be built where the new line crosses one of the other approach roads to the town. This might explain the rather rudimentary facilities presently provided.

OTHER CLOSED BRANCHES (now lifted)

The foregoing is an account of the lines on the FC de Mallorca which can still be traced with a little patience as they are still in existence, although the derelict parts are becoming more hidden with every passing year, and have been omitted from the Firestone maps since 1991. To follow the trail of the old lines to Alaró, Santany and Felanitx requires even more patience as in some places the line has vanished completely following the removal of railway embankments to enlarge the neighbouring fields. This is certainly true of the former line to Alaró, closed over 60 years ago. Sometimes an echo remains with the discovery of a crossing keeper's hut, an old bridge or a pathway through the olive trees that is flatter and straighter than a road and yet carries no wheeled traffic.

A crossing keeper's hut, near the site of Montuiri station. (AUTHOR)

We have already noted at Santa Maria the old Felanitx line curving away in a south-easterly direction. The first stop was **Santa Eugenia** (22kms) where the station was situated on a curve. The platform was on the right-hand side with the loop opposite. Behind the platform a facing siding served a loading bank. Today the tracks have gone, and the station building houses the bar for the municipal swimming pool. After this came **Algaida** (31kms), whose station layout was almost identical to Santa Eugenia, though with the addition of a goods shed at the end of the single siding. Near the site of the station a crossing keeper's hut survives. The station has now been converted and has become a private dwelling. Further on at **Montuiri** another hut can be found on the old main road near the bottom of the hill leading up into the town. A short way across the fields is the old station (38kms), now part of a farm complex, though the station name is still displayed over the doorway. Opposite the tree-shaded platform was the usual loop while the goods siding ran in behind the platform and faced Felanitx. Despite having no goods shed, merely a loading bank, the station saw plenty of traffic both in full wagonloads as well as small consignments. Where the siding joined the main line there was a water tower, although this was only to be used in emergencies as the water was acid and tended to corrode the locomotive boilers; indeed an early metal tank suffered problems with rust and had to be replaced with a stone example. The station was down-graded to halt status in 1965.

Further on at **Porreras** (45kms) there was until recently a large, solid two-storey station though in recent times this has fallen into a ruinous state. All traces of the two facing sidings behind the platform have disappeared along with the loading bank, which served the Can Reus wine-producing company. Beyond the station is a bridge over the road leading to Campos. In former days unfenced fields of barley bordered this part of the line, with the crops coming to within half a metre of the rails. The next stop was at **Canteras** (51kms), although the site of this halt is no longer marked on maps, possibly because it has become a private house. Originally the station was situated between two level crossings and had a goods loop with a loading bank as well as an additional spur at each end. The platform was situated just beyond the loop, although the station building was only added in 1903.

The terminus at **Felanitx** (58kms) is now hard to recognise, although the large factory on the edge of town makes a good landmark. The site of the yard has become a combination of scrap dump and stable yard and in contrast with much of the old remains, which have a wistful air, Felanitx seems merely sad. In the old days there was a loop line opposite the platform with a couple of sidings on the side of the tracks nearest the town. One of these served the goods shed, and the Can Tejedor factory also had a private loading dock. On the other side of the loop a facing siding ran in beside the engine shed and served an open loading dock used by the local wine shippers as the station was an important source of wine traffic. Access to the two-road shed was by a trailing connection off the inner end of the loop, and the turntable was gained from this

Felanitx station, with the inevitable De Dion railcar, in 1960.   (M. SWIFT)

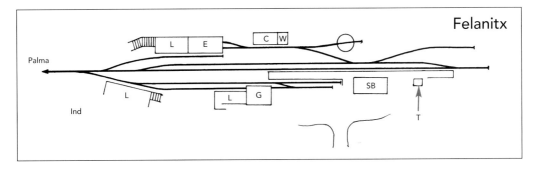

line, which was also provided with a water tank. There was a short facing siding running off the inner end of the loop, while the station building has been demolished since closure, and a block of flats built in its place. All the sidings originally at Felanitx, those at Porreres and Canteras, and a total of 7.5kms of the running lines on the branch remained laid with 20kg. rails until closure.

With the planned re-opening of the Felanitx branch it may not be long before this site is radically altered, as preparatory work begins.

The trail of the former branch to Santany is equally elusive, the more so following road building developments near Palma in the 1970s and 1980s, the site of the track having been covered by the motorway to Santany and the Continente supermarket.

Extensions to the airport have hidden the next kilometre or so, however a little further on a low three-arched viaduct can still be seen from the main road. In the centre of **Coll** (6kms) the station has become the Municipal Library. Further on there were formerly a number of halts, including **San Francisco,** and other stopping places not all of which gained timetable status, but which were added with the start of the island's tourist boom as the beaches around the Bay of Palma were only about a kilometre away from the line at this point. In this section was **Es Pil.lari**, the only halt hereabouts to be provided with a passenger shelter, which still stands, though in a ruinous condition. It was the usual open-fronted building, whose roof sloped down towards the track. The front wall had three arches giving onto the platform. Just beyond the platform there was formerly a short tunnel, which has now been filled in. The last of these halts was at **Las Cadenas** (11kms), which was originally a level crossing but became a recognised stopping place. The name comes from the chains that were strung across the road on the approach of the trains. Formerly there was a siding here, active in the 1940s, serving a supplier of building stone.

Further on towards **Arenal** itself the site of the line becomes more obvious as it is used as a footpath that uses the high bridge, the Pont des Jueus, which once took the single track over the deep valley of a small stream. Beyond here new streets and houses have obliterated the course of the line, though a straight row of trees betrays the location of the former platform (14kms) and nearby the old water tank survives in the middle of a car park. Final evidence is provided by the Bar Estación across the road. All this is hard to reconcile with a picture of the station taken shortly before closure.

The Santany branch had three halts with similar buildings. This one at Es Pil.lari has now lost its roof but is still recognisable. Others were situated at El Palmer and Llomparts. (AUTHOR)

This shows that there was a loop on the left of the line while the station building was on the right. Both loop tracks have a platform – an indication of the level of passenger traffic. Significantly there is no sign of the town in the photograph, which looks towards Santany. A turntable was provided as some services terminated here. At the far end of the station there was formerly a works producing concrete blocks. Beyond and slightly behind the platform the water tank can be seen, apparently standing in the goods yard so presumably there had been a water crane at one time, although it had gone by 1960. Further on was the goods shed and a coach siding that appears to run into a tunnel mouth in a stone embankment. Leaving the station there was a long climb, and a substantial viaduct over a dry river valley, followed by a rocky cutting at kilometre 17. The land here was undulating and cutting and embankment alternated. At the summit a long, high curve provided a good view over the Bay of Palma, before the line turned away inland towards Lluchmayor.

Development in the town of **Lluchmayor** (30kms) has covered all traces of the former station, which was the largest intermediate station on the entire system. It was also the highest point on the branch, and from here the line fell for the next 18kms. The next clue can be picked up at **Campos** (34kms) where the former station is nowadays providing housing accommodation, although there is a crossing keeper's house to be found on a minor road leading to the coast via Ca'n Vaca; however this building is currently under threat of demolition to make way for road improvements. Further

The station at Baños is now a private dwelling, but still betrays its railway heritage. (AUTHOR)

The station at Salinas was sold shortly after this picture was taken in 1988. The building is now a private house.   (AUTHOR)

south the line ran through a fertile plain, though traces of the halt at **El Palmer** (48kms) are hard to locate. Further on however at **Baños** (52kms) the station building still stands in splendid isolation beside the road leading to Ses Salines (formerly Salinas). Nowadays it too is a private dwelling, although it bears the unmistakable features of the Majorcan railway system. The actual spa is some distance away and a bus used to meet the trains, which only stopped when the baths were open. Once again the station in the middle of **Salinas** (55kms) was converted for living in 1993 and has lost its more obvious railway surroundings to make way for a garden. The local industry, which gave the village its name, is the production of salt, which is still taken from evaporation beds along the shore.

Little sign remains of the halt at **Llomparts** (58kms) which had a three-arched canopy similar to the shelter at Es Pil.lari, but further on at **Santany** (62kms) most of the railway building still exist, although they are somewhat mixed up with newer houses that have invaded the site, while the station has once again been converted into living accommodation, with the addition of a new external staircase. At the outer end of the yard a loop opened up on the left, and the engine shed on this side and the goods shed opposite once framed the tracks, which ran straight ahead into the platform situated on the right-hand side of the line. Opposite the platform was a large building providing living accommodation for the staff, including train crews on overnight lodging turns. On the same side of the line, which by now had opened out into another loop, were the water tank and a raised bank for coaling the locomotives. Beyond this a

Santany station has also gained a new life, again as a private dwelling – conversion work was under way in 1988 when this picture was taken. (AUTHOR)

turntable provided access to the two-road engine shed. The line leading straight across the turntable was provided with an inspection pit inside the building, and at the rear there were a couple of small rooms – perhaps a store/office and a workshop for minor repairs. The whole of the building is in a very bad state of preservation and may not remain standing for much longer.

Since closure those buildings that have remained at the more deserted sites have suffered from vandalism, and during the 1980s they were sealed with concrete blocks; however, after a few years these defences were pierced and the buildings have suffered further damage, graffiti and looting. Decorative features, such as the rather nice ornamental grille in the Ticket Office at San Lorenzo, and a handsome cast iron lamp bracket have seemingly found their way onto the "black" architectural market and it seemed that the remains of these old lines was doomed to descend slowly into squalor. The modernisation plans now in hand will be a welcome reversal of this trend.

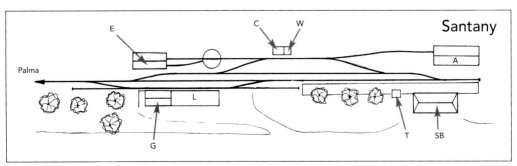

Chapter 6

Timetables and Train Working

The Early Days

A picture of the earliest days of the railway is provided by the Annual Reports, which include figures for the average train loading during these years. In 1877 the typical train consisted of three or four of the Composite carriages, a single Second and perhaps three or four goods wagons, mostly with a solitary brake van. Three years later one of the Composites had been replaced by another brake van in the average formation and the fourth goods wagon had become the rule rather than the exception. Records show that in 1877 none of the locomotives needed to work every day – sometimes remaining unsteamed for as much as ten days a month. That year the three passenger locomotives averaged just over 20,000kms each, compared with the goods locomotives' average of 14,100kms. With a main line round trip of 36kms, and allowing for shunting, an approximate total of 350 goods trips annually can be estimated, while taking into account the likelihood of there being three passenger trips a day. Indeed for

On an Autumn morning in 1957 MTM-built No. 9 prepares to leave Palma with the 8.40 am departure to La Puebla.

(L. G. MARSHALL)

Once the morning passenger trains had departed, Palma got ready to send out the daily goods trains. Here some last minute loading takes place, and the restricted height of the original goods vans can be appreciated. The open wagons in the right-hand train appear to be full of manure, a product of a city that still relied on animal power in the 1950s. (AUTHOR'S COLLECTION)

most of its independent life the railway ran a service of three trains on each of the four lines, with departures in the early morning, afternoon and evening being made from the outer termini with corresponding return trips from Palma. An exception was the Santany line, which saw some extra "short" workings to Arenal, working out of Palma which originally left the city at 10.00 am and 12 noon, returning at 3.30 pm and 5.15 pm. In steam days these required a turntable and watering facilities to be provided at Arenal.

Until the doubling of the main line to Inca it was common to work the branches to Felanitx and La Puebla as separate entities, involving a change of train at either Santa Maria or Empalme, although at least one daily train made the complete trip in both directions. Sometimes trains were combined and portions were added or detached at the junctions. As the Santany branch left the capital on a separate line all its services were worked to or from Palma. From the mid-1930s the railcars came to provide most of the services on the Felanitx and Santany lines. The De Dion cars often towed some of the four-wheeled carriages, and this was certainly a feature of the summer services on the Santany line, when trains to Arenal were well patronised. Two Third Class coaches would be added to the trains between Palma and Arenal, where one or both trailers would be uncoupled while the railcar continued to the terminus. Off-season a Postal/Second Class coach was often used to strengthen the railcar services on the two southerly branch lines. Both these branch lines would therefore have required separate goods workings, whereas the steam-hauled services to La Puebla and Arta were run with mixed trains. Additional goods trains were run on the main line when traffic dictated it, as the time needed for shunting at every wayside station would have been too great to sustain a reliable passenger service, even in more unhurried days. Goods trains tended to leave Palma around mid-day, returning when required; at busy times the amount of shunting could mean that the train did not arrive back in Palma until the early hours of the following day.

Operating Rules and The Train Crew

Until the time that railcars took over most of the train services the FC de Mallorca operated four classes of trains: – Rápidos, Correos, Mixtos and Mercancias. These are roughly equivalent to: – Express, consisting of passenger vehicles only, with a top speed of 50km/hr (31.25mph); Mail trains, containing a limited number of wagons, able to run at 45km/hr (28.12mph); Mixed trains, perhaps performing shunting duties en-route, with a running speed of 37km/hr (23.12mph) and Goods trains whose maximum permitted speed was a mere 30km/hr (18.75mph). When the railcars were first introduced, those travelling alone were classed as Rápidos and timed at 60km/hr (37.5mph), while towing up to two trailers classed the train as a Ligero limited to 50km/hr (31.25mph).

The extremely slow speed of the goods trains is a reminder that no continuous brakes were fitted to freight vehicles. This was covered by an operating regulation stating that unfitted trains should contain one vehicle in six fitted with a screw-brake. The practice of running with a brake van at each end of the train may stem from this rule, and perhaps also explains why some 1950s era pictures show brake vans marshalled in the middle of passenger rakes. In any case it would have been operationally convenient to have a rear brakeman, able to reset points at the tail of the train after the completion of any shunting manoeuvres. The Jefe del Tren (Guard) would ride in the front brake van, and be responsible for the dealing with the paperwork relating to loads being picked up and dropped off along the way; he would be accompanied by a junior brakeman to assist with shunting duties. As a number of wagons and vans were fitted with a brake standard and an open-air seat for a brakeman it is possible that they were used to augment the brake vans when required. It must be said that a journey from Palma to Arta perched on one of the roof-top seats can hardly have been a pleasant experience! However, the brakeman were not the only staff working outside the train. Travelling ticket inspectors (Revisors) formerly visited each coach while the train was in motion by walking along the running boards, and providing the reason for the provision of long horizontal hand-rails that were fitted to the four-wheeled stock. During their journey they might have to negotiate their way past passengers who had moved out onto the running board to converse with a friend in another compartment. Then again it was not unknown for ticketless passengers to hide outside on one side of the train while the Revisor visited the far side of the compartment. The practice of external ticket checking which was perhaps a hangover from British methods dating back to the line's Victorian origins (a similar scene occurs in 'Alice Through the Looking Glass'), but nevertheless survived until the four-wheeled carriages were laid aside at the end of the 1950s.

Other operating regulations gave the maximum loads that could be attached to the various classes of engine, according to the route or the type of train; where a train was above the appropriate tonnage then extra time was allowed on the more steeply graded sections of the line, at a rate of 30 seconds per kilometre per 10 tonnes of excess weight. In snowy or wet weather the loads had to be reduced to the next lower category. When double-heading was employed the train's tonnage was to be 90% of the total capability of the two locomotives. With goods trains comprising 20 to 30 wagons in the railway's heyday double-heading was a not uncommon occurrence. Finally, wagons whose loads weighed more than 4 tonnes were not allowed to travel at more than 40km/hr, thus relegating them to the mixed or goods services.

LLUCMAYOR and an unidentified Babcock locomotive get off to a rousing start on a stormy day in 1957. The train is a heavy one, and, as was the case in bad weather, an extra engine has been added as stipulated in the operating rules.   (AUTHOR'S COLLECTION)

The Nationalisation Era

After the State take-over in 1951 the Arta and La Puebla services were each reduced to two daily trains for some years, although by 1954 the service frequency had been increased and the working pattern was quite complicated, and it is obvious that there were substantial changes to the schedules from year to year. The steam-powered Correo had taken $3^1/_2$ hours to reach Arta including a 25 minute stop at Manacor; while part of this would have been to take on water, it seems that the section beyond Manacor was almost treated as a separate branch with an end-on connection. Passenger trains dropped carriages at Manacor before continuing on to Arta, and while this be mainly due to the poorer traffic potential, the fact that the smaller goods locomotives could not carry sufficient water for the final uphill slog to reach the far terminus meant that mixed trains were the rule on this section, at least until the arrival of more powerful engines in the 1930s.

By 1959 the published timetable shows what an impact the new diesel railcars were making. Without the need to perform shunting duties, the journey time between Palma and Arta was cut to just 2 hours and 8 minutes. Similarly the journey times of the first inward service from Manacor to Palma was reduced from 2 hours and 9 minutes to 1 hour 35 minutes. On all the lines the last train on public holidays was held back to depart one or even two hours later than usual. In 1959 the railcars were generally based at the outer termini. The traffic pattern on the La Puebla branch was different with

Krupp-built No. 35 splashes through the puddles on its way out of Palma on a wet winter's day in 1955. Four of the first five vehicles are brake vans.   (AUTHOR'S COLLECTION)

No. 51 at rest, having brought the Atra train into Palma, 1957.   (L. G. MARSHALL)

some of the services being locomotive-hauled while others were worked by railcars. These mixed trains were perhaps dictated by the amount of agricultural produce the line handled – perishable traffic that needed to be moved as soon as possible. The Arta services, also shared by steam and diesel, were even more complicated with some trains only working from Palma to Manacor. Lodging turns for the train crews were common and accommodation was available at the station at Arta, and also at Inca, Manacor, Felanitx and Santany as well as Palma. At one time staff quarters were also available at Empalme but this may only have been the case while the branch was run as a separate entity. Trackside workers on this branch were catered for at Llubi.

Changes in the 1963 timetable included the substitution of a railcar on many erstwhile steam services, including the afternoon Palma-Arta Correo. This railcar now left the capital one hour later than the old steam departure time, but reached Arta only a few minutes later than previously. The same railcar was then booked to return to Palma after a short wait at Arta. Two of the round trips between Arta and Palma are not marked AUTO (Railcar) so may have been diesel hauled, possibly providing mixed workings although the timings are as tight as the railcar schedules and would allow little or no time for shunting en-route. One Creusot diesel would have been required for these services.

The Santany line experienced minor re-timings, as did the La Puebla branch, which was now provided with four daily return services, worked by one railcar. The main beneficiaries of the new timetable were the users of the Felanitx branch who regained an extra railcar service in each direction thus helping to fill the service gaps in the morning and afternoon that had existed for some years. The first railcar from Palma now left at 9.25 am instead of 2.15 pm as previously, with an extra departure from Felanitx at 12.30 pm. Because of the existence of 20kg rails on part of the branch, it was never served by the Creusot diesels.

By 1965 a major change had occurred with the closure of the Santany branch. To compensate there were now several trips between Palma and Inca, which would have absorbed the Santany drivers, though their home shed would perforce have moved to Palma. Crew rosters on the lines to Felanitx and La Puebla would have been unaltered, but the working pattern on the Arta line could have been simplified with only one Creusot diesel being based there to work the twice-daily runs to the capital.

Two years later the end came for goods services and with it the need for locomotive-hauled trains, as the railcar fleet was able to cope with all services following the closure of the Felanitx branch. Although two of the Creusot locomotives were retained for a time, they cannot have been much employed. The 1975 timetable shows the railcars making five daily round trips to both La Puebla and Arta, though it is possible that the Arta line returned to three trips before its eventual closure in 1977. The following year the timetable included no less than eighteen services linking Palma and Inca, with four of these continuing on to La Puebla. In 1960 the steam train timings between Palma and La Puebla had been almost 2 hours, with 1 hour 14 minutes allowed for the railcars. By 1978 the latter timings had been cut by 8 minutes to 1 hour and 6 minutes. Contemporary travellers tell of the railcars being taken up to the maximum speed allowed despite the fairly poor state of the track, which gave a somewhat rough ride. This was certainly borne out by an examination of the track at La Puebla shortly after closure, which came in March 1981. By this time the 3ft gauge might be described as nominal, at best. Track improvements including the use of continuous welded rail helped to shorten journey times on the remaining section of line, and speeds at least on the straight sections between Palma and Inca were increased to 120km/hr (75mph).

From Visitors' Diaries

The transitional years between steam and diesel power attracted the attention of a few intrepid enthusiasts and the following accounts of the contemporary scene are of interest. (Other, more generalised accounts appear in the Appendix). The first was written by the late Kenneth Hartley, who spent an afternoon on the railway in 1957 just before the widespread introduction of the new diesel railcars. The author is grateful to the Editor of 'THE NARROW GAUGE' (the journal of the Narrow Gauge Society)

The evolution of a train in the 1958 timetable:- Having left Arta at 4 pm, No. 50 takes on water at Manacor. Prior to the 5.12 pm departure it seems that the extra coach on the left was added to the train... (D. W. WINKWORTH)

Shortly afterwards, at 5.33 pm, No. 51 left La Puebla with a train of Brown Marshall coaches and a string of open wagons, arriving at Empalme at about 6.20 pm. Here the engine and front brake van draws away from the train, just short of Empalme station... (D. W. WINKWORTH)

for permission to include it here, as it paints a graphic picture of the line in the last days of steam.

"There were many unusual features to note, sketch or photograph, not to mention the very basic train service of three trains a day from Palma to anywhere except Inca – which was served by eight, including expresses – that one needed a week or so to cover the lines then in operation. However, the steam railway was by no means the only attraction in Majorca, although it was the best. Hence, to see as many trains as possible in a limited time, I decided that Santa Maria was my best choice, as the double track main line ran through this junction en-route to Inca, as well as to La Puebla, Arta and Felanitx. In fact the only passenger trains not serving Santa Maria were those on the Santany branch, which left the main line soon after leaving Palma station. On 3rd July, 1957 I got a Second Class return and travelled on the 12.30 pm departure for Inca. This consisted of 2-6-0 tank number 9 with two of the superior bogie coaches, numbers 111 and 112, and brake van F20. The Guard saw that I was trying to get a shot of our train, and with customary Spanish courtesy held it back until I had got aboard. Soon after stopping at Pont D'Inca we passed De Dion railcar A3, and without stops at either Marratxi or a small halt further up the line arrived at the junction at 1.05 pm, my intention being to catch the 2.55 pm back to Palma. The first arrival was the 1.30 pm from Inca; Krupp 2-6-0 tank 33 with four First and Second Class four-wheelers and a brake van at either end. A few minutes after this train left for Palma, No. 21 SANTANY came in with a light load of three four-wheelers and brake F1 – again for Palma.

At 6.23 pm the Arta train headed by No. 50 arrived (having shed its vans since leaving Manacor). It then backed onto the La Puebla train, ready for departure at 6.38 pm. Arrival at Palma was timed for 7.39 pm. 6th May, 1958.

(D. W. WINKWORTH)

There was a pause until about 2.35 pm so I went into the village in search of a cold drink, returning to the station in time to see No. 30 arrive with a four-wheeler of each class – First, Second and Third. The whistle on this engine was deep toned, like the old Great Central railway. As the train departed No. 9 returned with its two bogies and brake van, and I was so intent on getting a shot of this, that I failed to note the time. Also almost before I had time to turn my film to the next exposure a most exciting train came into view, going "hell for leather" and bound for Manacor and Arta. It belted through the station at express speed, headed by 2-6-2 tank No. 55 – the load was two or three bogies, six goods vans and a couple of brakes. It was quite a few minutes after this exhilarating sight before I realised that I'd missed my train to Palma – and that the next one was not until about 7.00 pm.

It was a long wait, but by no means entirely wasted. I had another ice-cold orangeade in the village; was shown the process of making various types of coloured tiles in a little works adjacent to the station; and initiated into the art of drinking, more or less successfully, from a Spanish drinking vessel. Also there were several interesting arrivals and departures, first of which was 2-6-2 tank No. 51 with one bogie, six four-wheelers, six goods vans, a cattle truck and two brakes. By way of contrast the next arrival was the little 0-6-0 tank No. 5 with a train of a dozen assorted goods wagons headed and tailed by one of those old 3rd/brake composites – the only time I ever saw one in use. This halted on the centre track, to allow railcar A3 – without trailers – to pull into the platform a few minutes later, pause briefly and then turn off for Felanitx. After this, No. 5 had quite a busy time, rearranging her train, and inserting a waiting flat truck loaded with peaches. Finally with a shrill whistle, she slowly moved off with her load, curving away down the line to Felanitx.

Hardly had No. 5 got out of sight when No. 15 ALARO brought in a 24-wagon goods train from Palma. The 4-6-0 spent some time shunting various loaded and empty coal wagons, picked up a flat wagon loaded with barrels, and finally departed for Inca. About half-an-hour later a train for Palma arrived – earlier than I'd expected – and I was happy to join it. Krupp 2-6-0 No. 30 was our motive power for the three coach train, and seemed to be running on a whiff of steam, as the gradients were mostly favourable – the fireman in fact travelled for much of the journey on the edge of the footplate, hanging onto the cab handrails at arms length. We arrived at Palma at 7.00 pm, a busy time with railcars A2 and A4 – this latter with two well-filled trailers – in the station. 4-4-0 tank ARTA was shunting coaches, No. 21 tank was on a train bound, I think, for Inca; and No. 31 Krupp was in steam in the locomotive yard. A fitting end to a very satisfactory outing over a small part of the Majorcan Railways."

Another visitor to the island was K. P. Plant who made several journeys over the system in June 1960. By this time the change to diesel haulage was well under way, although steam power was still holding its own. After spending the morning of 10th June recording the locomotives in and around the sheds and workshops at Palma, K.P.P.

Krupp No. 31 pauses at Algaida with a Felanitx-Palma goods train in 1960. (M. SWIFT)

caught the 2.15 pm service to Felanitx. This was composed of railcar A-4 towing one of the Correos/Second Class carriages, number 34. The train left a few minutes late and arrived at Felanitx at 3.45 pm. Here there were about eight wagons in the yard, plus the partially dismantled remains of No. 11 ALGAIDA in the engine shed. At some stage of the afternoon another train must have arrived as by the time the railcar returned to Palma at 5.30 pm, Krupp No. 31 had appeared and was making up a goods train of six wagons bracketed by a brake van at either end. The goods was supposed to follow the railcar back to Palma but apparently used to leave "when the Maquinista (driver) felt like it". K.P.P. hitched a lift in the front brake van in the company of the Jefe del Tren and a youth who operated the brake wheel, while another brakeman rode in the tail-end van. Departure from Felanitx was delayed until 5.56 pm, while about half-an-hour later the train was leaving Porreres, Montuiri being reached about ten minutes later at 6.37 pm. Some smart shunting appears to have taken place as K.P.P's notes mention "very good traffic in small consignments and full wagons". Despite this the train was on its way again at 6.45 pm and reached Algaida at 6.54 pm. A visit to a nearby cafe for a drink with the crew ("not allowed to leave the train, really") seems to have delayed departure until almost 7.07 pm. Santa Eugenia was reached fourteen minutes later and here station work only took three minutes – possibly a small consignment being loaded into the front brake van. The main line junction at Santa Maria was reached at 7.34 pm and the train rested for twenty minutes, probably to allow other traffic to clear the main line. There was no work to do at Marratxi, which was passed without stopping, while a pause at Pont D'Inca added another two minutes to the journey. The train finally arrived back at Palma at 8.19 pm. This was presumably the homeward leg of the daily Felanitx goods turn. Railcars left Palma at 9.25 am, 2.15 pm and 7.15 pm, arriving at Felanitx at 10.56 am, 3.46 pm and 8.46 pm so the outward goods probably departed around mid-day. This should have resulted in a mid-afternoon arrival at the outer terminus in plenty of time for a "booked" departure around 5.45 pm – though this was obviously flexible.

The next day saw K.P.P. sample the service to La Puebla aboard the 9.00 am departure from Palma. This train was made up of one of the new railcars, No. 2001 and trailer No. 5001. As well as the driver, the train crew consisted of the Jefe del Tren and a Conductor, unlike the previous day's service, which only carried a crew of two. Nevertheless there was room for K.P.P. to sit on the second seat beside the driver. At Inca a permanent way gang were busy with some welding work, and had arrived at the site aboard a yellow petrol trolley. Further on at Empalme the driver "an apprentice of about 40" left the train and the Conductor took over the controls. Up to now speeds had been about 55-60km/hr, but the new man took the train up to 70km/hr almost its maximum permitted speed, despite the somewhat indifferent state of the track. After Llubi the line had been re-ballasted and the riding was easier. An ancient blue bus belonging to the railway company met the train at Muro, the connection to the town and other outlying villages. For the last couple of miles the line passed through fields of beans and potatoes watered by what seemed like hundreds of windmills. These were set on a base of stone blocks and had large 10-bladed wheels with a large arrow-shaped tail to keep them facing into the wind; only a few of these are left on the island today. Refreshments were available on this journey as the railcar's luggage area carried a supply of crated beer and soft drinks selling at 5 pesetas a bottle.

The terminus at La Puebla was reached at 10.15 am and there was time to note the old double engine shed, though one track had been lifted. Meanwhile the railcar ran round its trailer and made ready to leave. Departure time was 12.35 pm (5 minutes late) with a 1.05 pm arrival at Inca where K.P.P. left the train to await the connecting service to Manacor. This arrived shortly afterwards and was formed of Creusot diesel No. 1101 hauling four bogie coaches and a brake van. This train left Inca at 1.27 pm and ran non-stop to Sineu with K.P.P. aboard the rear coach, a 1st/2nd composite. Along the way the train's progress was watched by crossing keepers who carried a stick with red and green flags at opposite ends. Sineu station saw a large exodus from the train, and at Petra a 16-seater bus marked Petra-Ariany could be seen in the station yard. Speeds between stations were fast on this section and the well-sprung coach bounced its occupants around, there being no arm-rests separating the seats. Manacor was reached at 2.12 pm.

K.P.P. left the train and explored the surroundings. A Nasmyth 4-6-0T No. 12 SAN JUAN was discovered in the locomotive shed in good condition along with the derelict chassis of railcar A-1. In another shed were two Maquinista-built 2-6-0Ts, both derelict and rusty and with all identification removed, though one had 7 chalked on it. In the station yard was a 25-seater bus bound for Porto Cristo; built by General Motors it was owned by a private bus operator.

Later 2-6-2T No. 53 arrived with a train of a brake van, five bogie coaches and five vans. After much shunting the train was whittled down to the brake, two coaches and eight assorted goods wagons, and although due to leave for Arta at 4.23 pm all this activity delayed departure until 4.40 pm. Further up the line a wagon of timber was dropped off at San Lorenzo, and there was time to take some photographs during a pause at Son Servera. Arta was finally reached at 5.43 pm (5.20 pm). Rapid shunting soon disposed of the wagons, while two more bogies were picked up to strengthen the return working. Nevertheless the train managed to depart at 5.56 pm, only 6 minutes behind schedule. Back at Manacor another bogie carriage was added to the train, which left for Palma at 6.47 pm, overtaking a Palma-bound goods headed by Creusot diesel No. 1102 at Petra. The passenger train arrived at Palma at 8.21 pm, having taken 2 hours and 25 minutes for the journey.

At Palma 0-6-0T No. 5, seen complete the previous day, had now had its tanks removed, and the underframe of railcar A-3 was noted – the body apparently in the carpenters' shop undergoing repairs.

The following day was taken up by a trip on the Santany line. The train was again composed of railcar No. 2001 and trailer No. 5001, and left Palma "packed to the boards" a few minutes after the scheduled time of 9.20 am. At Coll d'en Rabassa there was a cheese factory next to the line and a military airfield (the present commercial airport) was visible on the left-hand side. Arenal saw a massive disembarkation, but despite this the train only managed to reach 45km/hr when climbing the gradient out of the station. Second gear was needed on this stretch. The summit was reached at kilometre 24 and by this time fields had replaced the scrub and woodland that had persisted since Arenal. After Lluchmayor a long straight stretch allowed the speed to reach 75km/hr on a well-maintained length where the railcar rode well. From Lluchmayor to Campos the line was on a falling gradient while beyond Campos was another stretch through the fields.

Santany was reached at 10.50 am. In the shed was a partly dismantled and anonymous 4-6-0T, thought to be No. 13 LLOSETA. The rest of the station was picturesque, with a very attractive garden surrounding the well. There appeared to be little goods activity, as by this time the branch freight only ran three times a week, on Mondays, Thursdays and Saturdays, leaving Palma at 9.30 am and returning when ready. The railcar left Santany at 12.45 pm for the return to Palma. The 9km long climb from Campos to Lluchmayor was a steady grind in second gear at speeds of 45-50km/hr. One motor got extremely hot under this treatment, the temperature gauge showing 85 degrees, with 90 degrees marked DANGER. The second motor remained

Creusot diesel, No. 1102, leaving Palma in 1960 with a light train bound for Santany.   (M. SWIFT)

at 75 degrees although the paintwork of both was blistered. (The Bussing motors often gave trouble and several railcars suffered fires; later, Pegaso engines were fitted to overcome this problem.) At intermediate stations flagmen were in attendance on the loop points, as trains were not allowed to enter a station until signalled by flag or lamp. Incidentally, flag signals followed former British practice with Red for Danger, Green for caution and White for All Clear. At Lluchmayor three more anonymous locomotives were found in the locomotive shed; two were 4-4-0Ts (thought to be No. 22 SALINAS and No. 27 ARTA) while the other was a Maquinista 2-6-0T (possibly No. 9) which was lacking its centre wheels. Back aboard the railcar speeds of 80km/hr was achieved coasting down the long slope to Arenal, and the arrival back at Palma was made at 2.11 pm.

Goods Workings

Freight traffic charges on the FC de Mallorca were divided into two categories: – Gran Velocidad and Pequeña Velocidad (roughly equivalent to Fast Traffic – by passenger/mixed train, and Slow Traffic – by goods train), with rates set according to the speed of delivery. The Gran Velocidad service mainly consisted of parcels and other small consignments, as well as goods in cans. Pequeña Velocidad traffic was divided up into three classes. First Class included items of value but small volume, among them acids, arms, fruit and vegetables, meat, manufactured products, furniture, jewellery, perfume, musical instruments and cotton. Second Class traffic was of medium value and volume, including oil, olives, shoes, sugar, lignite and dried fruit, while Third class (low value/high volume) covered adobe, coal, cement, and other building materials. The tariffs for the carriage of live animals varied according to their size, thus cattle and horses were rated as First Class, pigs Second, while goats and sheep were Third Class.

The discovery of the Freight Consignment Book for Llubi, plus a few scattered recollections of visitors allow one or two comments to be made concerning goods working on the system. Important stations were provided with a Stationmaster, a Goods Clerk and two Porters. Small stations had to get by with only a Stationmaster and a single Porter to cover all the duties, which included a considerable amount of paperwork. Each month was divided into 10-day periods and the proceeds from all categories of goods and passenger traffic, including the various taxes paid, thus had to be entered up three times a month with comparative figures produced at the month's end. With a station the size of Llubi, some of the sums displayed, for instance in the tax columns, were little more than a handful of cents, and in the days before calculators the task must have needed considerable arithmetical and book-keeping skills.

At Llubi almost all the outgoing goods wagons were filled with mixed consignments. The main exception was a van that carried milk to Palma every day. This was such a regular traffic that in the summer of 1939 van number C208 was habitually thus employed. Although milk was the only load for this vehicle, a large number of consignments to be shifted on 29th July that year resulted in the unhappy combination of milk and soap being placed in the wagon; hopefully both consignments were kept well apart! On the same day open wagon number B121 was sent away loaded to Pont D'Inca, but also carrying apricots bound for Manacor. Presumably one of these consignments was off-loaded en-route while the train waited. Open wagon A10 was dispatched to Palma with several consignments of mixed fruit, but also potatoes for Santa Maria, apricots for Porreres and fruit for Arenal. Loads travelling up the branch towards La Puebla are rare and when they occur a wagon number is rarely given. This is probably because the items travelled in the brake van, or were loaded into a wagon with spare capacity, but whose number was not known until the train's arrival.

A special check was kept on consignments of alcohol in any form, which were obviously entered up in a separate book, as their docket numbers are included in the Freight Consignment register. As well as fruit and vegetables, Llubi's main exports were soap, milk, liquor and eggs – all usually travelling in class C vans, but occasionally dispatched in open wagons. Livestock was also dealt with on a regular basis; horses, pigs, goats and calves were commonly carried, while on 22nd December 1939, eighty-eight turkeys were sent to Palma! Other loads that have been observed are class A wagons containing coal, B class opens carrying bundles of firewood, stone blocks or manure, the latter being sent out to the country stations from the stables of Palma for use as fertiliser. Carboys of olive oil, large barrels of wine or fruit in baskets were also handled in B class wagons, which were also used for ballast or sleepers when the Vias y Obras needed a train to help with track renewals.

Gran Velocidad traffic was suspended in 1972 when locomotive-hauled passenger trains were replaced by new railcars, which had limited on-board goods capacity, and were unsuitable for hauling a tail load of freight vehicles. In any case G.V. receipts had declined over the previous ten years from 340,000 pesetas in 1955 to 81,000 pesetas in 1962, with a sharp drop in 1959. The receipts from Pequeña Velocidad traffic were seven times that of the faster service in 1955, and by 1963 receipts had reached a total of 2,250,000 pesetas. That same year the faster service managed a slight revival to 114,000 pesetas, but this was not enough to prevent its withdrawal. The trend seems to have been a slow decline in goods traffic, as the next year goods receipts amounted to only 1,944,000 pesetas. The reasons for this are probably twofold:– those shippers who needed a guaranteed speedy service would have had to turn to road haulage, while the railway – now that steam power had been laid aside – had less potential motive power available for a full range of goods and mixed trains, while the latter were gradually disappearing from the timetable. The trains not designated as Auto (railcars) would still have been enough to cover the four routes. However, by this time all services to Santany and Felanitx were by railcar, and with dwindling goods traffic freight services may have been worked on an "as required" basis, hardly justifying the retention of all four Creusot locomotives. It is thus hardly surprising that two of the diesels were returned to the mainland around 1968, the others being scrapped soon after. As goods working diminished during the 1960s wagons were laid aside and slowly scrapped, although a large number were left at Palma for some years afterwards.

In earlier times FC de Mallorca wagons also occasionally ran through to Soller, despite the different couplings on the two railways. At least one FC de Mallorca van was provided with a Soller-style screw coupling in addition to its "chopper" and it may be that this was allocated to the Soller line and used as a converter wagon – otherwise the staff may have trusted merely to hooking the safety chains together. Apart from this vehicle noted on the FC de Soller, at least one other FC de Mallorca wagon followed it onto the neighbouring line. This was open wagon B132, which was converted into a weed-killing tank wagon and could be seen stored in a siding at Soller during the 1980s.

Goods traffic on the Alaró tramway was at first handled in small wagons and had to be transhipped at Consell. Later it seems FC de Mallorca wagons were used, particularly in the case of coal being loaded at the mines along the tramway, and this is certainly the case when part of the line was reinstated temporarily in the 1940s.

A final word on freight traffic – in this case a highly unofficial working. In the past the Spanish Government sought to raise money by taxes on a number of everyday commodities, including tobacco and coffee. Naturally the inhabitants of the coastal villages, where there were secluded bays well away from prying eyes, were up to landing the occasional cargo of contraband, the area around Santany being particularly well known for this activity. Some of this illegal freight was carried by passengers, and tended to be thrown to lineside accomplices on the outskirts of the capital at the point where the train began to slow down for its arrival at the terminus. A less risky approach was to make more intimate use of the railway's facilities. Steam locomotives lend themselves quite well to small-scale smuggling operations, particularly as they can legitimately begin and end their journeys away from curious eyes around the station platform. Favourite hiding places have resulted in contraband being placed under the coal in the bunker or, suitably wrapped, suspended in the water tanks. The story is told of a consignment of coffee beans that had to be delivered to Palma. One can imagine their night-time arrival at the station where somebody, possibly not too familiar with the workings of a steam engine, hid the bags in the locomotive's smokebox. By the time the train arrived at its destination the presence of the coffee must have been anything but a secret – ready roasted, indeed.

Signalling and Safety

K. P. Plant's memories earlier in this chapter raised the subject of flag signals, and it has been the case that for the majority of its existence the FC de Mallorca and its successors have employed no fixed signalling equipment, relying on flag or hand-held lamp signals at each station and staffed level crossing, as well as the employee's knowledge of the timetable. Trains were dispatched by telephone from station to station, and the "puede" (permission) would be given to the Stationmaster by his counterpart ahead, and this would be passed to the Jefe del Tren, in the early days at least, by the ringing of the station bell three times. The Jefe would then signal the driver with a long blast blown on a horn, to which the driver would respond with a whistle. Other signals made by the Stationmaster gave warning that an expected train had left the previous station, or was just about to arrive. While the Red, Green and White flags may date from the earlier era, by the time of FEVE control the signal to start would be given by the Stationmaster showing the driver an upright furled red flag (or even a wooden rod, the upper part of which was painted red.)

The furled flag as a signal to proceed was also used by level crossing keepers, who in the earliest days had to close their barriers 5 minutes before the expected arrival of the train, as a protection against the uncertainties of operations – a reminder of a more leisurely past, or perhaps even of the local spirit of "mañana". Later some of the crossings on the main line were connected to the telephone system and so could predict the coming train with more accuracy. During the 1950s level crossing barriers situated near some stations were put under the control of station staff, who would lower them using a windlass adjacent to the station building; in passing, one wonders how they knew if anyone was underneath as the barriers descended, as they were not fitted with any kind of audible warning. In the deep country, and especially at farm crossings the public was expected to listen out for the approaching train, and the roadside signs read "Ojo al Tren" (literally: – Keep an Eye on the Trains). This relaxed approach was ended after the INECO report, when automatic half barriers appeared between Palma and Inca; these are timed to close 60-90 seconds before the arrival of the train. With the reinstatement of the remainder of the line the situation has changed yet again, and modern safety rules state that no new level crossings may be installed or old ones reinstated, hence the provision of new overbridges in several locations. This has also dealt a deathblow to the occupation crossing, and many small semi-private farm tracks crossing the line have been fenced off and diverted beside the line to the nearest bridge. While probably causing immense aggravation to the local farmers, this has helped the enthusiast to reach parts of the system hitherto hard to find, Empalme station and the nearby bridge over the Torrente Major being but two examples. (Be warned however, a car with a high clearance underneath and good springs will be needed to cope with some of the back lanes that twist around the boundaries of the ancient fields, the junctions innocent of any signposts.)

Engine drivers in the steam era had a host of signals, differentiated by the numbers or length of whistles. The various messages covered events including "Train about to depart" (as outlined above), and also messages to the train crew:– "Screw down the brakes", or "Release the brakes", as well as a general warning whistle.

Returning to the subject of train safety, the re-gauging of the 1980s also saw the installation of a colour light signalling system, though once erected the signals remained inoperative for a while. With the recent changes to the Palma terminus, the addition of Son Rullan workshops to the track plan, not to mention the work needed to integrate the line to Sineu and Manacor, things have altered again, and in early 2003 the system was out of use with the latest modifications only partially complete. Meanwhile, train control had reverted to the traditional method of telephone blocking. At present the system is divided up into four "cantons" or blocks:– Palma-Son Rullan, Son Rullan-Marratxi, Marratxi-Inca and Inca-Sa Pobla, though at weekends Son Rullan-Inca is worked as a single block. There are four types of signal on the system, mostly located adjacent to the stations:– Advance (distant) signals give warning of the station approach, while Entry (home) signals and Exit (starter) signals protect the platform area. The last type of signal gives an indication of the state of the next level crossing – a green X shows "all clear" to the train, while a flashing green X shows barriers down but a fault in the system – approach with caution. A red X means the barriers are still open for road traffic.

(L. G. MARSHALL)

A view of the FC Soller's station at Palma, showing a van from the FC de Mallorca with a Soller-style coupling.

Part Two

The Soller Railway and Tramway

Chapter 7

A History of the Soller Railway

Although a road, climbing over the Sierra de Alfabia to link Palma and the north coast had been opened in the 1840s, it was clear by the end of the century that a more rapid means of communication was essential to serve Soller. In 1892 a proposal was drawn up for a railway linking the town with Palma running west of the mountains via Valldemosa, Esporles and Son Sardina, however the cost of this circuitous route was too great to be economically viable, and the scheme lapsed. In 1903 the Town Council of Soller again discussed the possibility of a rail link, this time by tunnelling through the mountains, but the plan failed as it was felt that the technical difficulties were too great. Despite this the idea was revived a year later and an engineer, Pedro Garau, was appointed to draw up plans for the line including a tunnel 2.8kms long at the summit of the railway. The total length of the proposed line was 27kms.

On 31st July 1905 the Compañia Ferrocarril de Soller S.A. (Soller Railway Company Ltd.) was formed to build the line with a capital of £131,500 divided into 7,000 shares.

Ornamental archway at the Soller Railway's station at Palma. (AUTHOR)

An early view of Bunyola, with No. 2 and train heading for Palma. (J. WISEMAN COLLECTION)

Such was the enthusiasm for the proposed rail link that the entire share issue was subscribed by local inhabitants within a couple of days. The scope of the plan was enlarged slightly in 1908 to include an extension to Puerto Soller. As originally conceived the railway's length would have been too short to attract a subsidy that would be payable to the builders of lines over 30kms long, following the passage of the Law of Secondary Railways of 1908. However, despite the subsidy, more money had to be raised for the extension and the total amount of the share capital was increased to £163,000, though later it had to be augmented yet again to a total of £208,700. This worked out at £6,732 per kilometre, mostly accounted for by the expenses of tunnelling. A gauge of 3ft was proposed so as to match the island's existing rail systems. Steam haulage was planned between Palma and Soller while the extension was to be built as an electric tramway.

The construction of the railway was undertaken by Luis Borio who contracted to complete the track-bed in thirty-four months, work starting in June 1907, though eventually tunnelling difficulties extended the construction period until August 1910. In all, thirteen tunnels were required plus a long viaduct and a number of bridges to bring the line through the mountains. At the northern end of the main tunnel the line was at an altitude of 210 metres above sea level, while the station at Soller was set at only 40 metres; thus the railway was obliged to descend in a series of loops almost amounting to a spiral for the last 9kms into Soller. Even so, the ruling gradient of this section is a challenging 1 in 45.

Track laying began in Palma in April 1911, and the contractor acquired a small four-coupled engine, which may previously have worked on the Palma Tramways. Named MARIA LUISA on its arrival on the Soller line, it had been built by the Brush Electric Works in Loughborough (Works No. 198 of 1891) to an earlier Falcon design. Once track laying started the work proceeded speedily, the original sleepers being pine or oak, spaced at 600 per kilometre. The permitted axle-load was 9 tons. Towards the end of July 1911, the rails reached the northern end of the Alfabia tunnel and on 25th July a special train carrying the Directors, shareholders and various dignitaries was run to the new railhead. Construction trains reached Soller on 19th August, and attracted great crowds. Work at Soller was sufficiently advanced on 17th October for the running of another special train, this one consisting of the MARIA LUISA with a saloon coach hired from the FC de Mallorca, carrying Eusebio Estada, Pedro Garau and a local politician, Antonio Maura, on a special inspection tour. The line opened officially on 16th April 1912, although goods trains had been running for the previous month.

The company had taken delivery of three 2-6-0 tank locomotives built by La Maquinista, two of which double-headed the inaugural train over the line. Shortly afterwards another similar locomotive was obtained and the Falcon tram was taken into the company's stock. To cater for passengers ten bogie coaches were obtained from Carde y Escoriaza, together with twenty assorted goods wagons from Orenstein & Koppel.

Having opened the railway to Soller, in 1912 the Directors considered a possible extension westwards from Palma, into an area as yet untapped by existing railways, to serve the town of Andratx. The route would go via Génova, Calvià, and Es Capdella and there would be an extension from Andratx to Puerto Andratx. The FC de Mallorca was considering a similar route, but despite negotiations with the local authorities at Andratx neither scheme progressed further than the planning stage, despite the proposed line being classified as having strategic importance in 1915.

The tramway extension to Puerto Soller was completed in September 1913 and services started on 4th October that year. At first they were run with three tramcars, obtained from Carde y Escoriaza at a cost of 10,000 pesetas each, as well as two trailers. Later more vehicles were added to the fleet. A small power station was established at Soller, the tramcars' motors picking up the 600v dc current via bow collectors from the overhead cable.

The railway company had under-estimated the line's traffic potential and it was not long before extra goods wagons were required, bringing their total up to thirty-six. After such a good start, there were some setbacks. A period of extremely heavy rain in 1919 caused services to be suspended for a while, following the collapse of an embankment on the mountain section. Luckily the driver of the first train to encounter the washout managed to stop his train safely, but while repairs were carried out independent services had to operate on either side of the gap while a replacement, the present Sa Llema viaduct, was constructed. This partial service lasted for over three months. Meanwhile the extra traffic demands also brought problems as it was found that the locomotives were somewhat underpowered. The almost continuous up-grade for some half the journey in either direction limited the potential loads, without recourse to double-heading, to something under 100 tonnes and added to this was the inconvenience of having to stop to take on water en-route. This double-heading made a nonsense of the economics of running the line, and no doubt the engines were driven harder to offset their shortcomings. Because of this, maintenance costs were soon higher than had been anticipated and the company began to operate at a deficit. Steam power was proving something of a liability, and by the mid-1920s it was clear that a major change was needed.

As early as 1915 the railway company first studied the possibility of electrifying the line, and sought the advice of German experts who suggested a plan costing £73,600, but this was more than the company could afford without State help. Finally in July 1926 the Consell Superior de Ferrocarriles (the government's Railway Council) gave permission for the plan to be implemented, and the new services commenced three years later on 14th July 1929. The electrified services were provided by four bogie motor saloon motor coaches, which hauled trains made up of the original carriages. At the same time four new carriages were added to the stock list, along with three bogie brake/luggage vans which arrived in 1931.

Electricity for the trains was at first obtained from the island's power station at Palma, via a sub-station at Bunyola, which supplied the 1200 volt dc traction current through Mercury-arc rectifiers. The inaugural electric train service to Soller was double-headed and this caused teething problems with the power; eventually this was traced to a breakdown in communication between Siemens, the suppliers of the train motors, and AEG who had supplied the power generating equipment. The outcome was a temporary return to steam working while the problem was sorted out. Electric haulage resumed in November 1929, after which the steam locomotives were laid aside at Palma until 1944 when all were transferred to the FC de Mallorca. Once the locomotives had gone, the company had no further use for the running shed, which was demolished in 1947. The line that had led to the turntable was then extended to make a direct approach to the goods shed, which up to now had relied on wagon turntables for access.

Despite the fact that the new trains ran on 1200 volts, while the tramway was rated at 600 volts, the equipment seems to have made it possible for the trains to reach the port, as shown in a photograph dated 1929. In the early days at least occasional trips were run in connection with the arrival at Puerto Soller of passenger shipping from Barcelona, but owing to the sharp curves on the tramway and the eventual growth of trees alongside the tracks the practice was discontinued. At times of great traffic

No. 4 and train at Palma. Note the goods shed and vans to the right of the train.   (K. TAYLORSON)

demand it was not unknown for the trams to tow trains of railway coaches instead of their usual trailers.

The development of tourism in the 1950s brought an upsurge in passenger traffic as visitors discovered the magnificent scenery through which the line passed. In 1955 the railway carried 331,000 passengers and the tramway 800,956; by 1960 this had risen to 421,570 railway and 861,194 tramway passengers. The same year 17,000 tons of goods were carried. Assuming that freight was only moved on six days a week, this is a daily average of 54½ tons or perhaps half a dozen wagon loads. The 1950s saw the end of several city tram systems in Spain, and the Soller Tramway was thus able to benefit with the purchase of four surplus "toast-rack" trailers from the Palma system in 1956, at a price of 15,000 pesetas each. Another tram and trailer arrived shortly afterwards, having been obtained second-hand from Bilbao, though conversion to 3ft gauge delayed their introduction until 1959. These new arrivals must have helped to take the pressure off the original tramcars and trailers, which by now were getting rather elderly.

In the early 1960s American forces were employed in the construction of an early warning system on Puig Major. While this may not have swelled the company's freight receipts, special trains – no more than a motor coach and one passenger carriage – were occasionally run between Bunyola and Palma for service personnel. Also at about this

143

No. 2 (complete with passengers) runs round its train at Palma in 1988. (AUTHOR)

A visit to Bunyola in 1984 revealed this special train – a rare shot of D-1 in action, as it propells a brake van towards Palma in the wake of a scheduled passenger service. (AUTHOR)

144

time the Mirador lookout station above Soller was being built and passing trains would occasionally drop off loads of supplies at the site, which was on an open section of the line. Once the wagon had been unloaded, the men would freewheel down to Soller using the wagon's screw brake when necessary.

In 1962 railway services once again had to be suspended due to a washout on the main line, but happily the interruption only lasted for three days on this occasion. Bad weather could however cause other problems. While the railway's power was now obtained from the national grid via Palma, there were nevertheless occasional problems with the overhead power supply, which was vulnerable to lightening strikes, resulting in train services being suspended during thunderstorms. To overcome this the Company purchased a diesel in 1968 to act as stand-by motive power. Built by Ferrotrade in Spain, D-1 was a 29 ton B-B locomotive, an Autotrade 500 type, fitted with a Deutz engine and Voith transmission delivering 470hp at 2000 rpm. It was thus theoretically capable of maintaining services with a five coach train, but proved to be not well suited to the line and unpopular with the drivers; in consequence it was little used.

During the following decade the passenger figures continued to increase, though the Tramway's returns declined slightly between 1967 and 1970. By this time the railway's running costs had risen to the extent that the whole future of the line was in doubt. In 1971, despite an increase in railway travellers to almost 575,000, the company posted a deficit for the first time. For a while closure rumours started to circulate, and it was even suggested that if the line were to close, the tunnel could be used by road traffic, on payment of a toll. However, the Ministry of Public Works undertook a study of the line and eventually allowed fares to be increased to cover the rising costs. Luckily, the gradual rise in passenger numbers continued, while economies were introduced, notably the cessation of freight traffic in 1972. A policy of catering more and more to the tourist industry was established, and visitors have been encouraged to visit Soller by railway, with the running of a "Tourist Special" departing from Palma at 10.40 am. All this succeeded in raising passenger numbers by 1978 to 656,208 on the railway, and to 716,476 on the tramway. In consequence the Company's official returns showed an operating profit of 6.2 million pesetas, and dividends were once more paid to the shareholders. At the same time improvements were made to the track and infrastructure. However, despite the railway's passenger success, the number of Tramway passengers started to decline, only relieved by an upturn for a couple of years in the 1980s. In 1983, 715,193 passengers were carried and this figure marked a peak on the Tramway for a while; that same year the railway carried 754,590 travellers. For the rest of the mid-1980s the Tramway continued its decline, perhaps due in part to increasing local car ownership.

A Government report on the island's transport systems was published by INECO and provides a useful view of the FC de Soller at the beginning of the 1980s. Installations and maintenance facilities, as well as rolling stock, were described as

A winter shot taken in the 1950s. No. 3 at the head of a mixed train heads along the street in Palma.

(AUTHOR'S COLLECTION)

No. 3 waits to depart from Soller, flanked by one of the trams.

(AUTHOR'S COLLECTION)

obsolete – although it was admitted that the antique motive power was one of the reasons why the line was popular with tourists. Ordinary fares were 3.20 pesetas/km for Second Class – more than either the FEVE line or even the national average, but given the special nature of the line they were not considered unreasonable. Workers, students and season ticket holders paid half the normal fare, while a special return fare of 160 pesetas applied to the daily "Tourist Special" departure from Palma. In general track maintenance was being carried out with 1000 – 1500 sleepers being replaced every year. New rail was needed in places, but it appeared that none of a suitable weight (35km/metre) was currently available. The report recommended work to improve safety on the urban section of the line in Palma, the urgent need of relaying the Palma to Bunyola section with 45kg/metre rail – to be completed as soon as possible, as well as immediate renovation work on two of the longest tunnels. The workshops also needed to be brought up to date as a matter of urgency, and a five-year plan was suggested to modernise the rolling stock. Finally, the railway's telephone system needed to be upgraded at once.

This work was carried out and on the whole did not change the look of the line appreciably. In general the motor coaches receive a general overhaul every four years, and the coaches are also rebuilt in turn. Early renovations to the carriages had given some of them 'bus style' windows with chrome edges, but these were gradually phased out as the vehicles came round for their next overhaul, and the original all-wooden look is being retained.

Over the years several local tourist operators have offered dedicated trips over the line, often combined with a boat connection along part of the scenic north coast. There was usually enough spare stock on the railway to cater for these extra trains, which often ran only between Soller and Son Sardina where there was more room for the passengers' transfer to their waiting coaches than at the Palma terminus. In 1991 a new coach interchange station, with a greater capacity for road traffic, was built at Son Reus. This halt has been given a passing loop, and the loop at Son Sardina has been removed, the station being reduced to halt status. This development followed the introduction of an alighting station, known as Can Tambor, which is situated a short distance outside Soller station. Because of the steep gradient at this point the stop is only used by trains travelling to Soller. Returning tourists, who have normally arrived by tram from the port, usually join their trains at Soller station. In order to provide corresponding extra capacity on the tramway, several trams were obtained from Lisbon. The original batch consisted of two four-wheelers (numbers 725 and 734) plus two bogie cars (numbers 334 and 807), however the latter were found to be unsuitable and were exchanged for more four-wheeled cars. After a period when they were stored awaiting restoration, they have now emerged in a smart maroon and white livery. The destination boards read "Servicio Agencias" when used for charter trips, or "Soller – Port Soller" for normal duties. To accompany them the workshops at Soller have turned out eight new bogie trailers, which are usually run in pairs with one of the new tramcars. As originally built, these were open-sided, but one pair was rebuilt during 2002 with enclosed and glazed sides for winter use. Perhaps to deal with this new programme of construction, the old goods shed at Soller was demolished in 1998, and a new erecting shop with three roads was completed in its place in 2000. The lines to the new building cross the tracks leading to the old running sheds and workshop buildings, resulting in several new crossings, most of them on a curve. All these tracks have been set into a concrete apron in front of the new shed that has inspection/work pits between the rails. Meanwhile, to help with the increasing demand for tourist traffic the company acquired a bogie electric locomotive from Euskotrebindeak (Basque Railways) in 2000. This is a Brown Boveri "Crocodile" B-B locomotive that was originally supplied for the Bilbao-San Sebastian line and, having been built in 1929, is thus an exact contemporary of the Soller's motor coaches. This interesting purchase is at present awaiting rebuilding to run on 3ft gauge, and at the time of writing its bogie frames could be seen stored beside the roadway at the rear of the platform at Soller station.

Some Minor Mishaps

The early years of the new century have seen a number of small out of the ordinary incidents to mar the normal smooth running of the line. In early November 2001 motor coach No. 2 had arrived at Palma, and the driver started the usual run-round move. Unfortunately the train was an extra coach longer than normal and the driver had not allowed enough room (there is some suggestion that the points were also set for the shorter loop option) and the motor coach side-swiped the last coach of the train, so that it ended leaning over at an angle of about 40 degrees. Although there were several passengers aboard, only superficial injuries were caused, and services were not suspended for more than a few hours. Subsequently the turnout at the mouth of the yard was moved out towards the street to give more room for shunting, a task that took two nights and a day to accomplish, and so caused a short interruption of service. Not long afterwards the driver of an all-terrain vehicle misjudged the clearance between a roadside wall and an approaching tramcar and was squeezed between the two. Once again the rail vehicle was canted over half off the track, although it did not fall, and luckily there were no injuries; after an hour the service was once more in operation. Then in September 2002, a fault developed in the new power station at Son Reus, which had been installed the previous summer. The generating company's engineers were forced to disconnect several circuits with the result that part of Palma suffered black-outs, and the 9.15am train from Soller was stranded in Calle Balmes for an hour, causing a traffic jam, which lasted until the power was restored.

In the past there have sometimes been problems with part-time staff recruited to help with the extra Summer traffic. One inexperienced tram driver dropped off his trailers at the port and moved off down to the end of the line at the dockyard gate, where he got stuck – the line was covered in a layer of sand and dirt which had insulated the power circuit from returning via the rails. After an agonised telephone call to the depot at Soller, the Chief Mechanic came down, driving a spare tram ahead of the scheduled service. He lowered the bow collector and turned off all the power on the stricken tram, then borrowed a bucket of water from a nearby bar, which he sluiced over the affected rails. The tram, presumably with a red-faced driver, was then able to make the return trip without further assistance.

Trouble Ahead?

The Soller Railway's monopoly of easy access to the town was broken in 1997 when the road tunnel linking Palma and Soller was finally completed. The effect was insidious, as despite the tolls being charged locals began to use their cars or buses to reach Palma, taking less time than the train's journey. The effect on the tramway was less noticeable, as it still catered for locals wanting to visit the market in Soller or travel to the port, in effect offering a door-to-door service without the need to worry about the limited parking available at either end of the journey. The railway's response was to try to increase its tourist traffic, with the acquisition of extra trams, the building of new trailers and the purchase of another locomotive. All this was a heavy drain on the company's capital. The events of 11th September, 2001, dealt a swift blow to travellers' confidence, and at the end of the year the company was showing a deficit of 230,000 Euros, mainly due to the recent acquisition of new rolling stock. Tourist bookings suffered during the following year to such an extent that it became apparent that the company was facing a grave financial crisis. An appeal to the government to increase fares by between 24 and 30% was turned down, although a 2.9% increase was approved. The managing director resigned, and in an effort to save money some staff in the workshops were dismissed. As one local newspaper report put it:– "authorisation could not be given for the purchase of even a single screw." For a while the railway continued to operate on something of a day-to-day basis, in the hopes of an improvement in the future, and further work on the Basque "Crocodile" seems unlikely for a while. In 2002 a new share issue was offered and successfully raised 168,700 Euros, which together with the fare increase has been enough to secure the situation for the time being. However, a new hazard to the company has been the announcement by the Mallorcan Transport Minister that in 2003 the tunnel tolls will be reduced for Soller residents, forcing the company to become more reliable on the potentially fickle tourist market. It is to be hoped that this will continue to sustain the railway and its tramway until the end of the concession in 2015.

MARIA LUISA, seen here at Palma after withdrawal. (AAFB ARCHIVE)

No. 1 SOLLER on the turntable at Soller (AAFB ARCHIVE)

Chapter 8

Locomotives and Rolling Stock

The Steam Locomotives

A slight mystery still surrounds the origins of the MARIA LUISA, the first locomotive to work over the FC de Soller. It is known that the engine came from the contractor who built the Soller line and may have been previously owned by the Palma Tramways, though this seems in doubt. Contemporary visitors who saw it before it was scrapped have reported its Falcon builder's plate, the Works No. 198 and the fact that it was fitted with Stephenson's valve gear. The engine had an almost totally enclosed body constructed of metal, rather resembling a passenger tramcar but without the end platforms. The buffer beams extended downwards to track level and at one time metal skirts had covered the wheels and motion, although on the Soller line these were removed. A simple stove-pipe chimney emerged above the arc roof, which in the early days was devoid of any other equipment. At a later date a large housing appeared on the roof, possibly the addition of condensing gear. Fuel capacity was 500kgs and the water tanks held 1,000 litres. MARIA LUISA continued in service, despite being rather under-powered for general use, and was employed mainly on the occasional engineering or works train until the arrival of the fourth locomotive from MTM. She was more useful on the Soller Tramway, both during the electrification of the line, and later bringing up wagon loads of coal from the port to the gasworks at Soller, and also on occasional passenger specials. Once the electrification of the main line was completed the five steam locomotives were moved to the roundhouse at Palma, where they remained until they were taken over by the FC de Mallorca during World War II.

The locomotives supplied by La Maquinista have already been covered in the section dealing with the FC de Mallorca. While employed on the FC de Soller they carried the following names:– No. 1 SOLLER, No. 2 PALMA, and No. 3 BUNYOLA (all completed by 3rd March 1912 with Works Nos. 58-60) and No. 4 SON SARDINA (completed on 15th September 1912, Works No. 65). These locomotives were a little smaller than the later engines that La Maquinista supplied to the FC de Mallorca. They carried 800kgs of coal and 3500 litres of water and their weight in running order was 30.5 tonnes. Numbers 1-3 eventually passed to the FC de Mallorca, while number 4 and the tram were scrapped in 1944. While running on the Soller line they carried large European-style brass locomotive lamps on the front buffer beam though these did not survive the move to the neighbouring system, where a less flamboyant British pattern of lamp was carried. Livery in the early days was quite elaborate, being a bright green (a shade similar to the shutters on the island's houses has been suggested) with a broad black outline to the tanks, which were divided into two panels by a thick black band. This was separated from the green by thin pale lining (possibly yellow). Quite how long this lasted with the locomotives blasting their way up through the long tunnel on each trip is open to speculation, and photographs of the engines out of use at Palma appears to show a plain all-over colour.

The Motor-Coaches

When electrification was being contemplated in the mid-1920s it was first planned to convert three of the existing carriages to become motorised units. However, when the change in motive power was finally agreed, the railway ordered four motor-coaches from Carde y Escoriaza (numbers 1-4) and all are still in use today, thanks to a rolling programme of general maintenance. The bodies of these vehicles measure 14.350 metres and they are mounted on Brill type bogies constructed by the French firm of Gallardon, and powered by two Siemens 120hp motors. The latter firm also supplied the pantographs, both of which are used in the raised position when running. The control gear was supplied by Schuckert. With a total load of 120 tonnes, a top speed of 45km/hr can be achieved on the line's ruling gradient; maximum permitted speed elsewhere is 50km/hr. The total weight of the motor-coaches is 35 tonnes.

No. 2 shunts a coach into the carriage shed at Palma in 1988. (AUTHOR)

Behind the driving compartment at each end is an open-sided platform providing passenger access. The driving compartment doors are set off-centre to allow the unused trailing compartment to be shut off; access to the rest of the train is then possible via the central doorway in the carriage end, and by fall plates above the buffer/couplings. All four motor-coaches offer both First and Second Class accommodation in separate compartments. First Class has twelve padded leather seats and in the case of No. 1 the original leather armchairs and settees have been retained. These are given cotton slip covers during the summer season. The Second Class compartments seats thirty-two passengers on slatted wooden seating. Externally the cars are finished in varnished teak, and the railway's crest appears on a metal plate, while the running number and class details are shown by individual metal numbers.

Between 1991 and 1996 all four motor coaches were given more modern electrical gear; the voltage of the control was stepped down from 1,200 volts dc to 24 volts dc and the necessary equipment was housed in a new compartment which took the place of a pair of seats on one side of the aisle in the centre of the vehicle, the window being panelled over.

The Diesel Locomotive

As early as 1937 the company had hoped to be allowed to purchase a diesel locomotive, however as this was during the aftermath of the Civil War the necessary permission was not granted. However, the period 1940/45 was marked by many electrical power-cuts and the company sustained a loss of traffic and revenue; clearly a solution had to be found. Under a modernisation plan of 1963 permission was granted for another electric locomotive or railcar, but no firms could be found who would build one for 3ft gauge. The company therefore decided to purchase a diesel from Ferrotrade, which arrived in 1968.

It was a diesel hydraulic machine with a Deutz engine and Voith transmission. Maximum speed was 60km/hr and the weight empty was 31 tonnes. The other main dimensions were:– Length over buffers 11,380 metres; the bogie centres were 4.860 metres apart and the bogie wheelbase was 2.240 metres. Overall width was 2.400 metres and the height above the rails was 3.280 metres. Because this came rather close to the overhead wiring in the long tunnel a couple of insulated roof bars were added after its arrival, both to protect the driver, and to help scrape ice off the overhead power lines inside the tunnel during the winter.

In service the machine was never popular with the Soller's drivers, who found the controls complicated after the simplicity of electrical power. It was also unsuited mechanically to a railway with such steep gradients and thus was little used. Indeed it has been said that its purchase was perhaps a strategic move to blackmail the electricity supply company into improving their service to the railway, for which use it seems to have been wholly successful. In the light of this, it is interesting to note that at some stage the FC de Mallorca were persuaded to allow one of their diesels to make a trip to Soller "to see whether it could get through the tunnels", when one might have thought that a less risky option would have been to construct a wooden mock-up to test this theory in practice. Nevertheless, one Creusot diesel made the journey, towing three of the company's Carde coaches. Again the economic sense of the result of this exercise is difficult to ascertain, as these vehicles were much heavier than the Soller's passenger stock, so perhaps this too was a veiled threat to the power company.

D-1 has now been retired, and for a while was stored in the open at Bunyola where it suffered at the hands of graffiti artists. In 2001 it was repainted and has been taken over by the AAFB (Friends of the Balearic Railways), a club of local enthusiasts with close ties to both the island's railways, who loaned it as a static exhibit for the 125th anniversary of Mallorcan Railways when it was exhibited at Palma station. These days D-1 can be found stored at the SFM's new running sheds at Son Rullan.

The "Crocodile"

While the demand for tourist traffic on the line continued to increase during the latter years of the 20th century, the four motor coaches were already being worked to capacity, and with the disposal of the Ferrotrade diesel there was no longer a back-up locomotive available. The decision was therefore taken to obtain another locomotive. A

Bogies for the "Crocodile" stored beside the station wall at Soller in 2003.   (AUTHOR)

1929 vintage Brown Boveri B-B electric locomotive has been bought from the metre gauge Euskotrebindeak (Basque Railways), which arrived in Majorca during March 2000. The new locomotive is 11.22 metres long and weighs 45 tonnes. As bought it has four 192hp motors using 1,500 volts, and these are being rebuilt to match the Soller line's existing standards together with the necessary re-gauging work. At the time of writing there is no definite date for the completion of this work.

Other Internal Combustion Vehicles

The FC de Soller owns two unusual items of rolling stock, both being rail conversions of 1930-era road vehicles. The first is a Hispano Suiza lorry mounted on a short wheelbase railway chassis, which was built in Barcelona in 1931 by Sabata-Ubach, and entered service the following year. The vehicle is 5.2 metres long, and has a wheelbase of 2 metres with 350mm diameter wheels. Behind a conventional lorry bonnet and cab, the rest of the body resembles a large wooden box with small toolboxes slung outboard on either side, pannier fashion. The body has a one tonne goods capacity and can carry seven people, and also supports a telescopic platform which is used for maintenance access to the overhead power wires. The original engine was a

The "Climent" beside the new workshop at Soller in 2003. (AUTHOR)

The Hispano-Suiza tower lorry was discovered lurking in the carriage shed at Palma during a visit in 2003. A Portuguese tram, awaiting conversion, is visible at the rear. (AUTHOR)

15hp Hispano Suiza four cylinder model, and it is reported that it ran with the same set of spark plugs from 1932 until the 1960s, though the fact that the vehicle had a very high petrol consumption (15 litres to make a one way trip over the line) may have had something to do with this, as it was not often used. The vehicle has mechanical transmission giving four forward and one reverse gear, providing a reason for the retention of small wagon turntables at both Bunyola and Palma. Maximum speed was 50km/hr. In 1995 the motor was replaced with an Ebro 3610cc engine producing 66hp, and in 2000 the wooden bodywork was rebuilt.

The other inspection car was built in 1937 to overcome the fuel consumption of its companion, and uses only 4 litres of fuel per trip. It was produced by the Soller workshops, under the direction of Climent Hernàndez, by mounting a 1920s vintage Renault car on railway axles having small disc wheels. The rest of the body is somewhat primitive and box-like having two doors, though these only extend to waist height and are open above. The motor is an 8hp Adler with four gears (three forward, one reverse). Both these vehicles are painted green, and are still to be seen in occasional use.

Towards the end of the 1980s the conversion of another rail-lorry was started by adding a lorry motor to one of the later types of goods van. This does not appear to have been a successful project and was never completed. However, in 2000 the company acquired a new internal combustion vehicle when it introduced a Land Rover rail-lorry into service. Meanwhile, in 1993 the Vias y Obras department gained a small ballast tamper.

The Land Rover rail-lorry outside the sheds at Soller.   (AUTHOR)

The Soller railway now owns this small ballast tamper, seen here at Bunyola.   (AUTHOR)

The Carriage Stock

At the start six bogie saloons were provided for the opening of the line, with another four following shortly afterwards in 1913. They comprised three First Class, two Composites, two Second Class/mail coaches and three Second Class vehicles, and had end balconies with decorative wrought iron handrails; however, the main difference from their present appearance was the provision of oil lighting with large lamp pots visible on the roof. Today electric lighting has been added. Another change came with the arrival of the bogie brake vans in the 1930s; the mail compartments were then stripped out of the coaches and a First Class compartment substituted. Later in the early 1950s coach number 6 was given tram-style couplings and used on the Puerto Soller section on Sundays and public holidays, to augment the capacity of the trams, though this use ended when the company acquired some open trailers from the Palma system.

Towards the end of the 1970s increasing traffic called for more coaches, and two more were built in the Soller workshops, their wheels having been purchased from the FC de Mallorca, having originated on a couple of the Carde bogie coaches that had recently been scrapped on their home line. The new vehicles were characterised by having square windows with metal frames with rounded corners, and bus-style seating. Three more were built by Talleres Seguí, of Palma, in 1982 and they are numbered 11-15. The original coaches are 12.70 metres long and weigh 13,000kgs, while the newer vehicles are slightly longer at 13.10 metres, weighing about 12,500kgs. Livery is similar to the motor-coaches. In 1984 the older pattern coaches were numbered 1-5 and 8. Number 1 was by then the only remaining First Class saloon carriage, the others having been demoted to Second Class over the years; Number 1 has since followed suit, First Class today being only available on board the motor-coaches. The new-style carriages were numbered 7 and 10-15, showing that some of the older carriages had been rebuilt in the more modern style over the years. Coaches 6 and 9 were not recorded on this visit and may have been undergoing conversion in the workshops.

During the 1990s the demand for seating grew and it was decided to add an extra coach to the trains. At the same time the three brake vans were found to be in need of major overhaul and the opportunity was taken to replace them with some new vehicles with passenger accommodation as well as a small brake compartment and one for the travelling ticket collector. These new coaches, numbered 16-18, were also built by Seguí and went into service in 2000/2001.

Brake Vans

For the opening of the line two brake vans were ordered from Carde y Escoriaza, but as the firm's order books were full the Soller company was forced to patronise another supplier, placing an order with Orenstein & Koppel. However, owing to the shortness

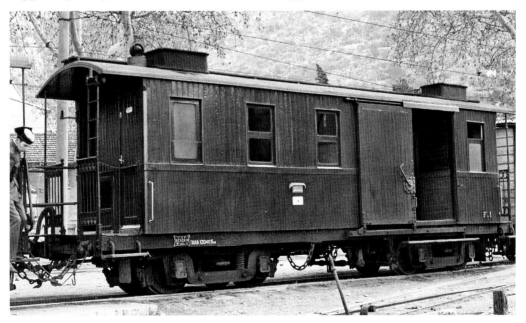

Brake van F1, seen here at Soller.   (J-L ROCHAIS – J. WISEMAN COLLECTION)

of time, the vehicles were not delivered before opening, and the company was forced to operate using ordinary vans as guards vans, though these needed the addition of extra ballast and internal brake equipment. The early regulations stipulated that a barrier vehicle was to be provided between the locomotive and passenger carriages, but there was no requirement for this to be a brake van. As the coaches had brakes on their end platforms and there were travelling brakemen who could also act as ticket inspectors this would not have been a problem in the short term, as regards safety. However, it must have been an inconvenient arrangement for the Senior brakeman (known as the Jefe del Tren), who might have needed to ride in the forward van to supervise the freight consignments, but who would have been cut off from his colleagues while the train was in progress.

Shortly afterwards the two delayed Koppel brake vans arrived. They were four-wheeled vehicles, 6.2 metres in length with end balconies and had a WC compartment at each end, and a dog box opening off the balcony at one end. There was a sliding door for freight and parcel loading in the centre of each side, and they weighed 7 tonnes. They had a fairly short working life, as they were made redundant by the later arrival of some larger brake vehicles some fifteen years later. The two smaller vans were then rebuilt as ordinary goods vans, and at first numbered C10 and C11; later they became C12 and C13.

Following the electrification CAF supplied three bogie brake vans in 1931; these were numbered F1- F3. As well as providing an office desk for the Jefe del Tren's paperwork there was also plenty of room for parcels and luggage with a large sliding door on each side of the vehicle to facilitate loading. There was also a small postal compartment which boasted an external letter box in which letters could be placed for onward despatch on arrival. Like the carriages the new vans had end balconies, though their ironwork was of a slightly simpler pattern – a length of chain providing protection above the fall-plate, rather than the small gates with which the carriages were provided. Like their predecessors they had a WC at each end of the van and a single dog-box. Unlike the carriages, the vans' end balconies had the distinction of being lit by electric light, and a ladder was incorporated into the end railing, allowing access to the water tanks on the roof that supplied the WCs. As the vans always ran at the Palma end of the train (the rule concerning barrier vehicles becoming obsolete with the end of steam power) lamp brackets were only fitted to one end of the vehicle, though lamps were not carried in service. Van F1 gained a window in its 'offside' sliding door.

In the final years of the 20th century there were problems with the bogies of these vehicles, which would have been uneconomic to replace. The brakes were therefore retired, and in 1998 F3 was sent to Barcelona to take part in an exhibition to celebrate 150 years of Spanish railways; it has not returned to Majorca. F2 remains at Soller, in a slightly run-down condition, while in 2000 F3 was removed from its bogies and erected in the town square at Soller to act as a ticket and information office.

Goods Stock

At the start of operations Orenstein & Koppel of Madrid provided twenty wagons. They could carry a load of 7 tonnes and comprised five vans C1-5), ten high-sided opens (A1-10) and five low-sided opens (B1-B5). It will be noted that each class of wagon was numbered in a separate series. To augment these vehicles there were also usually a number of FC de Mallorca wagons on the system. In 1929 the FC de Soller purchased a further batch of goods vehicles from Construcciones Metálicas del Llobregat. These wagons could carry 10 tonnes and indeed have a heavier look with additional ironwork strapping provided on the lowside opens, for instance. The new vehicles were four vans (C6-9), six high-sided opens (A11-16) and four more lowsides (B6-B9). The two ex-passenger brakes were rebuilt and became goods vans C10 and C11. At one time there was a crane mounted on bogies, and a tower wagon, though latterly a four-wheeled crane seems to have been in use. Almost the entire fleet survived until 1974 when there were still all the vans and twenty other wagons still in existence. Now only a handful of the lowsides remain.

The original type of open wagon is typified by B1 to B3 and number 4, which are one-plank dropside vehicles. B1 still retains a vertical screw brake handle while the others have conventional brake levers. Wagon B9, which is a one-plank wagon with fixed sides, typifies the later batch with disc wheels instead of the open spokes of the Orenstein & Koppel wagons. By 1988 wagons B2 and B9 had been fitted with 500kg hoists to assist with track laying duties. These hoists are topped with an electric lamp, though there is no sign of a generator being fitted to either wagon.

Goods stock at Palma. The vans display different styles of planking and ventilator-hatches, representing different building lots.
(M. ANDRESS)

Open wagons at Palma. Note the use of wagon turntables.   (M. ANDRESS)

The last of the high-sided opens appears to have been scrapped at some time after 1981 when it was seen at Soller loaded with scrap iron; by 1984 it had vanished. The body had five rather wide horizontal planks with central 'cupboard-style' doors and the axle boxes were similar to B1, hinting at its Orenstein & Koppel origin.

Only van number 8 survived latterly, though from its condition in 1984 it did not appear to have been used for some time, and may have been scrapped soon after. The body was interesting as the planks were of two alternating sizes and the panels on either side of the central doorways were not similar. With only one ventilation hatch, it appears to have been one of the later arrivals, the Orenstein & Koppel vans having two hatches on each side. It seems likely that its disappearance can be linked to the uncompleted project to turn a van into a self-propelled vehicle for maintenance work.

Goods wagon livery, if surviving at all, is a medium grey with all the ironwork picked out in black. The wagons still in service are fitted with continuous brake pipes as well as manual brakes. In service the wagons ran at the tail of the train, behind the brake van on trains bound for Soller. Side chains as well as centre couplings were used. On the Soller wagons a screw coupling was mounted below the large rectangular buffer, rather than the "chopper" type used on the FC de Mallorca. "Foreign" wagons running through to Soller presumably relied on the safety chains being hooked up, although there is anecdotal evidence that ropes were also sometimes used, particularly on the tramway. At least one FC de Mallorca van was fitted with a Soller-type screw coupling.

A weed-killing wagon has been converted from FC de Mallorca wagon B132, though little of the original body had lasted except for the metal strapping, and even part of the floor was missing when the vehicle was noted in 1988. A large rectangular tank had

In the 1980s the Soller line was using a Majorca Railways open wagon, B132, converted as a weed-killing sprayer. By 2003 the vehicle had been rebuilt as shown here. (AUTHOR)

Open wagon B9, one of the later series, with added hoist. Bunyola, 1988. (AUTHOR)

been fitted, and a small petrol motor at one end drove a spray which discharged through a perforated transverse pipe below the buffer beam. The wagon had retained its vertical screw brake and FC de Mallorca couplings, although these had been modified by the removal of the chopper hook and the fitting of a substantial link pin ending in a Soller style hook. The vehicle has recently been rebuilt with a metal floor and a cylindrical tank.

Apart from this service vehicle there are usually several trolleys of assorted types to be seen around the yard at Soller or Bunyola, at one time including a partly completed rail motor in the process of being converted from a flat trolley.

The Trams

If you listen to the guides on the tourist excursion coaches that visit Puerto Soller in the summer months, you may be told that the trams serving the resort date back to the turn of the century and that they were imported from San Francisco. This is a romantic story, but has little basis in reality. The fact is when the tramway opened in 1913 three four-wheeled trams were supplied by the same firms that eventually produced the railway's electrified rolling stock:– Carde y Escoriaza (bodywork), Siemens-Schuckert (electrical equipment) and Brill (running gear). The traction motors are rated at 35hp and air brakes are fitted, worked by a compressor. Electric current is picked up by a bow collector, though tram No. 1 has been fitted with a railway-style pantograph to enable

Tram No. 3 and two of the open trailers that came from the Palma tramways. Soller, 1996.

(AUTHOR'S COLLECTION)

it to work as station pilot at Soller. In the 1950s this duty was carried out by No. 3, but this has now reverted to having a bow collector. As the trams employ a link and pin coupler, a coupling adapter has to be temporarily attached so as to hook up to the railway stock. The trams have bodies of varnished wood, though the lower end panels have subsequently been covered with metal sheeting, painted a bright orange colour. The trams' official capacity is 18 seated passengers, but in summer this number is augmented by as many standing passengers as can cram themselves aboard.

Two closed wooden trailers were also obtained in 1913, and these were augmented in 1952 with the purchase of two open trailers from the Palma tramways at a cost of 15,000 pesetas each. These were also the products of Carde y Escoriaza and their design dated back to the 1890s, though they had actually been built as recently as 1922. Designed to carry 24 passengers on transverse bench seats, they were rebuilt with a central gangway and fall-plates at one end, to allow the Soller conductor to collect fares, and now run as a permanently coupled pair. This conversion delayed their introduction until 1954, but they were obviously a success as another similar pair was purchased in 1957. All four are now a staple part of summer operations on the tramway. The closed trailers now mainly work in the winter months, when one plus a tramcar is usually enough to cater for the off-season traffic.

Awaiting the conversion that never came – Portuguese bogie tram No. 607 at Soller in 1996.
(AUTHOR'S COLLECTION)

When the open trailers were to be moved to Soller they had to be run to the Palma tramway's terminus at the bull ring, and then dragged a few blocks across town to reach the Soller company's rails a short distance outside the terminus. The first pair's journey to Soller became something of a marathon as owing to a differing wheel profile on the tramcars, they kept derailing on the railway track, and only finally arrived at Soller in the early hours of the morning.

In 1957 the Tramway obtained another couple of vehicles, with the purchase of two tramcars for 120,000 pesetas from the Bilbao Tramways. They had basically similar dimensions to the earlier cars, but were metal bodied and metre gauge. Because of this they first went to the workshops of CAF to be converted to the Soller's 3ft gauge. However, alterations to the geared power trucks were found to be more difficult, and therefore more costly than anticipated and they entered service in 1958 as tramcar number 4 and trailer number 5.

At about the same time two cars (numbers 33 and 35) were purchased from the Palma tramway company, but these were merely cannibalised for their electrical gear, the bodies being exported to the mainland. Later, during the 1990s at the same time that the railway's motor coaches were having their control voltages altered, the trams were similarly adapted; while the traction current was kept at 600 volts, all control and subsidiary circuits were reduced to 24 volts dc. Tram number 3 was the last to undergo this work, emerging from a two-year rebuilding programme in December 2001.

Converted Portuguese tram in the new Soller Tramway colours. (AUTHOR)

A fully-laden "tourist" trailer leaves Puerto Soller behind one of the Portuguese trams.　　　(AUTHOR)

With the increasing demands placed on the line by tourism, and in particular the need to cater for coach-parties, some extra stock was needed by the end of the 1990s. Six four-wheeled trams, dating from the period 1931-39, were acquired from the Lisbon Tramways, their original running numbers being 710, 716, 718, 725, 729 and 734. After a period when they were converted to 3ft gauge and refitted, they emerged painted in a smart maroon and white livery, and numbered from twenty upwards. To go with them the company bought parts for eight new bogie trailers from Seguí, though their design can be traced back to similar vehicles built for the Santander tram system in 1923. They have waist-high wire mesh sides, and access is by end platforms. Internally they are fitted with paired seats on either side of a central gangway. These new trailers started work in 2000, although a pair has since been rebuilt with enclosed sides for winter services.

The arrival of these cars in service saw the retirement of No. 4 and its matching trailer, which have been returned to Bilbao for preservation.

Freight Vehicles

Another vehicle was formerly to be seen on the Tramway; this was a small open wagon used for general goods. Later it was rebuilt as a closed, almost cube-shaped, van and later adapted as an insulated van to be used for fish traffic on market days. It had a very short wheelbase and in its last incarnation was painted in two shades of blue. In use it was run at the rear of the trailers; fish was sent up the tramway from the docks behind the first tram, and the empty boxes were returned to the harbour when the market closed at mid-day. The van was destroyed in an accident during the 1980s.

During the line's freight carrying period goods wagons belonging to both the island's rail systems carried coal and other consignments through to the port, while the gas works at Soller was another customer. During the 1960s the loop nearest Puerto Soller was used as an unloading spot by the hotels situated at this end of the bay who received food and drink, as well as general supplies, via the tramway. At one time the dockside layout contained a loop line, the site of which was later enclosed within the Naval Base that was established on the dockside after the demise of the passenger ferries to Barcelona. Armaments for the base were stored inland at a depot near Santa Maria halt, and were brought down by goods wagons, the sight of a lowside wagon carrying a couple of torpedoes loosely covered by a tarpaulin being not uncommon. On one occasion there was a mishap and the torpedo load ended up on the roadway near the harbour, to general consternation. At the dockside a steam crane carried out any necessary shunting, as the overhead wires stopped at the dock gates. Because of the differing coupling standards, railway wagons could sometimes be found tied to the rear of the trams with odd bits of rope. This was presumably particularly the case with FC de Mallorca vehicles that found their way to Puerto Soller.

Chapter 9

The Soller Line Described

The Palma terminus of the FC de Soller is situated in the Plaza España next to the SFM station, however the Soller station is more attractive than its neighbour, the entrance archway with its decorative lettering being shaded by a tall palm tree. The whole site is narrow and constricted, and there is just room for a single platform with a pleasant station building of brick faced with stone. The running line splits into three loops opposite the station, and there was formerly a line leading to a three-stall semi-roundhouse. Latterly the stub end of this line terminated in a wagon turntable used to turn the Permanent Way Department's motorised vehicles. Beside the station is a two-road brick shed which used to house the motor-coaches, and which these days shelters the occasional spare carriage. There was formerly a goods shed and a couple of short sidings for freight at the outer end of the yard, all reached by a trailing siding and several wagon turntables. Goods wagons would have been manhandled on these sidings, as there was no locomotive access at first. All steam facilities were removed after World War II and a more direct connection to the goods shed was provided. When freight services ended the goods shed was demolished and the site is now used as a car park.

At the end of the station yard is a colour light signal, and beyond this the single line passes out through a gateway into the street where it runs along a central reservation,

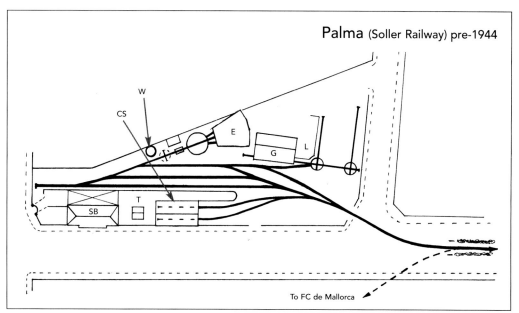

Palma (Soller Railway) pre-1944

To FC de Mallorca

Palma station drowses in the summer heat in this picture dating from the 1950s.   (AUTHOR'S COLLECTION)

Son Sardina station, seen in 1988.   (AUTHOR)

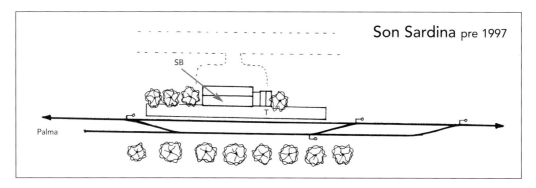

Son Sardina pre 1997

once flanked by low bushes. Several side streets cross the line in the first few 100 metres, and the train's whistle is in fairly constant use along this section of the line. There follows a mile or so of running through the city's high-rise suburbs and trading estates, which have proliferated in this area since the 1980s.

Leaving the city outskirts and passing beneath the motorway, the railway regains a more timeless feel as the track runs through fields of crops and scattered olive trees. Five kilometres after leaving the terminus the station of **Son Sardina** is reached. Here there is a single platform on the left of the line, and a simple single-storey station building sheltered by trees. There was formerly a loop track with an extra cross-over part of the way along it, plus a short dead-end siding, though these were removed when the station was down-graded to halt status. The building has been handed over to the AAFB as a club-room, replacing their earlier use of the upper floor at the Palma terminus. Leaving Son Sardina the gradient stiffens slightly as the line runs on through the fields, passing a newly laid loop and the tourist station at **Son Reus** (opened in 1997 on the site of an earlier halt), after which the climb stiffens again to 1 in 50. There are a couple of 'request stop' halts in quick succession, short platforms with a simple shelter where the line crosses a minor road; the first and smaller halt is **Santa Maria,** while the other is named **San Caubet** and serves a nearby sanatorium. Just beyond Santa Maria halt is the site of the former military depot, once a guarded, walled enclosure containing several buildings, but today in ruins.

Soon after this the gradient flattens out and the train arrives at **Bunyola**, the mid-point crossing station on the railway. The station yard is most attractively situated on

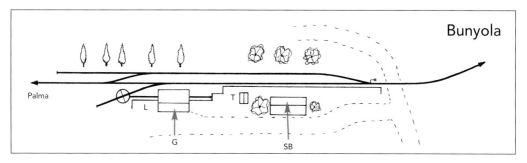

Bunyola

San Caubet halt. Note the traffic lights that now protect road users at the level crossing beyond the platform.   (AUTHOR)

General view of Bunyola station. The goods yard is now used to store track-laying supplies.

(AUTHOR'S COLLECTION)

the edge of the town and is flanked by a row of pine trees. Approaching the station the train passes the small electrical sub-station where the 15,000 volt national power supply is converted to the railway's traction current of 1,200 volts dc. Just after this the station loop opens up on the left, while on the right there is a trailing siding leading to a wagon turntable providing access to the modest goods shed and a small yard nowadays used as a store by the Permanent Way Department. Originally another siding ran off the turntable at right angles to the running line, crossed the road and ran into a cement works. The station building is on the right-hand side and the large clock overhanging the platform is worthy of note as it is shaped like a giant pocket watch, complete with winder. Opposite the main platform there is also a short, narrow island platform between the two tracks of the loop. As with the other station on the line the turnouts are marked by point indicators, picked out in red and white paint.

As the train leaves Bunyola it passes over another ungated level crossing and curves to the left. Ahead are steep hillsides covered with pine trees, the lower slopes terraced for the cultivation of olives, and the valley through which the line runs becomes increasingly steeper and narrower forcing the line to twist and turn through the woods in order to find the easiest path. Soon afterwards two tunnels, both short in length, are encountered. Two kilometres beyond Bunyola the summit tunnel is reached, the line's highest altitude of 238.8 metres being attained about halfway through. Shortly afterwards the line reaches a passing loop, added since 1988, and the platform (Mirador) where the daily Tourist Special pauses for 10 minutes for the passengers to

No. 2 picks up passengers bound for Palma at Bunyola, while the "Climent" heads back to Soller; a view taken in 1974.   (J. L. ROCHAIS - J. WISEMAN COLLECTION)

A winter arrival at Soller in 1992 – no lack of passengers, despite the season. (AUTHOR)

The new carriage shed which has been built at Soller on the site of the former goods shed. The partly completed carriage is one of the new brake/2nds, seen here awaiting the fitting of balcony ironwork in 2000. (AUTHOR)

admire the view. The line is now on a steadily falling gradient and descends in a series of horseshoe curves round the lower slopes of the mountains. Ten more tunnels of varying lengths are passed on the descent, as well as the long viaduct known as the Cinq Ponts, which has featured on many a railway postcard. Eventually the resin-smelling pine woods of the summit give way once again to terraced cultivation and ultimately the line passes through lemon groves whose trees are so close to the train that one can almost pick the fruit from the carriage window. With the town of Soller visible a short way below there is a new stop for excursion trains at a halt named **Can Tambor** (opened in 1990). Here coach parties de-train to continue their journey by road. After this the line runs through a last tunnel and as houses appear beside the track, the line squeezes between them and a large running shed on the left to enter the station yard at Soller, which is built on a shelf on the side of the hill, supported by a stone retaining wall. The railway's motor coaches and the trams that continue the journey down to the port share this shed. On the opposite side of the line are the old steam roundhouse and the line's workshops.

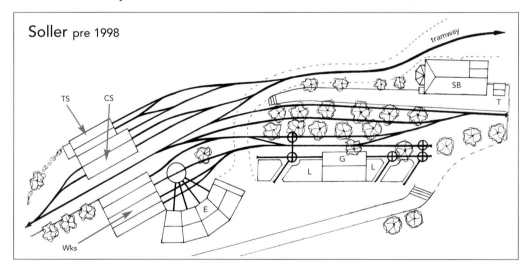

The station yard at Soller is planted with rows of plane trees, beneath which are several loop lines used for storing spare carriages. The single platform curves in front of the station building, which was converted from a house that dates back several hundred years; passengers descend an imposing internal stairway from the platform to gain the ticket hall where there is a plaque commemorating the opening of the railway.

At the far side of the station loops was the goods shed, which as usual with the FC de Soller was only accessible by negotiating several wagon turntables. Behind this was once a large stone tank supplying water to the locomotives and workshops. Nowadays this is the site of a new erecting shop where several of the railway's ongoing projects can be seen, although public access across the running lines is no longer allowed.

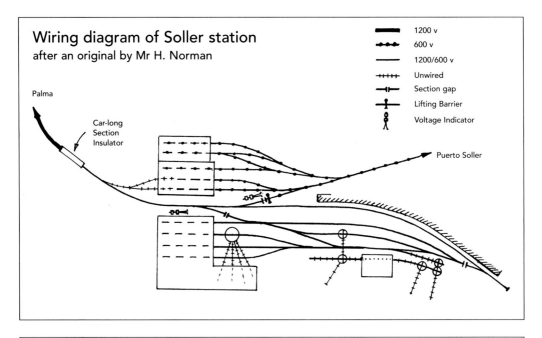

Wiring diagram of Soller station
after an original by Mr H. Norman

Palma

Car-long
Section
Insulator

Puerto Soller

	1200 v
	600 v
	1200/600 v
	Unwired
	Section gap
	Lifting Barrier
	Voltage Indicator

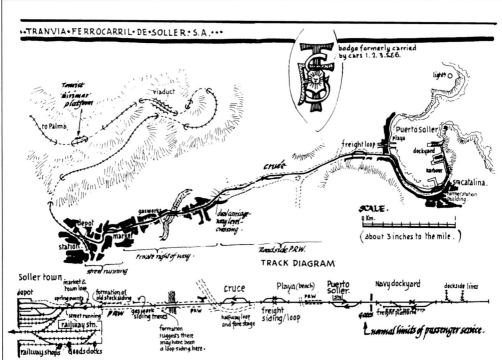

·•·TRANVIA·FERROCARRIL·DE·SOLLER·S.A.···

badge formerly carried
by cars 1. 2. 3. 5 & 6.

light

Tourist
'Mirimar'
platform

viaduct

to Palma

Puerto Soller
Playa

freight loop

dockyard

harbour

cruce

sa catalina
former station
building

gasworks

dual carriage-
way level-
crossing

SCALE.
0 Km.   1
(about 3 inches to the mile .)

depot

market

station

private right of way

street running

Roadside P.R.W.

TRACK DIAGRAM

Soller town

depot

market &
town loop
spring points

formation of
old stock siding

street running

railway stn.

formation
suggests there
may have been
a loop siding here.

railway shops   goods docks

gas work
siding traces

P.R.W.

P.R.W.

halfway loop
and fare stage

cruce

Playa (beach)

freight
siding / loop

P.R.W.

Puerto
Soller.
stn.

gates

Navy dockyard

freight platform

L normal limits of passenger service.

dockside lines

*This charming map and diagram of the Soller Tramway was drawn by Herbert Norman, a lifelong 'Soller' enthusiast,
A version of the map appeared in 'Modern Tramway' and is featured by kind permission of the Editor, Modern Tramway, now Light Rail
and Modern Tramway, jointly published by the LRTA and Ian Allan Ltd.*

The Soller Tramway

From a running shed at the station throat several tracks combine to form a loop which is used by the tramcars to run round their trailers. Two tracks (formerly one) drop down steeply to the street outside the station, where passengers for the port are picked up. Leaving this stop the tramway, now a single line, crosses a small Plaza that contains some notable buildings testifying to the town's past prosperity. The old brake van/ticket office is situated here, and the trams almost seem to run between the tables of a pavement cafe before slipping into a side street. Here is a loop line where the trailer cars are sometimes left if the incoming service does not connect with one of the trains, while the tram continues to the station alone. A little further on to the left of the line is the site of a pair of sidings, one facing the station yard, the other the port. The second formerly served the local gas works and must have been the destination of a good deal of coal traffic in the past. Shortly after this the line squeezes between two houses to cross a side road which is the site of a request stop, following which the town is soon left behind and the line crosses the course of a small river by means of a substantial girder bridge, before dropping down a short, sharp incline. Travelling through the fields a passing loop is reached which marks the mid-point fare stage of the tramway (shown on the tickets as Cruce), and shortly after this the main road to the port is encountered at an ungated level crossing where road traffic is protected by warning lights. Some way further on is another loop formerly used for goods transhipment, and now partially lifted.

Road and rail continue in close proximity until at length the tramway is running along the top of the sea-wall round the Bay of Soller, where there is another request stop, marked by a short platform. A loop line where the harbour jetty thrusts out into

Not going anywhere! Plinthed brake van F2 is now a Tourist office at Soller.   (AUTHOR)

Tram No. 3 and assorted trailers climbing the hill to the depot at Soller in 1953.   (D. TREVOR ROWE)

the bay marks the original terminal, and there is a cafe situated on the seaward side of the line. In the 1920s a 1km extension was made along the street to serve a naval base, developed at the outer end of the harbour, but these tracks have now vanished. As there are no run round facilities at the gate leading to the former base, the trams drop their trailers at the harbour station loop before continuing on to the end of the line alone. On the return trip a short halt is made at the station to pick up the trailers before the tram makes the return trip to Soller. At times this simple layout can get extremely busy as the service tram can be followed by two of the tourist tram-and-trailer sets running down empty to meet an excursion boat. These all need to perform quite a ballet to run round their trailers, and the manoeuvres can turn into a game of leapfrog, with the first tourist tram returning with the second set of trailers, leaving its companion to run round the remaining trailers when the loop is finally clear.

The tramway track is lighter than that used on the railway, and weighs only 22.7kgs/metre. Double check rails are used where the line runs through the streets of Soller and at the port. For the majority of the run through the countryside normal sleepered track is used, though the ballasting and maintenance is not always of a very high order. It is sufficient however for the light loads and low speeds employed, though the amount of shaking and swaying movements the elderly trams are capable of has to be seen to be believed, and one could be forgiven sometimes for wondering whether the body would disintegrate before reaching the end of its run. The steep gradient facing homeward bound trams approaching the station at Soller sometimes caused problems, particularly in wet weather with two fully laden trailers in tow. If the tram stalled it was sometimes necessary to persuade some of the larger passengers to move from the trailers into the tramcar to provide sufficient adhesion to get up the slope.

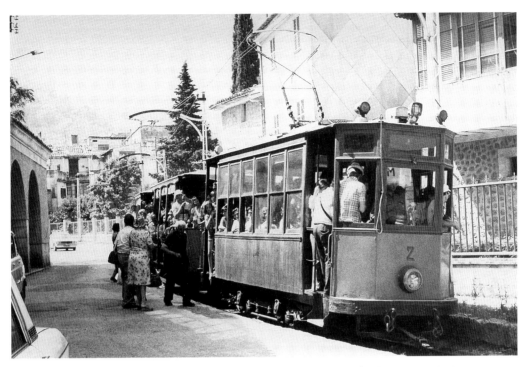

Tram No. 2 takes on passengers beside the market in Soller, en-route for the port in 1977.

(K. TAYLORSON)

PALMA Á SOLLER

PRECIOS			K.	ESTACIONES	2	4	6
1.ᵃ c.	2 ᵃ c.	3.ᵃ c.					
»	»	»	»	● PALMA .... S....	7.42	15. »	20. »
			5	Son Sardina......................	7.50	15.10	20.10
			15	Buñola...........................	8.10	15.30	20.20
			29	SOLLER.......................... Ll..	8.45	15. 5	21. 5

					1	3	5
»	»	»	»	SOLLER........................... S....	5.30	9.30	18. »
			13	Buñola...........................	6. 5	10. 5	18.35
			22	Son Sardina......................	6.25	10.25	18.55
			28	● PALMA.......................... Ll..	6.35	10.35	19. 5

Además de estos trenes, los domingos y días festivos saldrán otros dos de Palma para Soller á las 11.30 y 15.30 y otros dos de Soller para Palma á las 13.15 y 18.30.

1913

HORARIO DE TRENES

SECCION PALMA - SOLLER		SECCION SOLLER-PUERTO	
Salid. Sóller	Salid. Palma	Salid. Sóller	Salid. Puerto
5,45	7,—	5,—	5,20
8,15	9,30	7,—	6,30
10,45	12,—	8,5	7,30
13,30	15,—	9,—	8,30
17,15	19,30	10,—	9,30
		10,45	10,20
		12,5	11,30
		13,5	12,30
		14,—	13,30
		15,—	14,30
		16,5	15,30
		18,—	16,30
		19,—	17,30
c.1930		20,35	18,30
			19,30
			20,55

212 Palma-Soller 212

Km.	2 Cor. 1-2	4 Trn. 1-2	6 Cor. 1-2	8 Tra. 1-2	8 bis Trn 1-2.	ESTACIONES (1-IV-959)	1 Trn. 1-2	3 Cor. 1-2	5 Trn. 1-2	7 bis Cor. 1-2
0	8.—	13.—	15.30	20.—	20.30	S . Palma .... Ll ..	7.40	10.15	15.10	21 —
6	8.10	13.10	15.40	20.10	22.40	Son Sardina .... ↑	7.31	10.06	15.01	21.31
11	8.18	13.18	15.49	20.19	22.49	Santa Maria	7.23	9.58	14.53	21.38
16	8.28	13.28	15.59	20.29	22.59	Buñola	7.16	9.51	14.46	21.46
32	8.55	13.55	16.25	20.55	23.25	Ll . Sóller .... S ..	6.45	9.20	14.15	22.—

1958

Tram No. 2 runs along beside the beach, approaching Puerto Soller in 1992.   (AUTHOR)

Tram No. 2, its way to the dock gates blocked by parked cars, awaits its next departure from Puerto Soller.
                                                                                              (AUTHOR)

Part Three

Other Lines

Chapter 10

The Independent Railways
and Tramways of Majorca

The Harbour Tramway (1877/1931)

The first tramway in Palma came into being with the Majorca Railway Company's desire to gain access to the harbour. In 1874 the Railway's Engineer, Eusebio Estada, presented a report on a line linking the station with the harbour in order to save the time and cost of transhipping goods by road between the two points. Three projected routes were suggested, two tracing courses around the perimeter of the old city walls, the third to be built as an urban tramway through the streets of the capital. Not only were some of these narrow, but there was also a significant difference in height between the railway terminus and the harbour, both factors that led to the eventual route being rather circuitous. The third option was chosen, despite the fact that this would mean animal haulage being used, as steam locomotives were prohibited from the centre of the city. This was not a problem to Estada, as speed was not a consideration. In any case the two external routes would have involved more engineering works on the seaward side of the city walls and expensive expropriation of private land.

Work started in November 1875, and 7,800 metres of tramway rail were ordered from England in 1876, along with parts for seventeen turnouts. All this material arrived early the following year, and the track laying was completed between 1st February and the end of April 1877. The tramway started as an extension of one of the goods shed lines, and emerged from the station into what was then known as the Plaza de Eusebio Estada. (In those days the street beside the station was called the Calle de Infanta but the advent of the republic swept this royalist reminder away and the street was renamed after Eusebio Estada, leaving the square to become the present Plaça España). After passing the front of the station, the tramway ran a little way round the site of the old city walls to the former Puerta de Jésus. From here it entered the city centre and passed down the Paseo de la Rambla and the Calle Navarra, past the theatre where there was a sharp curve, and into the Plaza Weyler. It then ran along the Calle Unio (now known as the Calle General Mola) where the line turned left to run southwards to the port along the Paseo del Borne and the Avenida Antonio Maura. The distance between the station and the harbour was 2.9kms, with a further half kilometre of line on the

General view of Palma docks, 1914. (A. SANCHIS COLLECTION)

The imperfect quality of this photograph is regretted; nevertheless it has been included for its rarity value.

dockside. In the early days there were two passing loops in the city section and another at the entrance of the quays.

Once the route opened a few teething problems were soon encountered. Rubbish and dirt quickly accumulated in the rails, which in any case had very shallow grooves, barely compatible with the railway's wheel standards; this led to occasional derailments. The situation was compounded as the railway workers in charge of the animals were not experienced in the task, and in July 1877 a wagon derailed, killing one of the mules hauling the train. This led to the hiring of better skilled animal drivers, at an increased cost to that anticipated. Nevertheless, the amount of goods traffic destined for the docks must have grown rapidly as in 1879 the company applied to run a steam tram locomotive on the line. Spanish law had been passed in 1877 allowing such engines, but limiting them to 20km/hr in towns. The body had to be enclosed, the engine was to run silently with all the smoke consumed, while the driver had to have a good view of the track when travelling in either direction. The new tram locomotive came from the British firm of R. W. Hawthorn (Works No. 1836, built 1880), and had its cylinders arranged on the Brown system, which had been developed for use on unpaved streets. Rather than the normal method of attaching the cylinders below the footplate where the slide valves could get covered in dust or mud, they were mounted above the footplate and drove onto rocker arms, which transferred the motion to the coupled wheels via a connecting rod. As there was little lateral force transmitted to the piston using this method, the slide bars could be dispensed with. Some accounts of the line have suggested that this locomotive was bought "secondhand", on a tip-off from a Majorcan sea captain, and as it was 3ft gauge the decision on the island's railway gauge was thus decided. However, as the FC de Mallorca had already been built by this time this story must surely be apocryphal.

The locomotive arrived in 1881, but despite a trial run from Palma station to Pont d'Inca and back, with brake tests undertaken on the street track outside the station, the city council remained unconvinced. In any case the locomotive's passage through the city was at first prevented physically by the narrow archway at the Puerta de Jésus, so for a while longer animal traction remained in use. The street-running section was never particularly convenient for the operation of freight traffic, and it appears that in the early days at least this was seen as a temporary expedient. In 1886 authorisation was given for another route running round the edge of the city to the east, although this never progressed further, and the tram locomotive continued to hand over its wagons to the mule teams near the Puerta de Jésus, even after the gateway itself was eventually removed between 1911 and 1913. Despite the ban on the use of steam on the tramway, the company purchased a second tram engine in 1889. Once again it was an 0-4-0 tank engine, this one a product of Nasmyth Wilson's. The maker's photo shows it fitted with side buffers and a conventional hook coupling, which must have needed altering on arrival, when it apparently also acquired side skirts, though these were later removed again. Majorcan locomotives seem to have had nicknames bestowed on them by the staff, and the latest Nasmyth became known as "La Inglesita".

Meanwhile, in the city centre the mules soon learned that it was best to step outside the rails when hauling wagons round the sharp curves, but there is some anecdotal evidence that there was one spot on the tramway, in the Paseo del Borne, which was particularly troublesome and in the 1920s, when the city council had finally relented and allowed the company to operate its locomotives through the streets, the locomotives were prone to derail there. Passers-by soon got used to helping the train crew push the engine back onto the rails. Normally the tram was limited to a speed of 20km/hr in the streets, but this was reduced to 8km/hr at certain points on the line where there were sharp curves. In 1921 the company bought another locomotive for the harbour line, an 0-4-0 tank by Orenstein & Koppel, and by this time the Hawthorn locomotive seems to have reached the end of its life, as it was scrapped soon afterwards.

Considerable tonnages were dispatched over the tramway, which must have caused some inconvenience to both the city's inhabitants and the railway company. Finally, to ease matters, a military engineer, Luis García Ruiz, drew up plans in 1928 for a tunnel linking the station with the harbour and in April the same year work started, the contract having been awarded to Material y Obras, a construction firm from Barcelona. The new route was completed in 1931 and was 2.4kms long, of which 1.25kms was in a tunnel, nearly all on a falling gradient. The final cost was just over 2.5 million pesetas.

The material that had been excavated from the tunnel was used to reclaim part of the foreshore where it was planned to lay out a station with a passenger building similar in style to that recently erected at Sineu, and also a goods shed. Possibly because of the smoke encountered in the tunnel, regular passenger services never used the line and the new station was never built, a classification yard of five parallel loops being sufficient for freight use. Nevertheless, there is some evidence that occasional passenger trains may have been run in conjunction with the visits of cruise ships.

By this time there were a number of electric tram routes in the city centre, and the now obsolete goods route appears to have been wired up to become part of the passenger network.

Palma Docks (1877/1967)

Over the years that the tramway existed, the docks at Palma were extended several times. At first there was merely a single mole, 630 metres in length, with a triangular bulge halfway along which separated the Old and New wharves. In 1877 the original tramway merely ran the length of these wharves, but with several ships loading along the length of the mole this track arrangement was somewhat inconvenient, and soon a loop at the landward end of the wharves, and another more sharply curved loop line serving the wider central area were added, together with a siding at the outer end of the line near the lighthouse. The difficulties of working the harbour lines were also increased as the lines had been laid eight metres back from the edge of the wharves to allow room for cargo to be stacked during unloading. This led to a certain amount of

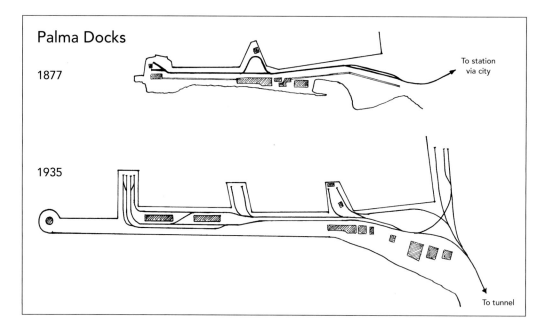

Palma Docks

1877

To station
via city

1935

To tunnel

double handling of materials in getting them to and from the railway wagons, and may have even needed the help of carts for some loads. The track layout remained unchanged until the early 20th century when in 1906 the New Wharf was extended, although extra sidings were not laid until 1910/11. However, the main problem remained one of railway access to the dockside. In late 1913 it was recorded that 15,647 tonnes of goods as well as 8,790 animals passed over the quays during a two month period, and this on a line which was still basically a single siding with a couple of passing places, fed by a street tramway. Between 1913 and 1922 a new jetty was constructed, provided with sidings, while later other lines were added up the spine of the wharf and along the La Lotje Quay, at the base of the harbour.

From the 1920s the small steam locomotives were able to bring wagons directly to the dockside, but for shunting the wharves the company purchased a couple of Fordson tractors, fitted with large wooden beams at the front, to move wagons around the quaysides, as these were more convenient. Only after the Harbour Tunnel was built in the 1930s were the original tight dockside curves eased so that the larger locomotives could use the quayside lines. In particular they needed access to the bottom of the main wharf and the line along the La Lotje Quay, which formed part of a triangle needed to turn the engines for their return trip to the main station.

From time to time the Junta del Puerto (Harbour Commissioners) laid down conditions that were not in the railway's favour, either limiting the times that trains could work on the harbour lines, or imposing tolls on the locomotives and wagons in transit, plus daily demurrage charges on stationary railway wagons. These were in force from 1929 until the early 1960s, but were not levied on the local road transport contractors. The five loop tracks at the seaward end of the tunnel, acted as a marshalling yard, and also provided a storage potential, able to minimise the time that

General view of the marshalling yard outside Palma docks, seen shortly after completion.

(A. SANCHIS COLLECTION)

Palma Harbour c.1930. By this time there are two lines of rails along the main wharf.

(AUTHOR'S COLLECTION)

No. 9 shunting the marshalling yard at the harbour in 1958. The heavy traffic in potatoes is evident.

(D. W. WINKWORTH)

company wagons used the harbour lines and thus save on the toll charges. This may also explain the use of the road tractors for quayside shunting, as they were toll-free.

Early plans had shown a station with goods facilities on the waterfront, though these were never built. Had the once-proposed line to Andratx ever materialised, such a station might have been needed as the new line would have had to run round the city walls before striking off for the proposed terminus to the west; this would have given the possibility of the railway company serving the southern side of the capital in competition with the city's trams.

Another possible westward extension that never became a reality was the linking up of the FC de Mallorca's dockside lines with those that were planned at the western end of the harbour in the late 1930s, to assist the building of a new harbour at Porto Pi. In the event the two systems remained separated, and the Porto Pi line was built to metre gauge.

The final extension on the dockside was the provision of additional tracks on an extension to the jetty made in the early 1950s, when large amounts of coal were being exported to southern Spain. However, by this time some of the other sidings were falling out of use, as lorries could reach the ships more easily than the railway. The end of goods working in 1967 brought about the closure of the harbour line, although by that date it had become almost completely derelict. The tracks were lifted or asphalted over, but nevertheless as late as 2002 about 20 metres of line could still be seen leading towards the start of the jetty.

The Palma Tramways (1891/1959)

The idea of a tramway system for Palma can be traced back to 1863, by which time a sufficiently large number of people living in the distant suburb of El Terreño needed an easy method of transport linking with the city centre. Despite this the Ayunamiento only issued the first concession to operate a tramway in 1874, although nothing came of this plan. In 1882 a new project was presented, this one linking Palma and Porto Pi, a little to the west of El Terreño. Once again these plans came to nothing, however, a few years later, in 1890, a horse bus route was established linking the city centre with the port.

A year later the Sociedad Mallorquina de Tranvias (Majorcan Tramway Company) was formed to build and work a tramway connecting the city centre with the area west of the main harbour, at Porto Pi. The route, which opened on 20th September 1891, started in the Plaza de Coll, and going via Calle Bolseria and Calle Colon reached Plaza Cort. From here it threaded its way along Calle Palacio (later known as Calle Conquistador) and ran round two sides of the gardens that today form part of the Plaza de la Reina, but was then known as the Plaza de la Libertad (which name was later changed to Plaza Isabel II). From here it ran down the Calle Marina (now the Avenida

Palma Tramways, Car No. 34, heads along the Establiments line en-route for the depot (the destination blind reads COCHERAS). (J. WISEMAN)

Palma Tramways, Car No. 40 on the Soledad route in 1958, shortly before closure. (J. WISEMAN)

Antonio Maura) to emerge from the city opposite the harbour. The last section along the Calle Marina may have shared tracks with the harbour freight line however, where this crossed an open space to reach the dockside, the Porto Pi route turned off to the right and ran along the waterfront, passing La Lonja, to cross the city moat by the Sa Riera bridge. From here it continued westward to serve the suburbs of Santa Catalina, El Terreño and Porto Pi, a total distance of 4.8kms.

The concession for the tramway stipulated that animal traction would be used, and at first nine open "toast-rack" trailers were obtained from Carde y Escoriaza to inaugurate the service, having canvas curtains hanging from the cantrail to protect the passengers from the sun. Soon after the total was increased by three more trailers, and later the number of vehicles was increased again to twenty-eight, some of these new arrivals being closed cars with end platforms for use during the winter months. At first twenty-eight mules were employed – a pair for each of the first twelve cars, plus extra animals for use where the route ascended a steep gradient and extra power was needed for a short distance.

At this point a mystery occurs, to which the answer has yet to emerge. The order books of the Brush Electrical Engineering Company (successors to Falcon) record that four tram engines (Works Nos. 198-201) were supplied to the Palma Tramways in 1891 supposedly for the Porto Pi route. Their running numbers were 2-5, and they were built to an earlier Falcon design. Despite the entry in the Falcon order books, the name of the tramway company is incorrect, and there seems to be little evidence locally that the steam trams were actually used for passenger haulage; indeed, at this date the City Council had yet to sanction the operation of a steam locomotive on the line connecting the railway station and the port. However, the fact that at least one of these tram locomotives arrived in Palma is not in doubt as one engine, Works No. 198, was later used by the contractor building the FC de Soller, and later passed into the ownership of the railway company.

A new method of propulsion was heralded in 1911, when the Compañia del Tranvia Electrico de Ca's Catala a l'Estacion de Palma was inaugurated to extend the existing line at both ends and convert to electric power. However, before the conversion work could be completed it was halted by the transfer of the concession to the Sociedad General de Tranvías Electricos Interurbanos de Palma de Mallorca (or TEIP) which was formed in 1914 to run, extend and electrify the Palma tramway system. The new company bought up the shares of the former tramway company and took over the mule-powered Porto Pi route where, following a two-year electrification programme, the first new trams ran on 1st July 1916. This was followed shortly afterwards by the inauguration of a new route, which linked Plaza San Antonio and ran along the Calle de Aragón to a new terminus at Ca'n Capas on the eastern fringe of the city. The engineer for these lines was Pedro Garau.

To work the services the TEIP ordered a total of fifty tramcars. They were built by Carde y Escoriaza with electrical equipment by Siemens, of a type similar to the Soller

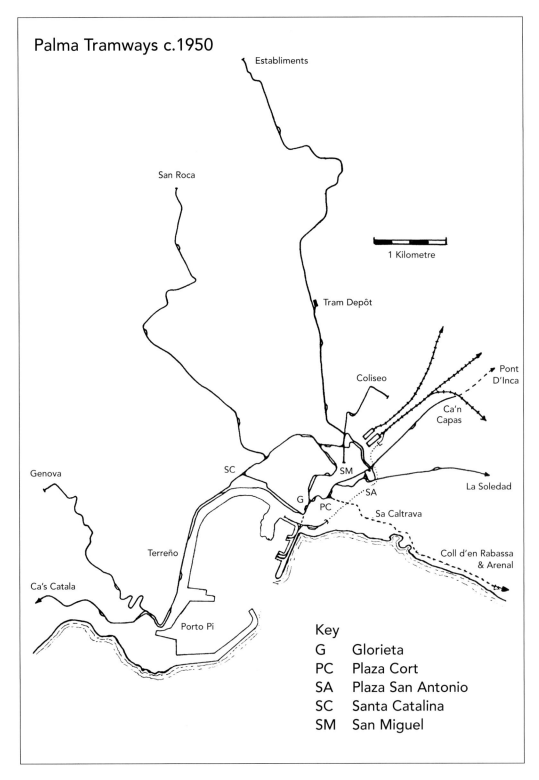

Palma Tramways c.1950

Establiments

San Roca

1 Kilometre

Tram Depôt

Coliseo

Pont D'Inca

Ca'n Capas

Genova

SC

SM

La Soledad

G

SA

PC

Sa Caltrava

Terreño

Coll d'en Rabassa & Arenal

Ca's Catala

Porto Pi

Key
G   Glorieta
PC   Plaza Cort
SA   Plaza San Antonio
SC   Santa Catalina
SM   San Miguel

Tramway, with three-sided ends and straight sides. On all the cars the running gear used French-built Brill trucks with a wheelbase of 2.20 metres, and the traction motors were rated at 35hp. This rating did not leave much spare power to haul a trailer and although some of the old mule cars were retained as trailers for use on the more popular routes serving Santa Catalina, Terreño and the bull-ring, most of the trams ran as single units.

Unhappily, the TEIP's first day of service was marred by a fatal accident when the brakes failed on one of the tramcars in the Calle Conquistador and the runaway vehicle crashed into a building in the Plaza de la Libertad, killing a teenage boy and injuring several other people The tram appears to have been written off by this incident as later reports only mention forty-nine cars in service. Other incidents blighted the electric tramways early days: – in August two cars, numbers 6 and 8 collided at almost the same place as the earlier accident. The site was a junction, and car No. 6 had halted to wait for the arrival of the incoming service from Terreño. Meanwhile, No. 8 was approaching along Calle Palacio, expecting to pass the waiting tram. However, just as No. 8 arrived, the driver of No. 6, believing he had been given the starting signal, moved off and struck the other tram. Both cars suffered damage. A few months later, in October 1916, an old woman was knocked down and killed in front of the Principal Theatre by car No. 5, on its way to Porto Pi.

The year 1920s saw the Porto Pi route lengthened to serve Ca's Catala, while the Ca'n Capas line was extended to Pont d'Inca. This involved a flat crossing with the FC de Mallorca's Santany branch at Ca'n Capas. Another new route was the circular line which linked the railway station with Santa Catalina and the Terreño branch, while in 1920 a line running east from Plaza Cort towards the Sa Caltrava district eventually reached Coll d'en Rabassa after a journey of 10kms. Here is made an end-on junction with a separate company, which had inaugurated a line linking the electric tramway terminus with Arenal further along the Bay of Palma (see The Arenal Tramway). Later the TEIP, which had declined the original concession for this line, bought out its rival and extended its wires as far as Arenal.

As well as extending along the bay of Palma in 1920, the following year saw the TEIP throw a long branch off the outer circle line, to reach the town of Son Roca to the north-west, while the next year saw the system extend still further, with a branch line from Porto Pi to Gènova, and another line from Plaza San Antoni to La Soledad, a manufacturing district on the main road to Manacor. As with the railways, the First World War had caused supply problems, and when the new routes demanded extra vehicles the company were forced to find a new supplier. Luckily the Barcelona Tramways had some surplus cars, about ten of which were purchased and transferred to Palma. They were numbered in the 100 series and had a different style of bodywork to the Mallorcan trams, with rounded ends and a wider body whose lower side panels curved inwards towards the bogie frames.

Car No. 26 passes the railway stations in 1953. (D. TREVOR ROWE)

Car No. 22, en-route to Porto Pi, runs through the centre of Palma. (L. G. MARSHALL)

At the same time as these easterly extensions, the TEIP also opened a new line 7.7kms long, from the railway stations northwards to Establiments. At first the system's tram depot had been situated in the Calle de Aragón near the city centre, but now a depot in a modern concrete style was built on the new branch at C'as Capiscol. At the end of the decade a bull-ring (Coliseo) was built to the north of the city centre and this was provided with a short branch, opened in 1929, running from a new central terminus situated near the market in the San Miguel district. It had been intended to extend this line to meet up with the Pont d'Inca route to create a new "outer circle", but this never materialised. For a short while, from 1935 to 1936, there was a 1km long electrified line serving the Moll de la Riba in the port of Palma, though this soon closed and may have fallen a victim to the loss of trade following the outbreak of the Civil War in 1936.

Despite this the tramway enjoyed several successful years, even in the uncertain period of the late 1930s,0 when power cuts were common. Passenger numbers climbed to an annual total of 14,197,304 journeys in 1939, and no doubt these totals were

An unidentified Carde-built tram poses in front of the later tram depot, inside which can be seen both original and ex-Barcelona cars.   (J. WISEMAN)

maintained due to the lack of available petrol for alternative transport during World War II. However, immediately after the war the annual total fell to 9,840,057 passengers. Paradoxically, the tramway's success was its own downfall. Many of the routes in the city centre ran through narrow streets where only a single line could be laid and consequently an intensive service was difficult to maintain, especially near the terminus of San Miguel and the area around the railway stations where many routes converged; this despite the fact that some of the circular route round the Avenues was double-tracked. The longer routes had only occasional passing places (four on the long Establiments line and three on the route to Son Roca), which must have made for fairly extended service intervals – perhaps one tram about every 15 minutes, based on early timetables. After the war the development of more route-flexible buses began to spell the end for the trams, and the first victims were the Coll d'en Rabassa to Arenal section which had closed in 1941, followed by the San Antonio-Coll section in 1948, while the outer end of the C'as Catala route was cut back to terminate at Porto Pi in 1954. The route cut-backs meant that some vehicles in the fleet became surplus to requirements, and in 1952 four open trailers were sold to the Soller Tramway.

An American visitor to Palma in March 1956 recorded his impressions of the local tramway system. The tramcars and the track were by then in a very poor condition and operations were conducted at a slow pace. At one spot on the Pont d'Inca route the rail had turned completely over on its side and the tram's wheels were running on the web of the rails for a short distance. Speed at this point was less than a walking pace, but even at normal speeds it was still possible to jump off a moving tram, run ahead to take a photograph, and then re-board the car as it caught up. Despite this state of affairs it was felt that much of the system would survive, if only because of the generally poor condition of the roads. In fact it was the Pont d'Inca route that was to suffer next, when in 1956 the line was cut back to terminate at C'an Capas, following a collision between a tram and a train bound for Santany. The tram driver underestimated the train's speed and failed to clear the crossing in time, though he and his passengers managed to jump clear before the actual collision, which totally destroyed the tramcar.

Despite these closures there was still a complicated network of routes serving Gènova, Porto Pi, Establiments, Son Roca, Santa Catalina, Coliseo and Soledad. Some of the lines ran out into the country, and there were intermediate turn-round points on the longer routes (e.g. Railway Stations – Terreño on the Porto Pi line.) The scenery on the outermost limits could be spectacular. The Gènova route climbed steeply up from the western end of the harbour with magnificent views over the city and the Bay of Palma. A series of sharp curves followed before the line reached an area of hill-top orchards and bluffs with Belver castle in the background. Beyond the city, the lines to Establiments and Son Roca still ran along bucolic unpaved roads to reach the small picturesque towns at journey's end. Competing traffic (at least in the country districts) was mostly horse-drawn, even in the late 1950s.

Car No. 30, "Marliyn", heads along the calle 31 Diciembre, on the Coliseo route.   (J. WISEMAN)

Although buses had by now replaced some tram services, little had been done to improve the roads themselves, and in consequence the buses rode worse than the trams and were just as crowded and slow. Thus as late as 1956, when tram number 30 was modernised with a streamline metal body, it still seemed possible that the network would survive. However, this proved to be a false hope and by 1957 it became obvious that the Tramway's days were numbered as the track had deteriorated badly, in some places spreading out of gauge. This state of affairs could not continue and the Company decided to implement the Alcover Plan (named after the President of the TEIP) under which the remaining tram routes were to be replaced by buses. 16th March 1958 saw the closure of the westerly routes that ran through the city centre to serve Porto Pi, Gènova, Santa Catalina and Son Roca, and by the end of the year the Soledad route had also changed to bus operation. This brought the number of operating trams down to ten, though their duties were now shared with buses on the remaining routes to C'an Capas and Establiments, where the presence of several textile factories had been instrumental in keeping this line operating into the late 50s. Tram working was finally suspended early in 1959, and the rails were removed from the streets.

As a post-script, 2 of the tramcars went to the Soller Tramway, to be cannibalised for spare traction parts, the bodies eventually finding their way to the mainland to be used as advertising hoardings.

The FC de Alaró (1881/1935)

There are several small lignite mines near Alaró and the town had originally hoped to be on the FC de Mallorca's main line. However, the railway company were unwilling to deviate from their planned direct route, and in consequence the FC de Alaró (Alaró Railway) was promoted independently by Jaume Comes Frau and Josep Sureda Villalonga, to link the town with the main line at Consell station, a distance of just over 2 miles from Alaró. Construction began in 1880, and the line was opened on 22nd May, 1881. Decauville track was used, and a gauge of 3ft was adopted to allow the interchange of vehicles with the FC de Mallorca.

The promoters found that money was harder than expected to raise, and although it had been hoped to provide steam locomotion there was only sufficient capital to provide two horse-hauled tramcars. One of these was a double-decker, built by Baucells & Sons (Barcelona) in 1880. It had an open upper deck enclosed by railings with a spiral staircase at the rear and a driving platform at the front; total capacity was forty-threee passengers, and two animals were needed to haul it. The company had intended to purchase a second passenger car and also a goods van, but owing to a shortage of capital the second car was constructed in Palma by Josep Mir in 1881/2, using iron parts imported from Britain. This car had an enclosed single deck body, arranged to carry both First and Second Class passengers, who were separated by a small central luggage compartment. The body was 6.6 metres long, and weighed 2,100kgs. A total of thirty-two passengers could be carried. The new vehicle was not a great success, and in 1884 there was talk of rebuilding it, while in 1888 there were discussions about purchasing another, lighter, car capable of being hauled by a single horse. It appears that finances were still too tight to enable this, and when extra capacity was needed, or when one or both tramcars were being repaired, the company had to hire Third Class coaches from the FC de Mallorca. This was certainly the case in the period of celebration when Alaró became the first town on the island to be lit by electricity (15th August 1901), and later in the 1930s, by which time the original tramcars were in a poor condition. For a while in 1919 the company obtained the use of tram number 43 from the Palma city system, although its wheels had to be altered to allow it to travel to Alaró.

In the beginning the company needed four horses to run its services, and a fifth was added in 1883, while by 1920 the number had increased to six. As the trip from Consell to Alaró is almost all uphill, the return trip was achieved by gravity, which saved having to turn the tramcars at each journey's end. The horses returned to Consell station, where their stable was located, by road. A limited goods service was run for the benefit of the local coalmines (the San Narciso and La Locomotora), both of which were quite close to Consell station, while a cement plant was established nearer the Alaró terminus. Most goods traffic was handled in wagons from the neighbouring company, allowing through running to destinations all over the island without the need for further transhipment.

At Alaró the station was situated at a lower level than the surrounding buildings. The approaching line split into three dead end roads, the left-hand one serving the passenger platform, with a staircase leading upwards to the small station yard, which was squeezed in next to the local Civil Guards' barracks. The middle road, which tunnelled under the yard to provide shelter, was used as the carriage shed, while the third line was used for unloading freight. At the junction, in the early days at least, the line ran behind the railway's station building, passing a goods loading bank that it shared with its neighbour before entering the station loop at a turnout facing towards Palma. There was also a small stable for the horses.

Early FC de Mallorca timetables did not include details of the Alaró services, though a timetable footnote read:– "Consell and Alaró. Between these two places there is a tramway 4kms long, on which services are run connecting with trains on the Palma-Manacor line. Fares are 30 cents First Class, 20 cents Second Class." Journey times were 15 minutes on the uphill leg to Alaró, and 10 minutes in the reverse direction.

The line seems to have been a success initially, as witness the hurried purchase of a second tramcar, and in 1921 the Company obtained the concession to carry mail. Then in 1922 animal haulage was replaced by two 18hp petrol driven rail motors, named SANT CABRIT and SANT BASSA after the canonised defenders of Alaró Castle, who died holding it against King Alfonso of Aragon. The rail motors were four-wheeled vehicles of the Champagne type, with a chain drive to the two axles. They weighed about 3 tonnes and had a top speed of 18km/hr, although the timings for the journey remained the same as previously. The units could tow 7,000kgs so trains could thus be made up with a tractor and both trams, or one tram plus one wagon, or three wagons. As the track layout remained unchanged, with the exception of an additional line at the junction running into the old stable which now became the rail motors' shed, it is assumed that goods vehicles were manhandled in and out of the various sidings at journey's end.

When the tractors needed occasional repairs they were run to Palma workshops, however, on at least one occasion they also hauled paying passengers along the main line. On 13th October 1929, on the occasion of an important bull-fight at the newly opened bull-ring at Palma, so many passengers travelled to Consell station that not all were able to board the connecting train to the capital. The tram then followed the main line train as far as Santa Maria, where additional coaches were available.

By this time the tramway was receiving fuller coverage in the FC de Mallorca's timetables, which now gave details of the service. Tramcars left Alaró at 5.35, 7.35 and 8.55 am; then at 1.00, 2.15, 3.00 and 6.55 pm with an extra departure on Sundays and public holidays at 8.30 pm. Homeward trips from Consell ran at 8.15 and 9.15 am, then at 2.45, 3.45 and 7.40 pm with a final run at 8.55 pm on Sundays and public holidays. These late runs coincided with the last train out of Palma, which was held back from its weekday departure time of 6.40 pm to leave at 8.10 pm – arriving at Consell at

8.55 pm. Normally the run back to Alaró took 15 minutes but for some reason an extra 5 minutes was allowed at the weekend.

The rail motors had been obtained with the proceeds of a 55,000 pesetas share issue, but after their purchase there was little surplus money to cover the operating costs.

The situation worsened in 1923 when some of the local mines closed, while at the same time road transport began to provide serious competition with the establishment of a bus service linking Alaró with Palma with fares lower than the combined tramway/railway journey. Both the trackwork and the two tramcars were in a bad state of repair by the start of the 1930s and the Directors of the line approached the FC de Mallorca in the hope of merging the two companies, however, the offer was declined. In August 1934 one of the rail-motors, the SANT CABRIT, required major work and it was laid aside. Soon afterwards the company lost its mail carrying concession. By this time there were three road transport companies based in Alaró and the tramway's days were numbered. Despite this, on 30th May 1935 the Alaró Railway was closed "provisionally", to allow six months for track renewals, and a bus connection was instituted linking the town with the railway at Consell. The outbreak of the Civil War coming shortly afterwards with the resulting downturn in the economic climate ensured that the closure became permanent, and the track was lifted in 1941. Later, between 1944 and 1951, part of the branch was reinstated as a long siding to serve the Isern mining company which had taken over the concessions of several of the local mines. During this period the line was worked by the FC de Mallorca and locomotives propelled empty wagons up to the mine for loading, after which they were returned by gravity to Consell station. However, after this short reprieve the line was closed and lifted again.

Today the remains of the tramway are ephemeral at best, but a few hints of its existence can still be identified. At the Inca end of Alaró & Consell station there is a dirt track into a field alongside the SFM line. About 20 metres from the level crossing a low elongated hump may be distinguished which, covered in long grass and tall weeds, curves away from the main line, its former route marked by a line of fencing. This is the beginning of the tramway whose course is also marked by parallel lines of trees. Drive away from the station and turn left for Alaró near the SFM's bridge which crosses the road and a small river, and you soon come to a narrow farm track on the left with some ruined buildings behind the trees which border the road. This is one of the mines formerly served, and the route of the tramway is just about visible where it once crossed the lane here and at other locations further on. Continuing towards Alaró the cement works still exists but from here on the course of the line is hard to trace owing to the expansion of the town. The old station can be found in the Plaça del Tren where it is the low house to the left of the newer building on the south-west corner of the square. It is just possible to peer across the garden wall at the rear and glimpse the archway that was the entrance to the tramcar's shed which is situated in the foundations of the station building; photography is however impossible.

While Alaró may seem a sleepy backwater today, it was formerly a more important place, not least because of the lignite mines nearby, and it is thus not surprising that it wanted to be connected to the island's rail system. Unfortunately the town's setting some way up a side valley, and away from the easier lower ground which the railway's engineers favoured, meant that it never benefited fully from its railway connections.

The Arenal Tramway (1921/c.1930) (then part of TEIP until c.1941)

Another independent line, known locally as the Carrilet de S'Arenal (Arenal Tramway), formerly ran along part of the Bay of Palma. Promoted in 1921 by Señor José Fontirroig, the line originally linked Arenal with a terminus near the former Café La Sirena in C'an Pastilla but was soon extended a couple of kilometres westward to serve Coll d'En Rabassa, where it met up with the electrified Palma tramway system. Work on the tramway proceeded quickly as there were no natural obstacles to be overcome, and the line was lightly laid with flat-bottomed rail spiked to the sleepers. Permanent way materials, costing 180,000 Francs, came from F. Beltjens & Guenebaud of Marseille, who supplied 11kms of rail, fourteen turnouts of 30 metre radius, and another four turnouts of 20 metre radius.

The opening ceremony, which took place on 14th October 1921, was described in flowery terms in the local newspaper, which made much of the beautiful views to be seen from the line, both looking inland and along the bay. The inaugural service,

The inaugural run of the Arenal Tramway pauses for an inspection of the Pontarró de Sa Siquia, 14th October 1921. Later the motor units and trams were combined to form four-wheeled motorised tramcars. (A. SANCHIS COLLECTION)

comprising a railcar hauling two tramcars, left Coll d'En Rabassa to the pealing of the local church bells. On board were José Fontirroig and the other members of the Tramway's governing body. A short stop was made at C'an Pastilla before the convoy moved on through a large crowd that lined both sides of the track so closely that speed had to be kept to a crawl. The arrival at Arenal was also met by the acclamation of the local populace, while the town band from Lluchmayor struggled to make itself heard above the din. A welcoming committee consisting of the Mayor and the Secretary of the Town Council together with the Civil Guard lieutenant and the parish priest met the tram, which was blessed on its arrival. In the speeches that followed the Mayor of Lluchmayor congratulated his Arenal colleague and expressed the hope that the tramway might soon be extended to link Arenal with Lluchmayor. However, although plans for this scheme were drawn up the following year and a share issue announced, the work never progressed any further.

The services were maintained by petrol railcars having a 12hp Citroen engine. They were obtained from the Badische Motor-Locomotivwerke AG of Mosbach (Baden). In the original form these vehicles resembled a primitive jeep on a solid railway chassis, while a later photograph suggests that they were rebuilt, and that each of the motorised chassis was married up with a tramcar body to produce a powered tramcar. Access was by means of the rear platform, the machine's bonnet being mounted immediately ahead of the body in place of the original front platform, shaded by the overhanging roof. The rest of the stock remained in use as trailer cars.

At first the timetable was ambitious, with departures from Arenal at 6.00, 7.15, 8.15, 10.15 and 11.00 am and then hourly until 6.00 pm with a final service at 7.30 pm. Return trips were scheduled at 6.30, 8.00, 9.30 and 11.30 am and then every hour until 7.00 pm with the final run being made at 8.30 pm. The two power units and a collection of single-deck tramcars (actually old mule-hauled enclosed trailers from the Palma system) were provided to work this timetable, and they were stabled at a new depot built at Arenal in a substantial building constructed from reinforced concrete to a traditional design, with three arched entrances. As well as housing the line's rolling stocks the structure also provided workshop facilities for light repairs as well as living quarters for a night-watchman.

While the Lluchmayor extension remained unbuilt, the combined tram journey must have been a more convenient way of travelling between Arenal and Palma, remembering the sparse train service; however, despite this tram services declined in later years. During the 1930s there were only six return trips daily, and while the tram trailers may have been more widely used at first, eventually they were only needed on Sundays and public holidays. At about the time of the Civil War the original concessionaires of the tramway appear to have ended their operations, and the line was apparently electrified and absorbed into the Palma Tramway network as the author has had sight of a photograph (now no longer accessible) of one of the TEIP's electric trams bearing a destination board marked Arenal. In 1941 the war appears to have caught up with the tramway, as the seaward end serving Arenal was closed, followed in 1948 by the section between Molinar and Coll d'en Rabassa. Following the closure the tracks were lifted, and subsequent development has covered all traces of the route. Today the site of the tramway is a concrete promenade, but in former times it was an unspoiled beach with no development apart from the small towns at either end.

INDUSTRIAL LINES

Apart from the public lines already mentioned there were formerly a number of industrial lines of various gauges to be found on the island. These were built to serve temporary engineering projects, as well as local industries as diverse as cement production, salt evaporation, coal extraction and glass making.

The Gènova Quarry Railway (1945/1956)

During the 1930s the increase in trade and the beginnings of tourism, in those days sea-borne, led to the planned development of a harbour to the west of Palma and the greater enclosure of that part of the bay by a breakwater. Studies established that the nearest supply of suitable stone could be found near the village of Gènova, some 5kms distant, but also considerably higher than the new harbour. A railway was therefore

Gènova Railway: Early days in the construction of the harbour at Porto Pi.   (A. SANCHIS COLLECTION)

necessary to link the two sites, and this would have to climb from a height of 4 metres above sea level, to an altitude of 110 metres at the quarries. The project was approved by the local military commander in 1937 and a scheme was drawn up later that year by the engineer Miquel Forteza to link the quarries with the new harbour extensions being planned at Porto Pi. As originally envisaged the railway would have had a double track main line, and would have been built to the "Mallorcan" gauge of 3ft. However, in 1940 the plan was finalised by the Engineer-Director of the Port of Palma, Gabriel Roca, and in its modified form became a single track line with a somewhat simpler infrastructure; only the three-arch viaduct needed to carry the line above the Palma to Andratx road was retained from the earlier plan, while the gauge was altered to one metre to make the supply of rolling stock easier. The actual start of construction was delayed by the shortage of materials resulting from the ongoing war, and although the line was operational by 1945, the last of the rails needed to complete the project only arrived in Palma during 1946.

At the quarry end the facilities were quite limited at first, being confined to little more that a small engine shed, a water tower and a weighbridge, though later a mess hall for the quarry workers was added, together with a workshop. At the lower end of the line, where the station was known as San Carlos – named after the nearby fort that protected the western end of the bay – there was a larger engine shed and another workshop to deal with most run-of-the-mill locomotive breakdowns, though the manufacture of new parts had to be farmed out to an engineering firm in Palma. In addition there were a number of sorting and storage sidings, while access to the excavators clearing the ground and the large construction cranes was by means of a separate system of

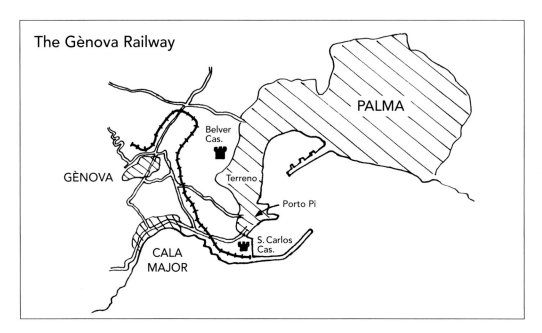

Decauville tracks. Later additions to the facilities at San Carlos included a power station, built to prevent the disruption caused by the power cuts that were a feature of the island's electrical supply.

As usual, a concession to build and operate the line was granted, being given to Dragados y Construcciones. Originally this firm requested 150 wagons from CAF, but because of the wartime conditions these could not be supplied, though eventually fifty wagons intended for the mines at Utrillas were diverted to Mallorca. Dragados made up the shortfall from their own rolling stock from other projects and supplied the locomotives. Few details of these remain, but there were two 0-6-0 tanks numbered L2 and L9, one or both possibly by Orenstein & Koppel, a 4-coupled locomotive numbered L18 from the same builder, and another engine thought to be a rebuild by Construcciones Devis SA of Valencia. At a later date some of the locomotives from the Gènova line are thought to have been moved by the contractor, who was also involved in the construction of a new harbour at the port at Alcudia.

During the construction work the line moved several million tons of stone, but by the time the work was completed, road traffic had become more viable and it was decided to close the line in September 1956, thereafter relying on lorries to carry any stone needed for future repair work. By 1958 the tracks had been lifted, and later road developments to the west of Porto Pi have swept away any traces of the railway, but despite this the site of the line remained marked on some maps as late as the mid-1970s.

Other Contractor's Railways – Alcudia and Puerto Soller

The port of Alcudia was always held back in earlier days by its lack of a railway connection with the rest of the island, the closest railhead being at La Puebla, some 15kms away. Finally, during the Civil War the line was deemed to be a military necessity and work started on the project. However, there was another problem as the harbour was too shallow for many vessels, leading to the added inconvenience of having to transfer cargoes into lighters to get them ashore. In 1933 studies had been made of ways of improving matters, which had concluded that a new mole 420 metres in length should be built, and that stone for the project could be obtained locally from a quarry on the nearby Alcanada estate. With the groundworks for the new connecting line from La Puebla slowly approaching the harbour, the decision was taken in 1941 to proceed with the harbour works, and the plans were re-drawn by the engineer Gabriel Roca, although they subsequently had to be slightly modified in 1943, at the insistence of the military, in order to provide better defences. At first some stone was taken from a small quarry opposite the harbour, but in 1942 work started on the construction of a 1.9km line linking the harbour with the Alcanada quarry.

Unforeseen difficulties soon emerged:– the contractor was unable to source any rails for the quarry line, although it had been hoped that either RENFE of the FC de

Mallorca might be able to help. However, the latter's stock of obsolete 20kg rails had been appropriated by the military authorities in order to build the La Puebla-Alcudia link. At the same time, the owners of the Alcanada estate entered into litigation with the authorities over the amount of compensation to be paid for the use of their stone, and the damage caused by the building of the tramway. This effectively stalled matters from 1943 until the case was settled in 1946, meanwhile the contractor found he was unable to continue and had to be released from the work. Eventually another company, Dragados y Construcciones, was appointed and work started again in 1947.

It was envisaged that two locomotives and sixty wagons would be needed, and Dragados provided one or perhaps both locomotives from its stock working on its Porto Pi harbour contract, including the Orenstein & Koppel 0-4-0T. There have been local reports that the second locomotive came from the FC de Mallorca, but as the harbour line was metre gauge any locomotive so provided would have needed a rebuild, and no details of such work appear on the company's records, this suggestion can almost certainly be discounted. (In passing, one does wonder about the "missing" Falcon engines, and whether a commercial workshop in Palma might have re-gauged them for work on the various Dragados projects. This however is pure speculation, at present). Work on the harbour modifications finished in 1953 and the line was lifted, little or no trace being visible today.

Earlier, in the 1920s, when the harbour at Puerto Soller was being extended, a short length of line was in use to shift the rocks forming the basis of the new breakwater and quayside. The wagons were wooden-bodied tipping trucks, with a high centre of gravity, not unlike those used in the English ironstone quarries. Animal power was used, as the line was only a few hundreds of metres long.

Cement Railways

The natural ingredients for cement making, a chalk-like rock and fuel to bake it, have always been present in Mallorca so it is no surprise to see that this was once a common industry locally. However, the cement produced was always liable to fluctuation in quality, depending on the rock and firing material in use. Nevertheless, up until the 1970s, when the Portland company established a large factory in Mallorca, there were several small producers at various sites throughout the island; after the new factory opened these lost much of their business and soon closed down. The need to move not only the quarried rock to the furnaces and crushers, but also the lignite needed for the firing, led to the use of short 60cm gauge lines, usually laid with Decauville track. Wagons with a 600kg capacity were commonly used.

The longest of these lines was situated a short distance outside Palma and served a quarry at Can Mascaró, linking it with the cement works at Can Fogerada situated further down the valley of the Torrente La Riera, at a distance of 2.4kms from the upper terminus. Despite this relatively short length this was a well-engineered line that crossed several bridges and three viaducts, including one 40 metres long and 6.5 metres high. The line sloped down towards the furnaces, and wagons were run down by gravity, with a brakeman to control the speed. The empty wagons were hauled back to the quarry by horses. The factory and the line closed in the 1970s but little evidence remains today as the line was taken up after closure; only the viaduct remains as evidence of this local industry.

Another 60cm gauge line existed near Sineu, and was in existence from the late teens until abandonment in the 1970s. Despite the fact that the cement it produced was not so reliable as other local factories, owing to the presence of pyrites in the rock being used, the factory nevertheless was the largest cement producer in the island at the end of the 1950s. There were two very short lines, one 400 metres long linking the quarry with the furnaces, while a shorter line 250 metres long ran in the opposite direction to a lignite mine.

Yet another line, 1,200 metres in length, was used at a cement works opened in 1917 situated near Sant Joan. It used very light Decauville track of 50cm gauge and weighing only 7kgs/metre, together with mule haulage, to bring rock from the quarry to the works known as Sa Farinera Vella de Sant Joan. As well as cement production the firm also ran a flour mill, hence the name of the works.

Another nearby firm which also combined cement production and grain milling was Sa Farinera Nova de Sant Joan. This was in production between 1924 and 1975, however, in 1945 the original workings had reached the nearest houses and could not be exploited further and a new quarry known as Sa Pedrera, was opened to the north of the town. This needed a line 300 metres long in order to reach the ovens, after which the rock was moved over part of the old line, past the abandoned quarry to reach the mills 700 metres away, passing through a tunnel under the road en-route. On this section of the line gravity was used to move the loaded wagons; on the reverse journey the wagons were pushed by hand. Although the ovens have gone, some of the track is still in place. It was the lightest rail in use on the island, weighing only 4.5kgs/metre. The sleepers were wooden, except at the turnouts where steel was used.

Salt railways

While most of the local salt production was based in Ibiza and Formentera, Mallorca still accounted for 20% of the Balearic's total output. During the 1950s there were five salt works on the larger island, and all used railway systems at one time or another. The salt pans were situated at Sa Vall (Colònia de Sant Jordi), at Campos, Ses Fontanelles (Playa de Palma), Sa Porrassa (Calvià) and the Salinas de S'Illot (Muro). Today only the first two survive, though the railways have gone. In contrast to the cement lines, a gauge of 50cm was used, and because of the corrosive nature of the salt, the wagons were made of wood, only the wheels, axles and couplings being of metal. Tipping trucks were used to move the raw salt from the evaporation beds to the works for processing, while salt that had been milled and bagged was transported on flat trucks. At the Campos works, the salt was transported in bulk using tippers, which ran some 4kms to a jetty at Sa Puntassa, which was in use from 1949 until 1958. At Colònia the line ran from the salt beds to the mill, which was situated close to the coast, from which a short extension took the wagons to the privately owned loading point, known as the Moll de la Sal (salt jetty). Usually animal power was employed on these systems, together with prefabricated track by Decauville, as this could be taken up and laid down according to varying needs of production.

Coalmines

At several places on the island there are lignite coal mines, and apart from the mines associated with the Alaró branch, which enjoyed connections with the main railway system for much of their working lives, there was a need for short "tramways" to move the coal out of the mine shafts to the stacking area. Once again a narrow gauge of 600mm was normal, with flat or low-sided wooden wagons in use at first, while metal colliery tubs were used in later years, usually with animal traction.

Industrias Alcasil, Palma

There was one other industry using a rail system on the island. This was Industrias Alcasil, which was concerned with glass making, and had a factory close to the shore at Palma. Although most of the necessary ingredients for the manufacturing process were obtainable in the island, carbonate of soda had to be imported from Marseille. Having been unloaded from the ships, it was transported by manpower the 70 metres to the factory over a line laid with 60cm gauge Decauville track. As much of the output was exported, it is assumed that the line was also used in the loading process. Glass making continued on the site between 1910 and 1920, while in 1922 the factory was converted to automobile production, which continued until final closure in 1929.

Annexe

Other Balearic Railways

Although Menorca, the second largest of the Balearic Islands, has no railway, the early years of the 20th century nearly provided one. Following discussions in the island, a line to link Mao (Mahon) and Ciutadella were included in the 1904 Law of Secondary Railways, and re-stated in the 1908 Law of Secondary and Strategic Railways. By 1911 a route 45.8kms long had been agreed linking the two towns at either end of the island, with intermediate stations at Alaior, es Mercadal, and Ferreries; in fact the route was pretty much the same as Kane's military road, built the previous century to link the garrison towns at either end of the island. However, just as it seemed that Menorca would enter the railway age, a local financial crisis forced the closure of a couple of important industrial concerns in the island and led to general loss of commercial confidence. This was followed shortly afterwards by the outbreak of war across most of mainland Europe, and the scheme lapsed never to be reactivated.

The smaller islands of Ibiza and Formentera, while hardly large enough to support their own common-carrier railways, were both formerly provided with industrial lines. These belonged to La Saliñera Española SA (Spanish Saltworks Company), and had a gauge of 750mm. Unlike the salt-hauling lines on Majorca, here locomotive power was employed, at first in the shape of several small tank locomotives mostly built by Decauville at their Petit-Bourg workshops. This French company built standard engines in three sizes, and eventually the saltworks owned at least one of each type, though other locomotives have also been recorded. As steam power was used from 1896 to 1966 some of the earlier locomotives may not have survived, although it seems that normally two were in use on each island. The details of the Decauville engines have been taken from the firm's order book, and it will be noted that the lowest numbered locomotive was not supplied first!

The Formentera system employed No. 2 (Decauville Works No. 242 – ordered 6.8.1896, despatched 12.10.1896). This was a 3 tonne 0-4-0T locomotive, similar to those working on the Volos narrow gauge line in Greece. Another locomotive used in later years was No. 3, an Orenstein & Koppel (Works No. 10436 of 1926). After 1966 the steam engines were laid aside and replaced by two Maffei four-wheeled diesels. These were painted in a red and blue livery and one carried the number 2. One locomotive worked at each end of the line shunting wagons, while main line trips were headed by a farm tractor that straddled the rails.

The system on Ibiza had a more varied complement of locomotives, although it appears that probably no more than two existed together at any one time. There appears to have been a small Decauville engine in use from 1896, but this was soon

Formentera saltworks. Locomotive No. 3 preserved at the local museum.   (AAFB ARCHIVE)

The imperfect quality of these photographs is regretted; nevertheless they have been included for their rarity value.

Formentera saltworks. The Maffei i/c locomotives that took over from steam after 1966.   (AAFB ARCHIVE)

Formentera saltworks. Tractor and train on the main line. (A. SANCHIS COLLECTION)

replaced by a 5 tonne machine from the same maker (Works No. 231, ordered 16.12.1897, despatched 9.2.1898) which was given the running number 3. Another locomotive in use appears to have been an 0-4-2T, possibly built by Couillet. At a later date, around 1963, another locomotive was acquired and by this time it is likely that one of the two earlier engines had reached the end of its life. The new locomotive was obtained secondhand from the Compañia Arrendataria de las Salinas de Torrevieja (Torrevieja Salt Company) on the Spanish mainland. It carried the name SALAS II

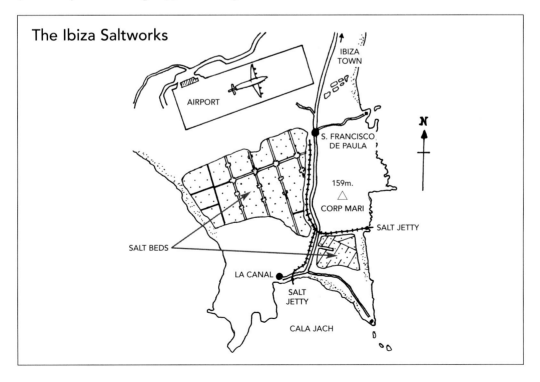

No. 6 and was a 7.5 tonne Decauville 0-4-2T (Works No. 305) originally ordered on 24.4.1899 and delivered to its first owners on 14.1.1900. After 1966 the line was worked by three Deutz four-wheeled diesels, Works Nos. 55689/90 (built 1958) and 57078. All were rated at 28hp and carried a green livery. Rolling stock on the line comprised a number of small four-wheeled tipping wagons, with metal underframes and wooden bodies.

The working method was the opposite to Formentera, as wagons were pushed by hand around the salt beds, whose sidings accounted for some 1,300 metres of track, as far as the main line where they were coupled to a waiting engine for transport to the jetties where shunting duties were performed by tractors. The main line, some 1,200 metres in length, originated at San Francisco de Paula, situated just to the south of the present airport, and ran south between the edge of the salt pans and the road leading towards Punta Roma. Where the road turned to cross the salt beds the line divided, an easterly branch swinging round the slopes of Corp-Mari to reach a salt-loading jetty at the northern end of Playa Cavallet. The southerly branch continued alongside the road to another loading point near La Canal, popularly known as "Es Gaufe", situated in Cala Jach. This small railway nevertheless managed to shift between 40,000 and 60,000 tonnes of salt each year, and by 1970 the two smaller islands accounted for 80% of Balearic salt production.

Both railways were phased out in the early 1970s, when road haulage took over, but despite this a few traces remain. On Formentera, locomotive No. 3 is preserved at the local Ethnographic Museum, while for some time the remains of some wagons were to be seen around the wharf at La Savina.

Ibiza saltworks. The salt jetty, showing the temporary nature of the track, and a pile of spare track pieces to the right of the white building. Small lighters are loading the salt to ferry out to the cargo ships waiting in the bay. (K. TAYLORSON COLLECTION)

A List of Majorca Railway Locomotives/Railcars

Steam Locomotives

a	last year locomotive known to be active	
d	month/year known to be derelict/withdrawn from service	
Rn	Rebuilt and re-numbered	
rn	re-numbered	
s	scrapped	
rb	rebuilt	
w	date recorded withdrawn from service	

Nicknames shown in parenthesis

NW	Nasmyth Wilson	MTM	La Maquinista	
OK	Orenstein & Koppel	H	Hawthorn	
P	Palma Works	NW/P	Nasmyth rebuilt Palma	
K	Krupp	BW	Babcock Wilcox	

No.	Name	Maker	Type	Series	Dates	Notes
1	MAJORCA	NW	4-4-0T	1	1874-1945	s by 1951
2	PALMA	NW	4-4-0T	1	1874-c.1948	s by 1951
3	INCA	NW	4-4-0T	1	1874-1951	w 1951 s 1960
4	MANACOR	NW	0-6-0T	4	1876-1963/4	w 1963/4
5	FELANITX	NW	0-6-0T	4	1876-1963/4	w 193/4
6(i)	SINEU	NW	4-4-0T	25	1877-1921	rb 1911 rn 25
6(ii)	"La Inglesita"	NW	0-4-0T	-	1917-c1951	w by 1951 s 1960
7(i)	LA PUEBLA	NW	4-4-0T	25	1877-1921	rb 1911 rn 26
7(ii)	"Koppel"	OK	0-4-0T	-	1921- c1957	w 1957 No number after 1944
7(iii)	-	MTM	2-6-0T	19	1944-c1960	a 1957 d 6/60 ex FC Soller
8(i)	SANTA MARIA	NW	4-4-0T	25	1877-1921	rb 1911 rn 27
8(ii)	-	MTM	2-6-0T	19	1944-c1960	w by 58 d 6/60 ex FC Soller
9(i)	BINISALEM	NW	4-4-0T	25	1877-1921	rb 1911 rn 28
9(ii)	-	MTM	2-6-0T	19	1944-c1960	d 6/60 ex FC Soller
10(i)	MURO	NW	4-4-0T	16	1877-1916	rb 1911 rn 24
10(ii)	SANTA EUGENIA	NW	4-6-0T	10	c1916-c1964	w 1959 d 6/60(?)
-	"Brown"	H	0-4-0T	-	1881-1920s	w 1920-1928 Never numbered
11(i)	PETRA	NW	4-4-0T	16	1881-1929	rn 18
11(ii)	ALGAIDA	NW	4-6-0T	10	1929-c1958	a 1955 w 1958 d 1960
12	SAN JUAN	NW	4-6-0T	10	1887-c1964	?a 6/60 w 1959-64
13	LLOSETA	NW	4-6-0T	10	1887-c1957	a 1957 w 1957/8 d 6/60
14	MARRATXI	NW	4-6-0T	10	1891-c1960	w? 1959 d 6/60
15	ALARO	NW	4-6-0T	10	1891-c1959/64	a 1957 w by 1964
16	PORRERAS	NW	4-4-0T	16	1897- 1960	w c51-54 d 6/60
17	MONTUIRI	NW	4-4-0T	16	1897-1960	w c1951-54 s 1960

Steam Locomotives – *continued*

No.	Name	Maker	Type	Series	Dates	Notes
18(i)	ALFONSO XIII	P	4-4-0T	16	1902-1916	rb 1911 rn 22
18(ii)	ALGAIDA	NW	4-6-0T	10	c1916-1929	rn 11
18(iii)	PETRA	NW	4-4-0T	16	1929-c1960	w 1958 d 6/60
19(i)	ESPAÑA	P	4-4-0T	16	1903-1916	rb 1911 rn 23
19(ii)	LLUCHMAYOR	MTM	2-6-0T	19	1917-c1962	w by 1/63
20(i)	ALGAIDA	NW/P	4-6-0T	10	1911-c1916	rn 18
20(ii)	CAMPOS	MTM	2-6-0T	19	1917-c1962	w by 1/63
21(i)	SANTA EUGENIA	NW	4-6-0T	10	1911-c1916	rn 10
21(ii)	SANTANY	MTM	2-6-0T	19	1917-c1962	w by 1/63
22	ALFONSO XIII	P	4-4-0T	16	1916-1931	re-named Salinas 1931
22	SALINAS	P	4-4-0T	16	1931-c1960	w 1958 d?6/60
23	ESPAÑA	P	4-4-0T	16	1916-1960	w 1951/54 s 1960
24	COLL	NW/P	4-4-0T	25	1916-1957	w by 1957 s 1960
25	SAN MIGUEL	NW/P	4-4-0T	25	1921-c1951	w c1951 s 1960
26	SAN LORENZO	NW/P	4-4-0T	25	1921-c1951	w c1951 s 1960
27	ARTA	NW/P	4-4-0T	25	1921-c1960	a 1953/57 d 6/60
28	SON SERVERA	NW/P	4-4-0T	25	1921-c1951	w c.1951 d 1957 s 1960
30-35	-	K	2-6-0T	30	1926-c1964	no. 32 d 1957 w 1958
50-55	-	BW	2-6-2T	50	1930-c1964	

FC de Mallorca Railcars

w	withdrawn	F	destroyed by fire
nc	not converted to metre gauge	ob	seen with body removed from bogies
A	exported to Argentina	s	scrapped

No.	Type	Rating	Engine	Type	Builder	Dates	Notes
A1	4-wheel	40hp	petrol	mechanical	Berliet	1926-1936	d 6/60
A2	4-wheel	40hp	,,	,,	De Dion/CAF	1930-1969	rb 1956 w 1969
A3	4-wheel	40hp	,,	,,	De Dion/CAF	1930-1969	F 14.4.52 rb 1954 w 1969
A4	4-wheel	40hp	,,	,,	De Dion/CAF	1930-1964	rb 1956 w 1964

EFE/FEVE Bogie Railcars

No.	Builder	Built	Arrival on island	In use from	Departure/ Disposal	Notes
2001	Esslingen	1956	1956	1956	19.07.66	F
2002	,,	,,	,,	,,	?w 1991	A 1997
2003	,,	,,	,,	,,	1.9.66	F
2004	,,	,,	,,	,,	?w 1991	A 1997
2005	Euskalduna	1959	1959	1959	?w 1991	A 1997
2006	,,	1960	1960	1960	?w 1991	A 1997

EFE/FEVE Bogie Railcars – *continued*

No.	Builder	Built	Arrival on island	In use from	Departure/ Disposal	Notes
2011	Euskalduna	1958	c1980	nc		ob 12/91 s 1990s
2012	,,	1958	1979	nc		s 1990s
2013	,,		c1980	nc		s 1990s
2019	,,		1959	1966		A 1997
2020	,,	1959	c1980	nc		s 1990s
2026	,,	1959	1971	1971	19.05.73	F
2027	,,	1960	1973	1973	?w 1991	A 1997
2028	,,		c1980	nc		s 1990s
2029	,,		c1980	nc		s 1990s
2314	MAN	1967	1992	1992		cab twds Inca A 1997
2334	,,	1967	1992	1992		cab twd Palma A 1997
2348	,,	1967	1992	1992		cab twds Palma A 1997
2354	,,	1969	1992	1992		cab twds Inca A 1997
2358	,,	1970	1991	1991		2 driving ends A 1997
2360	,,	1973	1991	1991		cab twds Palma A 1997
2364	,,	1973	1991	1991		2 driving ends A 1997
2365	,,	1973	1991	1991		cab twds Inca A 1997

EFE/FEVE Railcar Trailers

No.	Builder	Built	Arrival on island	In use from	Departure/ Disposal	Notes
5001*	Esslingen	1956	1956	1956		
5002#	,,	,,	,,	,,	?w by 1991	
5003*	,,	,,	,,	,,	?w by 1991	
5004*	,,	,,	,,	,,		
5005*	,,	,,	,,	,,		
5011	Ferrostahl		c1980	nc	s 1990s	
5013	,,		c1980	nc	s 1990s	
5015	,,		1982	nc	s 1990s	
5016	,,		1982	nc	s 1990s	
5017	,,		c1966			
5018+	,,		c 1969		?w by 1991	
5019	,,		c1980	nc	s 1990s	

*   fitted with postal compartment and toilet until c1980
\#   fitted with postal compartment and toilet until c1989
+   short trailer

EFE/FEVE Diesel Locomotives

No.	Type	Builder	built	Arrival on island	In use from	Withdrawn	Notes	
1101	B-B	SECN	1959	1959	1959	c1974	3ft gauge	s
1102	B-B	,,	,,	,,	,,	c1968	,, ,,	CR
1103	B-B	,,	,,	,,	,,	c1974	,, ,,	s
1104	B-B	SECN	,,	1960	1960	c1968	3ft gauge	CR
1207	0-6-0	Batignolles/CAF	1960	1981	1981	R	metre gauge	

R   undergoing protracted rebuilding   CR   transferred to Cantabrican Railways
s   scrapped

SFM Railcars

No.	Builder	Date	Arrival on island	In use	Notes
61-01	CAF	1995	1995	1995	m.u. with 61-02
61-02	,,	1995	1995	1995	m.u. with 60-01
61-03	,,	1995	1995	1995	m.u. with 61-04
61-04	,,	1995	1995	1995	m.u. with 61-03
61-05	,,	1995	1995	1995	m.u. with 61-06 & 62-03
61-06	,,	1995	1995	1995	m.u. with 61-05 & 62-03 (a)
61-07	,,	1995	1995	1995	m.u. with 61-08 & 62-01
61-08	,,	1995	1995	1995	m.u. with 61-07 & 62-01
61-09	,,	1997	1997	1997	m.u. with 61-10 & 62-02
61-10	,,	1997	1997	1997	m.u. with 61-09 & 62-02
61-11	,,	1997	1997	1997	m.u. with 61-12 & 62-04
61-12	,,	1997	1997	1997	m.u. with 61-11 & 62-04

(a) badly damaged in Sa Pobla accident, January 2002. Subsequently scrapped.

SFM Trailers

No.	Builder	Date	Arrival on island	In use	Notes
62-01	CAF	1997	1997	1997	
62-02	,,	,,	,,	,,	
62-03	,,	,,	,,	,,	
62-04	,,	,,	,,	,,	

SFM Diesel Shunter

No.	Builder	Date		Arrival on island	In use	Notes
14	CAF/GE	1971	c.2000	c.2000		

Table of Locomotive Dimensions

Locomotive Dimensions

	4-4-0T	4-4-0T	4-4-0T	0-6-0T	4-6-0T
	MAJORCA PALMA INCA	SINEU LA PUEBLA STA MARIA BINISALEM	MURO PETRA PORRERAS MONTUIRI ALFONSO/ SALINAS Plus 1911 Rebuilds	MANACOR FELANITX	SAN JUAN LLOSETA MARRATXI ALARO ALGAIDA STA EUGENIA
Cylinders Diameter/stroke	11"x 18" 0.280x0.455	13"x18" 0.330x0.455	13½"x19" 0.340x0.480	13"x18" 0.330x0.455	15"x20" 0.380x0.510
Leading wheels	2' 0" 0.610	2' 0" 0.610	2' 0" 0.610	none	2' 0" 0.610
Coupled wheels	3' 6" 1.067	3' 6" 1.067	3' 6" 1.067	3' 3" 0.990	3' 3" 0.990
Coupled w/base	6' 9" 2.055	7' 9" 2.360	7' 9" 2.360	12' 6" 3.810	12' 1" 3.685
Total w/base	14' 10" 4.520	16' 4½" 4.990	16' 4½" 4.990	12' 6" 3.810	19' 5½" 5.930
Length over Buffers	23' 7½" 7.200	26' 3" 8.000	26' 3" 8.000	24' 10½" 7.585	29' 0½" 8.850
Boiler length	8' 0" 2.440	8' 0" 2.440	8' 9" 2.665	8' 9" 2.665	10' 3" 3.125
Boiler diameter	3' 0" 0.915	3' 0" 0.915	3' 5½" 1.055	3' 5½" 1.055	3' 7" 1.095
Firebox length	3' 6" 1.065	3' 6" 1.065	3' 9" 1.145	3' 7½" 1.105	4' 8½" 1.425
Smokebox length	1' 11½" 0.600	2' 1" 0.640	2' 2½" 0.675	2' 2½" 0.675	2'2½" 0.675
Weight	15.8t	16.3t	see text	16.2t	

Locomotive Dimensions – *Continued*

	2-6-0T Maquinista	2-6-0T Krupp	2-6-2T Babcock & Wilcox	0-4-0T Nasmyth Wilson	0-4-0T O & K
Cylinders Diameter/stroke	13½"x19¹¹⁄₁₆" 0.345x0.500	14½"x21⅝" 0.370x0.550	14½"x21⅝" 370x0.550	10"x14" 0.245x0.356	
Leading wheels	2' 1⅝" 0.650	2' 4" 0.710	2' 4" 0.710	none	none
Coupled wheels	3' 5" 1.060	3' 7¼" 1.100	3' 7¼" 1.100	2' 6" 0.760	
Rear wheels	none	none	2' 4" 0.710	none	none
Coupled w/base	8' 2½" 2.500	9' 6¼" 2.900	9' 4¼" 2.850	5' 0" 1.525	
Total w/base	15' 1⅛" 4.600	16' 4⅞" 5.000	21' 11¾" 6.700	5' 0" 1.525	
Length Over buffers	28' 4½" 8.650	28' 11" 8.815	33' 4" 10.160	16' 8¾" 5.100	18' 4½" 5.600
Boiler length	10' 6" 3.200	9' 10" 3.000	11' 9¾" 3.630	5' 9" 1.755	
Boiler diameter	3' 9¾" 1.165	3' 11¼" 1.200	3' 11¼" 1.200	3' 1" 0.940	
Firebox length	5' 2" 1.575	3' 5¼" 1.050	3' 11¼" 1.200	3' 8" 1.120	
Smokebox length	3' 2¼" 0.975	4' 2¼" 1.275	4' 11" 1.500	1' 8½" 0.525	
Weight	30.75t	37.3t	46.4t	12.5t	13.2t

Timetables of the FC de Mallorca

SON BORDILS Á LA PUEBLA

PRECIOS 1.ª c.	2.ª c.	K.	ESTACIONES.	18 1-2	20 1-2-3	22 1-2
»		»	SON BORDILS (E.)....8....	9.16	16.12	20. 2
0.60	0.45	5	Llubí	9.27	16.23	20.20
0.80	0.55	9	Muro	9.38	16.32	20.83
1.05	0.75	13	LA PUEBLA....Ll.	9.44	16.40	20.41

PRECIOS 1.ª c.	2.ª c.	K.	ESTACIONES.	17 1-2-3	17 1-2	21 1-2*
»		»	LA PUEBLA....8....	6.55	12. »	17.25
0.55	0.35	4	Muro	7. 4	12.15	17.40
0.75	0.5x	8	Llubí	7.15	12.33	17.58
1.05	0.75	13	SON BORDILS (R.)....Ll.	7.25	12.46	18.10

SANTA MARIA Á FELANITX

PRECIOS 1.ª c.	2.ª c.	K.	ESTACIONES.	12 1-2	14 1-2-3	18 1-2*
»		»	SANTA MARIA (E.)....8....	8.24	14.47	19.19
0.70	0.45	7	Santa Eugenia	8.39	15. 2	19.3X
1.20	0.80	16	Algaida	9.18	15.25	20. 3
1.80	1.20	23	Montuiri	9.18	15.41	20.26
2.40	1.80	30	Porreras	8.34	15.57	20.46
2.85	1.80	36	Las Canteras	9.47	16.10	21. 5
3.35	2.10	43	FELANITX	10. 4	16.27	21.27

PRECIOS 1.ª c.	2.ª c.	K.	ESTACIONES.	13 1-2-3	13 1-2*	15 1-2*
»		»	FELANITX....8....	6.40	12.15	17. »
0.70	0.45	7	Las Canteras	6.65	12.35	17.18
1.05	0.75	18	Porreras	7.12	13. »	17.41
1.65	1.10	20	Montuiri	7.30	13.27	18. 8
2.31	1.50	27	Algaida	7.49	13.65	18.31
2.85	1.85	36	Santa Eugenia	8. 6	14.18	18.50
3.35	2.10	43	SANTA MARIA (E.)....Ll.	8.20	14.32	19. 6

PALMA Á MANACOR

PRECIOS 1.ª c. P.C.	2.ª c. P.C.	3.ª c. P.C.	K.	ESTACIONES.	2 1ª2ª	4 1ª2ª3ª	6 1ª2ª3ª	10 1ª2ª	8 1ª2ª
			»	PALMA....8....	7.40	14. »		18.15	14.40
0.65	0.30		4	Pont d'Inca	7.50	14.10		18.27	14.50
0.80	0.45		9	Marratxí	8. 5	14.25		18.45	16. 5
1.20	0.75	0.65	15	Santa María (E.)	8.24	14.44	14.46	19.10	15.24
1.55	0.95		19	Consell (E.)....Ll.	8.34	14.54		19.20	15.34
				S.	8.35	14.65		19.21	15.36
1.75	1.10	0.70	22	Binisalem	8.44	15. 4		19.30	15.44
2.05	1.25	0.85	26	Lloseta	8.61	16.11		18.37	15.61
2.15	1.35	1.00	29	Inca....Ll.	9. 1	15.21		19.47	16. 1
				S.	9.11	15.31		19.57	16.11
2.75	1.75	1.16	34	Son Bordils (E.)....S.	9.16	15.32		20. 2	
3.15	2.00	1.35	43	Sineu	9.34	15.60		20.89	
3.25	2.10	1.35	45	San Juan	9.41	15.57		20.48	
3.65	1.80	1.35	54	Petra	9.55	16.11		21.15	
4.00	2.65	1.35	64	MANACOR....Ll.	10.10	16.26		21.40	

PRECIOS 1.ª c. P.C.	2.ª c. P.C.	3.ª c. P.C.	K.	ESTACIONES.	1 1ª2ª3ª	3 1ª2ª3ª	5 1ª2ª	9 1ª2ª	7 1ª2ª
			»	MANACOR....8....	2.30	6.30		17.16	
0.55	1.05		10	Petra	3.10	6.49		17.34	
1.60	1.05		19	San Juan	3.40	7. 5		17.60	
1.10			21	Sineu	4. »	7.14		17.59	
2.40	1.60		30	Son Bordils (E.)....Ll.	4.25	7.29		18.14	
				S.	4.30	7.34	12.50	18.19	
2.75	1.85		36	Inca....Ll.	5.16	7.48	13. 4	18.33	
				S.	5.38	7.58	13.14	18.43	
3.05	2.05		38	Lloseta	5.53	8. 6	13.22	18.51	
3.25	2.25		42	Binisalem	6.15	8.16	13.31	19. »	
3.50	2.30		45	Consell (E.)....Ll.	6.18	8.16	13.32	19. 1	
3.55	2.4)		49	Santa María (E.)	6.33	6.25	13.41	19.10	14.46
4.00	2.65		56	Marratxí	6.66	8.40	13.56	19.26	16. 4
4.00	2.55		60	Pont d'Inca	7.18	8.52	14.12	19.37	16.16
4.00	2.55	1.35	64	PALMA	7.30	9. »	14.20	19.45	16.24

Los sábados sale de Manacor para Palma un tren á las 11.55 y de Palma para Manacor á las 4.46 tarde.

CONSELL Á ALARÓ

E.. estos dos puntos hay un tranvía de 4 kilómetros de extensión, por el que circulan trenes ascendentes y descendentes en combinación con la línea de Palma á Manacor, y cuyos asientos cuestan 30 á 25 céntimos, según sean de 1.ª ó 2.ª clase.

1913

LA PUEBLA, FELANITX Y MANACOR A PALMA

PRECIOS			K.	ESTACIONES	1	81-5	13	9	85-15	51-3	53-11	55-16	61-3	83-11	65-16
1.ª	2.ª	3.ª			1-2-3	1-2	1-2-3	1-2	1-2	1-2	1-2	1-2	1-2	1-2	1-2
P. C.	P. C.	P. C.		Desde La Puebla											
0,55	0,35	.		LA PUEBLA .....S.										7. .	12.15 17.18
0,75	0,50	.		Muro............										7.10	12.27 17.31
1,10	0,75	.	8	Llubi...........										7.20	12.39 17 50
			13	*EMPALME......Ll.										7.30	12.48 18. 3
				Desde Felanitx											
0,70	0,45	.		FELANITX......S.				8.45	11.50	17.15					
1,10	0,75	.		Las Canteras....				6.59	12. 4	17.29					
1,70	1,15	.		Porreras........				7.16	12.19	17.44					
2,40	1,55	.		Montuiri........				7.32	12.34	17.59					
2,95	1,90	.		Algaida.........				7.50	12.51	18.15					
3,45	2,15	.		Santa Eugenia...				8. 5	13. 7	18.31					
				*STA. MARIA....Ll.				8.19	13.27	18.45					
				Desde Artá											
1,20	0,80	0,60	10	Artá............S.	6.50	16.19									
1,60	1,05	0,70	17	Son Servera.....	7. 5	16.5									
1,85	1,20	0,80	21	San Miguel......	7.16	16.40									
2,75	1,85	1,20	30	Nata Lorenzo....	7.23	16.50									
				MANACOR........	7.42	17.15									
3,60	2,30	.		Petra...........	5.25	8. 1	11.30	17.23							
4,40	2,95	.		San Juan........	5.38	8.14	17.33								
4,50	3,00	.		Sineu..........	5.48	8.20	17.45								
			51		5.53		18.5								
5,25	3,50	.	60	*EMPALME....{ S.	6.14	8.43	17. .	11.30	18.19						
					6.20		17. 7	11.37	18.28						
5,85	3,95	.	65	Inca...........	6.28	8.54	17.14	11.44	18.33						
6,10	4,15	.	68	Lloseta.........	6.33	.	17.21	11.51	18.40						
6,35	4,20	.	72	Binisalem......											
			75	Consell.........	6.38	9. 4	17.27	11.57	18.46	18.50		8.27	13.29	18.50	
6,60	4,30	.		*STA. MARIA{ S.	6.39	9. 3	17.28	11.58	18.50			8.30	13.32	18.48	
6,85	4,45	.	86	Marratxí........	6.48	.	17.37	.				8.40	13.40	.	
6,95	4,45	.	90	Pont d'Inca.....	6.55	.	17.47	.				8.50	13.49	.	
6,85	4,45	2,90	94	*PALMA.........Ll.	7.1	9.25	17.52	12.20	19.12			8.58	13.55	19.15	

TREN 81-5.—Los viajeros cuyo destino sea el Empalme, se apearán en Inca, los que vayan a Lloseta lo harán en Benisalem y los que a Consell en Santa María para tomar el tren 6. Los que vayan a Marratxí y Pont d'Inca se apearán en Santa María para tomar el tren 7.—**TREN 53-11.**—Circulan los martes, miércoles, viernes, sábados y domingos.—**TREN 85-15.**—Los viajeros cuyo destino sea Marratxí o Pont d'Inca se apearán en Santa María para tomar el tren 17.

PALMA A ARTÁ, A FELANITX Y A LA PUEBLA

PRECIOS			K.	ESTACIONES	4-82	6-52	10-54	8	16-56	6-62	14-64	12-54	16-66	2
1.ª	2.ª	3.ª			1-2	1-2	1-2	1-2	1-2	1-2	1-2	1-2	1-2	2-3
P. C.	P. C.	P. C.		Desde Palma.										
0,55	0,30	.		*PALMA.........S.	8. .		8.25	14.15	13.45	14.45	14.15	18.30	18.30	7.15
0,80	0,40	.		Pont d'Inca.....			8.41		13.55	18.33		18.38	18.38	7.22
			9	Marratxí.......			8.41	.	14. 9	18 47		18.47	18.47	7.31
1,25	0,75	0,60	15	*SANTA MARIA..{ L.	8.20		8.59	14.45	14.24	18.59	8.59	18.59	18.59	7.39
				{ S.	8.22				14.25		9. 4		.		7.40
1,90	0,95	0,70	19	*CONSELL.......		8.33			14.35		9.21	15.25	19. 7	7.47
1,90	1,15	0,75	22	Binisalem......					14.45		9.31	15.35	19.14	7.54
2,10	1,30	0,90	26	Lloseta.........		8.45			14.52		9.40	15.42	19.21	8. 1
2,25	1,40	1,05	29	Inca............					15. .		2.30	15.50	19.28	8. 8
				*EMPALME......{ Ll.					15. .		9.43	15.59	19.36	.
2,85	1,80	1,20	34								9.48	15.59	19.37	
				Desde Santa María.										
				Siteu...........		9. 6						15.41	19.50	
3,25	2,05	1,40	43	San Juan........		9.12						15.47	19.55	
3,35	2,15	1,40	45	Petra...........		9.24						16. .	20. 6	
3,75	2,25	1,40	54	MANACOR........		9.43						16.20	20.17	
4,10	2,60	1,60	64	San Lorenzo.....		9.57						16.34		
5,00	3,35	1,80	72	San Miguel......		10. 3						16.40		
5,25	3,35	1,95	77	Son Servera.....		10.14						16.51		
5,95	3,85	2,20	84			10.28						17. 5		
6,85	4,45	2,80	94	Artá...........Ll.										
				Desde Empalme.										
0,70	0,45	.		*SANTA MARIA...S.			9. 5	14.46			9.49	16. .		19.38
1,25	0,80	.	7	Santa Eugenia...			9.17	15. 1			9.55	16. 6		19.51
1,85	1,25	.	16	Algaida.........			9.36	15.22	19.14		10. 2	16.13		20. 6
2,50	1,60	.	23	Montuiri........			9.50	15.35	19.34			16.18		20. 8
2,95	1,85	.	30	Porreras........			10. 4	15.50	19.49		10.16	16.26		20.15
3,45	2,15	.	36	Las Canteras....			10.16	16. 2	20.17					
			43	FELANITX.....Ll.			10.31	16.18	20.33					
				Desde Empalme.										
0,60	0,45	.		*EMPALME........S.										
0,90	0,55	.	5	Llubí...........										
1,10	0,75	.	13	LA PUEBLA.....Ll.										

TREN número 16-66.—Los domingos y días festivos, retrasa su salida de Palma hasta las 20.

1934

SANTAÑY A PALMA

PRECIOS			K.	ESTACIONES	71 Cor. 1-2-3	73 Míx. 1-2	75 Míx. 1-2
1.ª	2.ª	3.ª					
P. C.	P. C.	P. C.					
0,45	0,30	0,20	7	SANTAÑY.......S.	8.40	12.10	17.20
0,75	0,60	0,45		Las Salinas.....	8.51	12.21	17.35
2,00	1,25	0,75	18	Baños de San Juan.	6.58	12.27	17.41
2,05	1,30	0,85		Campos..........	7.13	12.47	18. 1
3,15	1,65	1,15	32	Lluchmayor......	7.52	13.31	18.29
2,50	2,10	1,30	44	El Arenal.......	8.23	14. 1	18.52
3,60	2,35	1,25	52	Coll d'en Rebasa.	8.38	14.16	19. 3
4,00	2,60	1,40	62	*PALMA.........	8.50	14.26	19.13

TREN 73.—Circula los jueves.

CONSELL A ALAROS

Entre estos dos puntos hay un tranvía de 4 kilómetros de extensión, por el que circulan trenes ascendentes y descendentes en combinación con la línea de Palma a Manacor y cuyo servicio cuesta 30 céntimos y 20 céntimos según sean de 1.ª o 2.ª clase.

PALMA A SANTAÑY

PRECIOS			K.	ESTACIONES	72 1-2	74 Cor. Míx. 1-2-3	76 Míx. 1-2
1.ª	2.ª	3.ª					
P. C.	P. C.	P. C					
0,40	0,25	0,15	6	*PALMA......... .S.	7.55	14.40	18.25
0,95	0,60	0,35	14	Coll d'en Rebasa.	8. 6	14.50	18.36
2,00	1,25	0,75	18	El Arenal.......	8.24	15. .	18.51
3,15	1,65	1,15	44	Lluchmayor......	9. 2	15.36	19.25
3,15	2,10	1,30		Campos..........	9.28	15.57	19.56
3,50	2,25	1,30	52	Baños de San Juan.	9.44	16.37	20.12
3,75	2,51	1,40		Las Salinas.....	9.50	16. 3	20.13
4,00	2,60	1,40	60	SANTAÑY........	10. .	16.12	20.33

TREN número 76.—Circula los jueves.
Trenes sólo paran en la estación de Baños únicament cuando está abierto el Balneario.

E.F.E. 1954

Palma ↔ Arta ↔ Felanitx ↔ La Puebla

Km.	ESTACIONES		4 Cor.	6 Cor.	8 Tm.	12-84 Cor.	14-84 Cor.	16 Lig.	16 bis Lig. ⊕✝	10-54 Cor.	Cor.	6-42 Cor.	16-56 Lig.	16-66 Lig.
—	PALMA	S.	8.00	8.40	13.25	14.15	14.45	18.30	21.00					
4	Pont d'Inca	S.	8.09	—	13.33		14.54	18.39	21.09					
9	Marratxi	S.	8.20	8.57	13.40		15.05	18.50	21.20					
15	SANTA MARIA	Ll.	8.27	9.12	14.05		15.19	19.06	21.36					
—	SANTA MARIA	S.								15.00			19.33	
7	SANTA EUGENIA	S.								15.20			19.48	
16	ALGAIDA	S.								15.41			20.11	
23	MONTUIRI	S.								15.54			20.28	
28	PORRERAS	S.								16.03			20.48	
30	LAS CANTERAS	S.								16.25			20.57	
43	FELANITX	Ll.								16.40			21.12	
—	SANTA MARIA	S.	8.37	9.12	14.05		15.19	19.06	21.36					
19	Consell	S.	—	9.20	14.15		15.28	19.15	21.45					
22	Binisalem	S.	8.45	9.28	14.25		15.37	19.24	22.04					
26	Lloseta	S.	9.03	9.44	—		15.46	19.34	22.11					
29	Inca	S.	9.15	9.54	14.34		15.58	19.50	22.35					
34	EMPALME	Ll.			14.42	15.10	16.06	20.05						
—	EMPALME	S.										9.55	16.08	20.03
5	LLUBI	S.										10.00	16.20	20.18
9	MURO	S.										10.18	16.32	20.33
13	LA PUEBLA	Ll.										10.25	16.41	20.42
—	EMPALME	S.	9.15			15.10		20.05	22.35					
3	Sineu	S.	9.40			—		20.19	22.49					
5	San Juan	S.	9.44			15.36		20.25	22.55					
7	Petra	S.	9.43			15.42		20.40	23.10					
...	MANACOR	S.	10.02			15.58		20.56	23.16					
...	San Lorenzo	S.	10.27			16.23								
7	San Miguel	S.	10.46			16.42								
84	San Servera	S.	10.54			16.49								
96	ARTA	Ll.	11.14 / 11.30			17.04 / 17.20								

El tren 16-66 retrasa su salida los domingos hasta las 20.—. Los trenes 16-66 y 68-11 son discrecionales.—El tren 16 retrasa su salida los sábados hasta las 19,50, y los festivos hasta las 20,50.

E.F.E. 1954

La Puebla <–> Felanitx <–> Arta <–> Palma

147

ESTACIONES	Km.	1 Tm.	61-3 Cor.	81-5 Cor.	11 Lig.	13 Tm. ⊕⊕	83-15 Cor.	15 bis +	51-3 Cor.	53-11 Lig. Cor.	55-17 Cor.	63-11 Mix.	65-15 Cor.
ARTA Ll.	10			6.35			16.00						
San Servera S.	17			6.50			16.19						
San Miguel S.	21			7.02			16.35						
San Lorenzo S.				7.09			16.47						
MANACOR Ll.	30	5.05		7.30			17.12						
Petra S.	44	5.22		7.50			17.32						
San Juan S.	47	5.37		8.05			17.48						
Sineu S.	51	5.44		—			17.59						
EMPALME S. ●	60	6.00		8.14			18.23						
LA PUEBLA Ll.	1		7.00										
MURO S.	4		7.13										
LLUBI S.	6		7.25										
EMPALME Ll. ●	13		7.35										
EMPALME Ll.	60	6.00	7.36	8.41	12.51	17.00	18.23	21.00					
Inca S.	63	6.15	7.55	—	13.04	17.07	18.38	21.07					
Lloseta S.	68	6.23	8.05	8.54	13.12	17.14	18.44	21.14					
Binisalem S.	72	6.31	8.15	—	13.20	17.21	18.55	21.21					
Consell S.	75	6.39	8.25	9.08	13.26	17.21	19.03	21.21					
SANTA MARIA S. ●	77	6.47	8.35	9.08	13.37	17.28	19.12	21.28					
FELANITX Ll.	1								7.00		17.20		
LAS CANTERAS S.	7								7.12		17.32		
PORRERAS S.	13								7.27		17.50		
MONTUIRI S.	20								7.44		18.00		
ALGAIDA S.	27								8.01		18.26		
SANTA EUGENIA S.	36								8.16		18.41		
SANTA MARIA Ll. ●	43								8.25		18.54		
SANTA MARIA Ll. ●	77	6.47	8.35	9.10	13.39	17.28	18.40	21.28				12.10	17.33
Marratxí S.	83	6.57	8.43	9.18	13.49	17.38	19.22	21.38				12.23	17.47
Pont d'Inca S.	88	7.06	8.54	9.27	13.58	17.47	19.31	21.47				12.38	18.04
PALMA Ll. ●	94	7.14	9.02	9.35	14.05	17.55	19.39	21.55				12.48	18.16

147

1959

FERROCARRILES DE BALEARES

502   PALMA A ARTA   502
(SERVICIO DESDE EL 1.º DE ABRIL DE 1959)

K.	ESTACIONES	132 Auto	62 Auto	134 Auto	104 Mix.	118 Cor.	64 Cor.	66 Mix.	138 Auto	112 Auto	66 bis Lig.	112 Auto
	,PALMA .... s.	8.—	9.—	12.30	13.25	14.25	14.46	18.40	19.10	20.10	20.30	22.—
4	Pons	8.06	9.06	12.36	13.30	»	14.54	18.39	»	20.16	20.39	22.06
9	Marratxí	8.11	9.10	12.41	13.38	»	15.05	»		»	»	»
15	°SANTA MARIA	8.19	9.18	12.49	13.49	»	15.19	19.03		20.29	21.03	22.19
19	Consell	8.26	9.24	12.55	13.55	»	15.28	19.11		20.35	21.11	22.25
22	Binisalem	8.31	9.30	13.—	14.01	»	15.37	19.19		20.41	21.19	22.31
26	Lloseta	8.37	9.36	13.05	14.07	»	15.46	19.27		20.47	21.27	22.37
29	Inca	8.44	9.43	13.10	14.12	15.10	15.58	19.37	19 48	20.53	21.37	22.43
34	°EMPALME	»	9.49	»	»	16.10	16.04	19 48		20.59	21.48	22.49
43	Sineu	9.02		13.25		16.36				20.05	21.10	22.—
46	San Juan	9.06		13.28		15.42				20.08	21.18	23.03
54	Petra	9.17		13.38		15.58				0.19	21.24	23.14
64	Manacor	9 30		13.51		16.23				.31	21.35	23.25
73	San Lorenzo	9.42		14.03		16.42				20.43		
77	San Miguel	9.47		14.08		16.49				20.48		
84	S. Servera	9 57		14.18		17.04				20.58		
94	ARTA .... Ll.	10.08		14.19		17.20				21.09		

K.	ESTACIONES	111 Auto	61 Cor.	121 Auto	63 Auto	133 Auto	103 Tran.	65 Cor.	135 Auto	137 Lig.
	ARTA .... s.			7.55		13.12			17.50	18.50
10	S. Servera			8.07		13.24			18.01	19.05
17	San Miguel			8.17		13.34			18.12	19.17
21	San Lorenzo			8.22		13.39			18.17	19.24
30	Manacor	6.—		8.36		13.56			18.29	19.41
40	Petra	6.13		8.47		14.08			18.41	19.58
49	San Juan	6.24		8.58		14.17			18.52	20.14
51	Sineu	6.30		9.08		14.21			18.56	20.21
60	°EMPALME	6.42	7.35	»	12.55	»		18.23	»	20.37
65	Inca	6.50	7.53	9.21	13.03	14.36	17.—	18.38	19.13	21.
68	Lloseta	6.56	8.01	»	13.05	14.41	17.06	18.46	»	21.07
72	Binisalem	7.02	8.09	9.32	13.16	14.46	17.12	18.55	19 24	21.14
75	Consell	7 08	8.17	»	13.21	14.51	17.18	19.03	»	21.23
79	°SANTA MARIA	7.14	8.25	9.43	13.27	14.57	17.24	19.12	19.35	21.28
85	Marratxí	7.23	8.35	»	13.34	15.05	17.33	19.22	»	21.38
90	Pons	7.30	8.44	9.56	13.39	15.11	17.40	19.31	19.48	21.47
94	°PALMA ...... Ll.	7.35	8 52	10.01	13.44	15.15	17.45	19.39	19.53	21.55

El tren 133 circula los festivos una hora después.

503 | PALMA A FELANITX | 503

(SERVICIO DESDE EL 1.º DE ABRIL DE 1959)

	K.	ESTACIONES	54 Auto	56 Auto	K.	ESTACIONES	51 Auto	55 Auto
I		•PALMA .... S..	14 15	19 15		FELANITX .... S..	7 30	17 30
D	15	•SANTA MARIA	14 39	19 39	7	Canteras	7 39	17 39
D	72	Santa Eugenia	14 49	19 49	15	Porreras	7 51	17 51
D	31	Algaida (165 m.)	15 03	20 03	20	Montuiri	8 04	18 04
I	35	Montuiri	15 13	20 13	27	Algaida	8 16	18 16
I	45	Porreras	15 26	20 26	36	Santa Eugenia	8 29	18 29
D	51	Canteras	15 37	20 37	43	•SANTA MARIA	8 39	18 39
D	58	FELANITX (86 m.) Ll	15 46	20 46	58	•PALMA Ll	9,—	19 —

El trayecto detallado entre Palma y Santa María y viceversa, véase en el itinerario 502.
Los trenes 55 y 56 retrasan una hora su salida los días festivos del 1.º de octubre al 31 de mayo, y después dos horas.

504 | PALMA A LA PUEBLA | 504

(SERVICIO DESDE EL 1.º DE ABRIL DE 1959)

		K.	ESTACIONES	52 Auto	54 Cer.	L. 56 Lig.	K.	ESTACIONES	51 Cer.	53 Auto	55 Cer.
24			•PALMA .... S..	9.—	14.45	18.59		LA PUEBLA .... S..	7.—	12.30	17.33
		34	•EMPALME .... {Ll / S..	9.47 / 9.49	16.06 / 16.08	19.43 / 19.48	4 / 8	Muro .... / Llubí	7.13 / 7.24	12.38 / 12.47	17.47 / 18.04
6	D	29	Llubí	9.58	16.20	20.03	13	•EMPALME ... {Ll / S..	7.34 / 7.36	12.55 / 12 55	18.16 / 18.23
		43	Muro	10.07	16.32	20.18					
15	I	47	LA PUEBLA Ll	10.14	16.41	20.27	47	•PALMA Ll	8 52	13 44	19.23

El tren 66 retrasa su salida los festivos hasta las 20.30.
El trayecto detallado entre Palma y Empalme y viceversa, véase en el itinerario 502.

505 | PALMA A SANTAÑY | 505

(SERVICIO DESDE EL 1.º DE ABRIL DE 1959)

		K.	ESTACIONES	72 Auto	74 Auto	76 Auto ✗	78 Auto ✠	K.	ESTACIONES	71 Auto	73 Auto	75 Auto ✗	75 Auto ✠
5	I		•PALMA... S..	9 20	14 30	19 20	20 20		SANTAÑY S..	7 30	12 45	17 30	18 30
9	D	6	Coll	9 28	14 38	19 28	20 28	4	Llomparts (ap.).	7 34	12 49	17 34	18 34
	I	11	San Francisco.	9 34	14 44	19 34	20 34	7	Salinas	7 39	12 54	17 39	18 49
	D	14	Arenal	9 40	14 50	19 40	20 40	10	Baños	7 44	12 59	17 44	18 44
136	I	30	Lluchmayor	10 01	15 11	20 01	2 01	18	Campos	7 54	13 09	17 54	18 54
	I	44	Campos	10 17	15 27	20 17	21 17	32	Lluchmayor ...	8 03	13 28	18 12	19 13
	D	52	Baños	10 26	15 36	20 26	21 26	48	Arenal	8 31	13 46	18 41	19 31
	D	55	Salinas	10 32	15 42	20 32	21 32	51	San Francisco.	8 36	13 51	18 36	19 36
	D	58	Llomparts (ap.).	10 36	15 46	20 36	21 36	56	Coll	8 43	13 59	18 43	19 43
	D	62	SANTAÑY Ll	10 40	15 50	20 40	21 40	62	•PALMA. Ll	8 50	14 05	18 50	19 50

Del 1.º junio al 30 septiembre los trenes 75 y 76 circulan los días festivos dos horas más tarde que los laborables.

1963

214 Palma - Artá 214

Km.	ESTACIONES 1-VII-960	132 Aut.	134	104 A Aut.	136 Aut.	138	136 bis	112 Aut.	112 bis Aut.
0	Palma .... S.	8.—	12.30	13.25	15.30	19.10 ✗	20.10 ✠	20.10 ✗	22.— ✠
4	Pont	8.06	12.37	13.30				20.16	22.06
9	Marratxi	8.11	12.44	13.38					
15	Santa María	8.19	12.55	13.49		19.34	20.34	20.29	22.19
19	Consell	8.25	13.01	13.55		19.40	20.40	20.35	22.25
22	Binisalem	8.31	13.07	14.01	15.58	19.46	20.46	20.41	22.31
26	Lloseta	8.37	13.13	14.07	16.04	19.52	20.52	20.47	22.37
29	Inca	8.44	13.19	14.12	16.10	19.58	20.58	20.53	22.43
34	Empalme	8.50	13.25			20.04	21.04	20.59	22.49
43	Sineu	9.02	13.36		16.27	20.15	21.15	21.10	23.—
46	San Juan	9.06	13.40		16.31	20.20	21.20	21.13	23.03
54	Petra	9.17	13.52		16.42	20.31	21.31	21.24	23.14
64	Manacor	9.30	14.04		16.55	20.43	21.43	21.35	23.25
78	San Lorenzo	9.42	14.16		17.07	20.55	21.55		
77	San Miguel	9.47	14.22		17.12	21.01	22.01		
84	S. Servera	9.57	14.33		17.22	21.12	22.12		
94	Artá .... Ll.	10.08	14.45		17.33	21.24	22.24		

Km.	ESTACIONES	111 Aut.	131	133 Aut.	135	137 Aut.	103 A Aut.
0	Artá .... S.		7.15	13.—	16.10	17.50	✠
10	S. Servera		7.28	13.12	16.23	18.02	
17	San Miguel		7.39	13 22	16.34	18.12	
21	San Lorenzo		7.45	13.27	16.40	18.17	
30	Manacor	6.—	7.58	13.39	16.54	18.29	
40	Petra	6.13	8.10	13.52	17.06	18.41	
49	San Juan	6.24	8.21	14.03	17.17	18.52	
51	Sineu	6.30	8.26	14.07	17.22	18.56	
60	Empalme	6.42		14.17	17.32	19.06	
65	Inca	6.50	8.44	14.24	17.39	19.13	21.—
68	Lloseta	6.56	8.50	14.30	17.45	19.19	21.06
72	Binisalem	7.02	8.56	14.36	17.51	19.25	21.12
75	Consell	7.08		14.42	17.57	19.31	21.18
79	Santa María	7.14	9.07	14.48	18.03	19.37	21.24
85	Marratxi	7.23		14.56	18.11	19.44	21.33
90	Pont	7.30	9.22	15.02	18.18	19.50	21.40
94	Palma .... Ll.	7.35	9.28	15.07	18.24	19.55	21.45

A Circula ⑤ ⑪ ✠ y visperas de ✠

1963

215   Palma - Felanitx   215

Km.	ESTACIONES 1-VII-960	52 Aut.	54 Aut.	56 Aut.	Km	ESTACIONES 1-VII-960	51 Aut.	53 Aut.	55 Aut.
				A					A
0	Palma .... S.	9.25	14.15	19.15	0	Felanitx .... S.	7.30	12.30	17.30
15	Santa María ...	9.49	14.39	19.39	7	Cameras	7.39	12.39	17.39
22	Santa Eugenia	9.59	14.49	19.49	13	Porreras	7.51	12.51	17.51
31	Algaida	10.13	15.03	20.03	20	Montuiri	8.04	13.04	18.04
35	Montuiri	10.23	15.13	20.13	27	Algaida	8.16	13.16	18.16
45	Porreras	10.36	15.26	20.26	36	Santa Eugenia	8.29	13.28	18.29
51	Cameras	10.47	15.37	20.37	43	Santa María ...	8.39	13.38	18.39
58	Felanitx .... Ll.	10.56	15.46	20.46	58	Palma .... Ll.	9.—	13.59	19.—

A Retrasan una hora su salida los días festivos, del 1-X al 31-V, y dos horas, del 1-VI al 30-IX.

216   Palma - La Puebla   216

Km.	ESTACIONES 1-VII-960	62 Aut.	64 Aut.	66 Aut.	68 Aut.	68 bis Aut.	Km.	ESTACIONES 1-VII-960	61 Aut.	63 Aut.	65 Aut.	67 Aut.
						✠						
0	Palma .... S.	9.—	12.10	15.—	18.50	20.30	0	La Puebla .. S.	7.30	10.20	13.30	17.30
34	Empalme . { Ll. S.	9.47 9.49	12.56 12.58	15.46 15.48	19.36 19.38	21.17 21.19	4	Muro	7.39	10.28	13.38	17.38
39	Llubí	9.58	13.07	15.57	19.47	21.28	8	Llubí	7.47	10.37	13.47	17.47
43	Muro	10.07	13.16	16.06	19.56	21.37	13	Empalme - { S. Ll.	7.59 7.55	10.44 10.46	13.54 13.56	17.53 17.55
47	La Puebla .. Ll.	10.14	13.23	16.13	20.03	21.44	47	Palma .... Ll.	8.44	11.33	14.43	18.43

213   Palma-Santañy   213

Km.	72 Aut.	74 Aut.	76 Aut.		ESTACIONES (1-VII-960)	71 Aut.	73 Aut.	75 Aut.	
			A					A	
0	9.20	14.30	19.20	S.	Palma .... Ll.	8.50	14.05	18.50	
6	9.28	14.38	19.28		Coll	8.43	13.58	18.43	
11	9.34	14.44	19.34		San Francisco (apd.) .	8.36	13.51	18.36	
12	9.37	14.47	19.37		Las Cadenas (apd.) ...	8.33	13.48	18.33	
14	9.40	14.50	19.40		Arenal	8.31	13.46	18.31	
30	10.01	15.11	20.01		Lluchmayor	8.13	13.28	18.13	
34	10.17	15.27	20.17		Campos	7.54	13.09	17.54	
44	10.23	15.33	20.23		El Palmer (apd.)	7.47	13.02	17.47	
52	10.26	15.36	20.26		Baños	7.44	12.59	17.44	
55	10.32	15.42	20.32		Salinas	7.39	12.54	17.39	
58	10.36	15.46	20.36		Llombarts (apd.)	7.34	12.49	17 34	
60	10.40	15.50	20.40	Ll.	Santañy .... S.	7.30	12.45	17.30	

A Retrasan su salida una hora los ✠, del 1-X al 31-V, y dos horas, del 1-VI al 30-IX.

473   Palma ⟶ Artá   1965

Km.	ESTACIONES	132 Aut.	102	134	104 Aut.	136 Aut.	138	106 Aut.	138 bis	112 Aut.	112 bis Aut.
0	PALMA............... S.	8.—	10.—	12.30	14.—	15.30	19.10	19.30	20.10	20.10	22.—
4	Pont....................	8.06	10.05	12.37	14.05			19.35		20.16	22.06
9	Marratxi..............	8.11	10.13	12.44	14.13			19.43			
15	Santa María	8.19	10.24	12.55	14.24		19.34	19.54	20.34	20.29	22.19
19	Consell	8.25	10.30	13.01	14.30		19.40	20.—	20.40	20.35	22.25
22	Binisalem	8.31	10.36	13.07	14.36	15.58	19.46	20.06	20.46	20.41	22.31
26	Lloseta	8.37	10.42	13.13	14.42	16.04	19.52	20.12	20.52	20.47	22.37
29	Inca.....................	8.44	10.47	13.19	14.47	16.10	19.58	20.17	20.58	20.53	22.43
34	Empalme.............	8.50	—	13.25	—		20.04	—	21.04	20.59	22.49
43	Sineu...................	9.02	—	13.36	—	16.27	20.15	—	21.15	21.10	23.—
45	San Juan	9.06	—	13.40	—	16.31	20.20	—	21.20	21.13	23.03
54	Petra...................	9.17	—	13.52	—	16.42	20.31	—	21.31	21.24	23.14
64	Manacor...............	9.30	—	14.04	—	16.55	20.43	—	21.43	21.35	23.25
73	San Lorenzo..........	9.42	—	14.16	—	17.07	20.55	—	21.55	—	—
77	San Miguel	9.47	—	14.22	—	17.12	21.01	—	22.01	—	—
84	Son Servera..........	9.57	—	14.33	—	17.22	21.12	—	22.12	—	—
94	ARTA................... Ll.	10.08	—	14.45	—	17.33	21.24	—	22.24	—	—

473   Artá ⟶ Palma

Km.	ESTACIONES	111 Aut.	131	101 Aut.	133 Aut.	103 Aut.	135	137 bis Aut.	105 Aut.	137 Aut.
0	ARTA................... S.	—	7.15	—	13.—	—	16.10	18.20	—	17.50
10	Son Servera...........	—	7.28	—	13.12	—	16.23	18.34	—	18.02
17	San Miguel	—	7.39	—	13.22	—	16.34	18.46	—	18.12
21	San Lorenzo...........	—	7.45	—	13.27	—	16.40	18.52	—	18.17
30	Manacor................	6.—	7.58	—	13.39	—	16.54	19.05	—	18.29
40	Petra....................	6.13	8.10	—	13.52	—	17.06	19.19	—	18.41
49	San Juan	6.24	8.21	—	14.03	—	17.17	19.32	—	18.52
51	Sineu...................	6.30	8.26	—	14.07	—	17.22	19.39	—	18.56
60	Empalme...............	6.42		—	14.17	—	17.32	19.51	—	19.06
65	Inca.....................	6.50	8.44	13.—	14.24	14.30	17.39	19.58	21.—	19.13
68	Lloseta	6.56	8.50	13.06	14.30	16.36	17.45	20.05	21.06	19.19
72	Binisalem	7.02	8.56	13.12	14.36	16.42	17.51	20.12	21.12	19.25
75	Consell	7.08		13.18	14.42	16.48	17.57	20.18	21.18	19.31
79	Santa María	7.14	9.07	13.24	14.48	16.54	18.03	20.24	21.24	19.37
85	Marratxi	7.23		13.33	14.56	17.03	18.11	20.32	21.33	19.44
90	Pont....................	7.30	9.22	13.40	15.02	17.10	18.18	20.39	21.40	19.50
94	PALMA................. Ll.	7.35	9.28	13.45	15.07	17.15	18.24	20.50	21.45	19.55

474   Palma ⟷ Felanitx ⟷ Palma

Km.	52 Aut.	54 Aut.	56 Aut. A		ESTACIONES		51 Aut.	53 Aut.	55 Aut. A
0	9.25	14.15	19.15	S.	PALMA	Ll.	9.—	13.59	19.—
4		14.20	19.20		Pont d'Inca	▲	8.55	13.54	18.55
9		14.28	19.28		Marratxí		8.48	13.47	18.48
15	9.49	14.39	19.39		Santa María		8.39	13.38	18.39
22	9.59	14.49	19.49		Santa Eugenia		8.29	13.28	18.29
31	10.13	15.03	20.03		Algaida		8.16	13.16	18.16
38	10.23	15.13	20.13		Montuiri		8.04	13.04	18.04
45	10.36	15.26	20.26		Porreras		7.51	12.51	17.51
51	10.47	15.37	20.37		Canteras		7.39	12.39	17.39
58	10.56	15.46	20.46	Ll.	FELANITX	S.	7.30	12.30	17.30

A. Del 1-X al 31-V, retrasan una hora en salida.

Palma ⟷ La Puebla ⟷ Palma   475

Km.	62 Aut.	64 Aut.	66 Aut.	68 Aut.	68 bis Aut.		ESTACIONES		61 Aut.	63 Aut.	65 Aut.	67 Aut.
0	9.—	12.10	15.—	18.50	20.30	S.	PALMA	Ll.	8.44	11.33	14.43	18.43
4	9.05	12.15	15.05	18.55	20.35		Pont d'Inca	▲	8.39	11.28	14.38	18.38
9	9.10	12.20	15.10	19.—	20.40		Marratxí		8.34	11.23	14.33	18.33
15	9.18	12.28	15.18	19.08	20.48		Santa María		8.27	11.16	14.26	18.26
19	9.24	12.34	15.24	19.14	20.54		Consell		8.21	11.10	14.20	18.20
22	9.30	12.40	15.30	19.20	21.—		Binisalem		8.15	11.04	14.14	18.14
26	9.36	12.46	15.36	19.26	21.06		Lloseta		8.09	10.58	14.08	18.08
29	9.43	12.52	15.42	19.32	21.13		Inca		8.03	10.52	14.02	18.02
34	9.49	12.58	15.48	19.38	21.19		Empalme		7.55	10.45	13.55	17.55
39	9.58	13.07	15.57	19.47	21.28		Llubí		7.47	10.37	13.47	17.47
43	10.07	13.16	16.06	19.56	21.37		Muro		7.38	10.28	13.38	17.38
47	10.14	13.23	16.13	20.03	21.44	Ll.	LA PUEBLA	S.	7.30	10.20	13.30	17.30

(3) Circula los sábados, domingos, festivos y vísperas.

F.E.V.E.

1972

PALMA - ARTÁ - PALMA

TREN 130	TREN 132	TREN 134	TREN 136	Kms.	ESTACIONES	Kms.	TREN 131	TREN 133	TREN 135	TREN 137
8,00	13,00	16,00	18,50	—	Palma	94	9,19	12,05	16,59	19,59
8,05	13,05	16,05	18,55	4	Pont d'Inca..	90	9,14	12,03	16,54	19,54
8,10	13,10	16,10	19,00	9	Marratxi.....	85	9,09	11,58	16,49	19,49
8,18	13,18	16,18	19,08	15	Santa Maria	79	9,02	11,51	16,42	19,42
8,23	13,23	16,23	19,13	19	Consell	75	8,56	11,45	16,36	19,36
8,28	13,27	16,27	19,18	22	Binisalem ..	72	8,52	11,41	16,32	19,32
8,34	13,33	16,33	19,24	26	Lloseta	68	8,46	11,35	16,26	19,26
8,40	13,39	16,39	19'29	29	Inca	65	8,41	11,30	16,21	19,21
8,46	13,45	16,45	19,35	34	Empalme ...	60	8,33	11,23	16,14	19,14
8,56	13,55	16,55	19,46	43	Sineu	51	8,23	11,13	16,04	19,04
8,59	13,58	16,58	19,49	45	San Juan ..	49	8,20	11,10	16,01	19,01
9,11	14,10	17,10	20,01	54	Petra	40	8,09	10,59	15,50	18,50
9,23	14,22	17,22	20,13	64	Manacor ...	30	7,57	10,47	15,39	18,39
9,35	14,34	17,34	20,24	73	San Lorenzo	21	7,45	10,35	15,27	18,27
9,39	14,38	17,38	20,28	77	San Miguel	17	7,40	10,30	15,22	18,22
9,48	14,47	17,47	20,38	84	Son Servera	10	7,31	10,21	15,13	18,13
9,59	14,58	17,58	20,49	94	Artá .	—	7,20	10,10	15,02	18,02

PALMA - LA PUEBLA - PALMA

TREN 160	TREN 162	TREN 164	TREN 166	Kms.	ESTACIONES	Kms.	TREN 161	TREN 163	TREN 165	TREN 167
9,00	12,00	15,00	19,20	—	Palma	47	8,33	11,33	14,18	18,48
9,05	12,05	15,05	19,25	4	Pont d'Inca..	43	8,28	11,28	14,13	18,43
9,10	12,10	15,10	19,30	9	Marratxi	38	8,23	11,23	14,08	18,38
9,18	12,18	15,18	19,38	15	Santa Maria	32	8,16	11,16	14,01	18,31
9,23	12,23	15,23	19,43	19	Consell ...	28	8,10	11,10	13,55	18,25
9,28	12,28	15,28	19,48	22	Binisalem ..	25	8,06	11,06	13,51	18,21
9,34	12,34	15,34	19,54	26	Lloseta......	21	8,00	11,00	13,45	18,15
9,39	12,39	15,39	19,59	29	Inca	18	7,55	10,55	13,40	18,10
9,45	12,45	15,45	20,05	34	Empalme ...	13	7,48	10,48	13,33	18,03
9,52	12,52	15,52	20,12	39	Llubi	8	7,40	10,40	13,25	17,55
10,00	13,00	16,00	20,20	43	Muro	4	7,32	10,32	13,17	17,47
10,06	13,06	16,06	20,26	47	La Puebla .	—	7,25	10,25	13,10	17,40

PALMA - INCA

ESTACIONES	Kms	TREN 100	TREN 102 (1)	TREN 104 (2)	TREN 130	TREN 160	TREN 106	TREN 108	TREN 162	TREN 132	TREN 116	TREN 164	TREN 134	TREN 112	TREN 114	TREN 136	TREN 166	TREN 116
Palma	—	6,15	7,35	7,45	8,00	9,00	9,30	11,00	12,00	13,00	14,00	15,00	16,00	17,00	18,25	18,50	19,20	20,00
Pont d'Inca	4	6,20	7,40	7,50	8,05	9,05	9,35	11,05	12,05	13,05	14,05	15,05	16,05	17,05	18,30	18,55	19,25	20,05
Marratxi ...	9	6,25	7,45	7,55	8,10	9,10	9,40	11,10	12,10	13,10	14,10	15,10	16,10	17,10	18,35	19,00	19,30	20,10
Santa Maria.	15	6,33	7,53	8,03	8,18	9,18	9,48	11,18	12,18	13,18	14,18	15,18	16,18	17,18	18,43	19,08	19,38	20,18
Consell	19	6,38	7,58	8,08	8,23	9,23	9,53	11,23	12,23	13,23	14,23	15,23	16,23	17,23	18,48	19,13	19,43	20,23
Binisalem .	,22	6,43	8,03	8,13	8,28	9,28	9,58	11,28	12,28	13,27	14,28	15,28	16,27	17,28	18,53	19,18	19,48	20,28
Lloseta....	26	6,49	8,09	8,19	8,34	9,34	10,04	11,34	12,34	13,33	14,34	15,34	16,33	17,34	18,59	19,24	19,54	20,34
Inca	29	6,53	8,13	8,23	8,40	9,39	10,08	11,38	12,39	13,39	14,38	15,39	16,39	17,38	19,03	19,29	19,59	20,38

TRENES ASCENDENTES.— Circulan diariamente con las variantes (1), solo DIAS LABORABLES y (2), solo DOMINGOS Y FESTIVOS

INCA - PALMA

ESTACIONES	Kms	TREN 101	TREN 103 (1)	TREN 105 (2)	TREN 161	TREN 131	TREN 107	TREN 163	TREN 133	TREN 109	TREN 165	TREN 111	TREN 135	TREN 113	TREN 167	TREN 115	TREN 137	TREN 117
Inca	—	6,55	8,15	8,28	7,55	8,41	10,15	10,55	11,30	12,00	13,40	15,00	16,21	17,45	18,10	19,10	19,21	20,40
Lloseta.....	3	7,00	8,20	8,33	8,00	8,46	10,20	11,00	11,35	12,05	13,45	15,05	16,26	17,50	18,15	19,15	19,26	20,45
Binisalem	7	7,06	8,26	8,39	8,06	8,52	10,26	11,05	11,41	12,11	13,51	15,11	16,32	17,56	18,21	19,21	19,32	20,51
Consell	10	7,10	8,30	8,43	8,10	8,56	10,30	11,10	11,45	12,15	13,55	15,15	16,36	18,00	18,25	19,25	19,36	20,56
Santa Maria	14	7,16	8,36	8,49	8,16	9,02	10,36	11,16	11,51	12,21	14,01	15,21	16,42	18,06	18,31	19,31	19,42	21,01
Marratxi	20	7,23	8,43	8,56	8,23	9,09	10,43	11,23	11,58	12,28	14,08	15,28	16,49	18,13	18,38	19,38	19,49	21,08
Pont d'Inca	25	7,28	8,48	9,01	8,28	9,14	10,48	11,28	12,03	12,33	14,13	15,33	16,54	18,18	18,43	19,43	19,54	21,13
Palma	29	7,33	8,53	9,06	8,33	9,19	10,53	11,33	12,08	12,38	14,18	15,38	16,59	18,23	18,48	19,48	19,59	21,18

TRENES DESCENDENTES.—Circulan diariamente con las variantes (1), solo DIAS LABORABLES y (2), solo DOMINGOS Y FESTIVOS

Eye-Witness Accounts of the Majorcan Railway

Impressions of the Railway

Apart from its official historians, the Majorca Railway has occasionally figured in the accounts of visitors to the island in a more generally descriptive form. Nevertheless, these 'snapshots' are interesting enough to quote here. Apart from anything else they show how little basically changed throughout the railway's ninety-year steam era. The chosen eyewitnesses are Charles Bidwell, who saw the first trains on the island, Gordon West, who describes a journey from Palma to Arta some fifty years later, and Lawrence Marshall who made a brief visit in the late 1950s.

1875

The ceremony of inauguration, which was an interesting and peculiar one, was performed on 24th February. The event was the occasion of a general holiday in the capital and in the towns and villages along the line of the railway. The station at Palma is situated at the Puerta Pintada, just outside the grand old city walls, which were partly pulled down when the Republican party first came into power. [..] Outside the station, on the passenger platform, was erected a temporary altar, where the preliminary religious ceremony of blessing the engine and carriages before starting took place. Invitations had been issued for 9 am. At that hour, in the presence of the Captain General of the Province, the Civil Governor, the Consular Corps, the Provincial Deputation, the Ayunamiento of Palma, the railway directors and authorities, and a number of other distinguished persons, and half the ladies of the city, the religious ceremony was performed. The chief vicar (in charge of the diocese vacant by the death of the late bishop), assisted by from thirty to forty priests in their vestments, and preceded by a large golden cross, arrived before the altar chanting the prayers used on the occasion, and when those prayers were over the chief priest walked along the line to each carriage and sprinkled it with holy water.

The religious ceremony over, the priests and gentlemen took their seats, many of them for the first time in a railway carriage. "But why are all the priests going?" innocently asked one of the bystanders who had not been invited.

"They are going to give absolution to the killed and wounded", replied his neighbour.

"And the doctors, too: why are they going?"

"Ah! They go to cure the maimed" was the reply.

"I don't believe it will go without mules," exclaimed a countryman in jacket and blue calico Moorish drawers, with a twinkle in his eye.

"How should it?" said his companion, a handsome, dark-eyed girl, probably his daughter. "Don't we put a fire on our hearth all the winter nights, and did any of us see the kitchen start off? I don't believe in it a bit!"

"They won't take me in with their smoke", said another grave countryman. "We have none of us been allowed to go near the train. What will you bet that the mules are not concealed between the wheels?"

Amid these commentaries, made partly in jest and partly in earnest, the last shriek of the engine mingled with the strains from the band of music stationed on the platform, and the train started. Nothing could be more agreeable than the trip across the pleasant country. The morning, although the weather had been cold and rainy for the previous days, was bright and sunny. The fields were covered with the vegetation of early spring, and the verdure of the ground crops formed a delicious carpet to the thousands of almond-trees now in full blossom, just before their budding leaf appears, while the reflection of the sun on the mountains, capped with the unmelted snow which had fallen during the late storm, formed a charming background to the landscape. All along the line the villagers stood in crowds to see what a real railway train in actual motion was like, for up to February 1875 they had not a notion. More than one yoke of mules which their too curious drivers had brought up in close proximity to the line of railway, started off at full gallop when they had had their peep at the unknown monster now first appearing among them.

The train proceeded to Inca without stopping, and arrived there in 64 minutes. At Inca it was received by two local bands of music. All the streets were decorated by means of cords of myrtle suspended from myrtle-covered posts, in the use of which the Majorcans display natural skill and taste on all their festivals and holidays. Here, too, were half-a-dozen more triumphal arches, primitive in their construction, but significant of their purpose. Thus, one dedicated to "Industry, Agriculture and Commerce" was adorned by actual implements and tools familiar to the eye of country people. Wine-casks, ploughs, baskets, brooms, hammers and such like were arrayed amid the myrtle leaves, flowers, emblems, and banners. Amid the crowded streets, hung with flags as they had probably never been before, and accompanied by the local musicians, the public functionaries and gentlemen walked to the parish church, receiving meanwhile the smiles and welcomes of the fair inhabitants from their draped balconies. At the church a Te Deum was sung in the presence of the congregation full to cramming. On return to the station a capital lunch was offered by the railway authorities, and after a number of speeches of more local than general interest, the party returned to Palma, calling on their way at the six intermediate stations. In the afternoon a second train conveyed the shareholders who could not be accommodated in the morning train. Although the nature of the land upon which the railway has been constructed has not given rise to engineering operations of great importance or of a difficult character, the line being carried for the most part over a comparatively level country, with insignificant watercourses, the necessary works have been carried out in a credible manner. [..]

The works connected with this railway have chiefly been given out in small contracts to local artisans and workmen, a system that has been found to answer very well; and the whole of the construction has been carried on first to last by native engineers and architects, as the necessary funds have been entirely raised among the inhabitants of the island. The total cost has been about 15,000 dollars (something over £3,000) per kilometre, on the twenty-nine now finished. It is contemplated to extend the line, if successful, to the port of Alcudia and to Manacor, the second town of the island, situated towards the eastern coast. Whether it is likely to be a paying concern is a question upon which it is too early to form an opinion; but this consideration, happily, did not deter the promoters and shareholders in their patriotic efforts towards advancement of the best interests of the island. [..] We have seen new railways established in many places; but nowhere had we seen a railway received by the inhabitants with a warmer welcome than at Palma. [..] We heard of one grave gentleman, who had probably never left the island, say that this sensation (of train travel) overpowered him. "The effect on me, Señor," he said "was to bring tears to my eyes."

1920s

To begin at the beginning of the train, the engine: it is a vast improvement upon Stephenson's ROCKET. It was made decades ago in the Midlands of England, and it is capable of an average speed of 18 miles-an-hour. It is a little engine, high funnelled, and it wears important tanks at its side.

You cannot gaze upon a Majorcan railway engine without feeling that it is trying to impress its passengers and the toy coaches that cluster behind it like humble and grateful dependants. Its manner says: "Watch me while I make ready, for without me you are lost. You are powerless without me. These coaches, poor helpless creatures, are useless without me. Yet I will condescend to pull them; I will have pity on them."

The engine that was to take us to Arta said all this and more as we reached the little terminus at Palma through the flowers and the palms that fill the station square. The day was Saturday, a busy one for the railway. Hoards of peasants have come from the furthest corners of the island into Palma in the early hours; they have crowded through the town, talked themselves into a fever in the market place, inspected the shops, spent a few of their hard-earned pesetas; and now in the early afternoon many of them are going home.

It is an event; everybody is excited; there is none of that calm acceptance of a railway journey as a common experience. There is a bewildering roar of hoarse voices that drowns the fussing of the bantam steam engine, so that it hisses and puffs more vigorously to emphasise the importance of its social position.

Shawled women whose faces are aglow with the thrill of travelling push their purchases into coaches, hurry away, rush back, scramble into the wrong coaches, into First Class coaches, scramble out, search for their purchases, find them, hurry with them to another coach where they have found friends and neighbours.

The station is a tumult of adventurous humanity. Nut-vendors struggle through the crowd, selling peanuts, walnuts and brazils at thirty and forty centimes a time. Nuts are the national sustenance for railway journeys; everybody buys them; we buy some; a vendor opens my pocket and pours then in. A wet, warm bulb is pressed into the back of my neck and a pitiful high-pitched bleat sounds in my ear; whereupon a brown giant of a man behind me apologises, laughing, and wades past with a ewe lamb tucked under each arm.

Here is a woman with a black hen imprisoned under her shawl; its head protrudes at her breast, its beak moves in hoarse and dreary protest, and its eyes have the expression of startled indignation of a hen with whom great indignities are being taken. Here is a man with two bundles of dried fish hanging round his shoulders; One of these bundles swings out and delivers a blow upon another man's ear, but everybody laughs, nobody cares, nobody falls into a rage.

A shrill warning from the preposterous bantam engine. A final scramble of humanity. Doors slam; and swing negligently open again as the train sways and grinds its way slowly out of the station. We have begun the great adventure: a journey of 45 miles!

The Majorcan railway coach is built for utility, not for luxurious travelling. We are in Second Class because there is no Third Class. The coach is divided into compartments by waist-high partitions; the seats are narrow planks 18 inches wide; and we cannot lean back, for the partition is so constructed that it catches the shoulders and forces the body to a forward incline. First Class compartments are upholstered in bright red, but give little comfort.

There is but one notice on the wall of the coach. We are not asked to refrain from any of those objectionable and dangerous habits that are invariably the subject of exhortation by railway companies; we are merely asked not to blaspheme! Travellers who blaspheme in the carriages of the railway company (says the notice) will be fined from 5 to 50 pesetas, and (adds the notice), if they cannot pay they will spend the rest of the day in prison!

The windows of the coach rattle vigorously, the wheels grind and bump, and small pieces of coal from the engine, which even now will not let us forget its existence, fly in at the window and sting our faces; but nobody cares, everybody is happy and talkative and friendly.

There are many diversions for the traveller on a Majorcan railway journey. The first appears soon after we leave the terminus. A swarthy unshaven fellow with a long thin cigar between his lips appears with disconcerting suddenness on the footboard outside and thrusts his head through the window.

"Buenas…Boletas…Boletas…Gracias, gracias, señor." He grins amiably as he thrusts his arm through the window and snaps his ticket punch. Tickets are handed along the compartment, he glances at them, clips them, collects those whose owners alight at the next station, then swings off along the footboard, hanging perilously onto the hand grips, the wind blowing through his hair and sending behind him a trail of vicious smoke from his cigar.

Nor is the footboard restricted to his use. Any passenger may open the door of their compartment and swing themselves from end to end of the train, if they should desire an airing or a conversation with some friend in another coach. We looked from the window when the guard had gone and saw half-a-dozen men standing on the narrow footboard, everyone with his head through the window, talking vigorously to an acquaintance while the train bumps its way across the island. The guard is an agile fellow; he does not drive the footboard conversationalists back to their compartments so that he may pass, but swings perilously round them and goes on without interrupting their social intercourse.

And all the while the railway winds through the valleys, avoiding the blue mountains, for tunnels are costly and difficult structures; why should one go through a thing expensively when one can so easily go round it cheaply? This must surely have been the argument of the engineers who built the railway, for you will see that they meticulously edge away from anything in the nature of a hill. They build economically, knowing that a railway in this island of peasants would not prove too profitable a venture; and everywhere one may observe the care with which they have eliminated the unnecessary.

The level crossing is a masterpiece of economy. There are many of them along the track, each with a small white cottage to hold the wrinkled old woman who is its guardian. When the train bumps its way towards the crossing you may see her emerging with a small flag in her hand. Her task involves little strength. She has no levers to manipulate, no heavy wood frame to swing out. She takes a cord that is attached to a post, walks across the roadway and hitches it to another post! That is her gate, and she has closed it.

When the train has passed she rolls up her cord and the crossing is clear. Sometimes the "gate" has little strips of coloured cloth or paper attached to it at intervals, like a bird-scare in the garden, for fear you should not see the plain undecorated cord! And the old woman is unfailing in her practice of her important ritual; there may be neither man, woman nor sheep within 10 miles of her, but she will still stretch her piece of string across the road.

The train stops at Inca, and when the grinding of its wheels has ceased we hear the sound of high words in the next coach; high words from a woman, and protesting, conciliatory words from a man. Then from the coach steps the man with his two bundles of dried fish.

He is one of the finest of island types: tall and lean and strong, eyes shining with his vitality, a quick flashing smile, features mobile, expressive, and stamped with the finesse of old Rome. He puts his head in at our window and speaks in the patois in a hoarse, rapid voice, with a laugh breaking through his words. The other travellers laugh and look at us expectantly, and one man asks me in Spanish if we object to travelling with fish. We sniff simultaneously. No, we do not object. Why should we? The fish is good.

"It is good, yes," he replies. "But there is a little trouble in the next coach with a woman from Alcudia, where her man was a fisherman. He was drowned, and now she will not suffer fish. She will not eat fish, or look at fish, nor travel with fish. Ai! It is a pity, with so much fish in Majorca, and so cheap."

Since we do not object, the fish is tossed under the seat. It is such dry fish that one imagines it would soak up a whole bucket of water; it is like very old parchment, crumbling and dusty, and in dust it lies under the seat.

We all begin to eat nuts, and in 10 minutes the floor of the carriage is half-an-inch deep in shells that rustle like autumn leaves with every movement of a foot. There are eight in the carriage, all men with the exception of my wife and the woman with the hen. She has taken the bird from beneath her shawl and is holding it in her lap, where it slowly droops off into a doze, awakening occasionally to utter a shrill protest. One of the men says that perhaps the hen is laying an egg. The woman replies that it couldn't start laying early enough for her; she lifts up the hen and looks in her lap, but there is no egg. Everybody laughs. So the journey passes until we reach Manacor.

Every time we stop at a town the train loses a coach, so that for the final stage to Arta we have but two small coaches packed with chattering, laughing, gesticulating humanity. The train emerges from a labyrinthine way through close-packed mountains, where it has been twisting for a quarter-of-an-hour; the engine screams; the hen clutters, the peasants begin to gather up their goods; our Roman friend swings himself along the footboard and claims his bundle of dried fish. Arta at last.

(Author's Note: This extract is taken from the Black Swan edition of JOGGING ROUND MAJORCA. While the Publishers have made every effort to discover the owner of the work without success, they would be pleased to hear from the author's estate.)

1957

"Where to Señor?" "Mallorcan Railways Station, please." "But, Señor," said the driver of my vast American taxi as we roared away from the hotel, "tourists always use the coaches for sightseeing, the trains are very slow and very dirty, only for soldiers and the poor Spaniards."

"Trains very slow and dirty – that must mean steam trains," I said to myself with a sigh of satisfaction. Soon we swung off the cobbled streets of Palma into a cross between a chicken-yard and an open-air market, and there in the background I saw the magic, if faded, words, "Estación de los Ferrocarriles de Mallorca".

Fighting my way through two huge queues of people patiently waiting for tickets for the two morning trains to distant Arta and La Puebla, I finally arrived on the platform. On the left-hand side of the departure platform stood two diminutive blue and white railcars, each with a wonderfully antiquated brown four-wheeled coach attached to take the inevitable overflow. These were the two morning departures to Santany and Felanitx, two branches now given over entirely to railcars for passenger working. The main departure platform was completely occupied with a ten-coach train of these four-wheeled coaches, followed by four vans and several open wagons. At the head of this delightful array stood a diminutive 2-6-0 tank endeavouring to raise the energy to move this cavalcade and obliterating the area in smoke at the same time; small wonder most of the Mallorcan engines are dirty, for they only burn coal dust! Like so many Spanish narrow-gauge lines, the Mallorcan Railways are run by the State, which means that it is essential to keep the line running, but as little money as possible must be spent doing so! The train for Arta was a far more presumptuous affair and consisted of six modern bogie corridor coaches hauled by one of the six Babcock & Wilcox 2-6-2 tanks, also in a woe-be-gone and paintless condition.

Once these four trains had departed, the railway's two little Nasmyth Wilson 0-6-0 tanks with stovepipe chimneys, Nos. 4 and 5, began the most vigorous shunting campaign I have ever seen, coaches, vans and wagons being treated with the utmost disdain – small wonder that the little coaches showed more bare wood than paint on their ceilings. Old Nos. 4 and 5, dating from 1876, are among the oldest British-built narrow-gauge locomotives still in use in Spain; these, together with No. 27, which appeared to be the last active survivor of the once ubiquitous 4-4-0 tanks – two of which were built in the island – seemed to share the Palma station pilot and shunting duties between them.

Time now for a look around the two locomotive roundhouses; the first and largest seemed to house all the active locomotives, and in steam were three of the large modern Babcock & Wilcox 2-6-2 tanks, two of the class of five Krupps 2-6-0 tanks delivered in 1926 and one of the four surviving Nasmyth Wilson 4-6-0 tanks. These latter engines are spending the remainder of their active lives on troop and freight workings, two of them dating back to 1887. The only other engine in steam was No. 9, one of four rather top-heavy looking 2-6-0 tanks built by the Spanish firm of La Maquinista Terrestre y Marítima between 1911 and 1917. These engines were some of the very first to be built by the firm and, as the heavy train to La Puebla had shown earlier on, they are still very capable little machines. No. 9, incidentally, was purchased from the neighbouring Soller railway when that line was electrified in 1929. The smaller roundhouse adjoining the workshops seemed to house all the less active members of each class, together with the little railcars. During 1956 two French-built railcars were delivered to the island, and these have proved the ideal answer for the less heavily loaded Felanitx and Santany trains. Scattered all round the area were the decaying remains of various locomotives, mainly 4-4-0 tanks, but including the sixth member of the Krupps 2-6-0 tanks, No. 32, and the tiny Orenstein & Koppel 0-4-0 tank No. 7, built as recently as 1921 for the harbour branch.

Leaving Palma the main line runs due north; at the far end of the yards the harbour branch makes a trailing connection from the right, and shortly after, the Santany branch, 18 miles long, curves away to the right. The main line, doubled in 1931, now bears to the north-east and passes through the most delightful scenery: vineyards, fig trees, giant prickly pear cactus and fields of bright red *pimientos* abound, while the line itself is bordered by great lines of almond trees. To enhance the picture still further, the landscape for the first few miles out of Palma is dotted with gaily painted little windmills, providing the necessary irrigation for the crops. At Santa Maria the 27 miles long Felanitx branch turns away from us to the east, and from here onwards the soil gradually becomes more barren and less fertile.

After Inca, the ancient capital of the island, the line becomes single and more tortuous, and at Empalme the La Puebla section swings off north while we continue across the centre of Mallorca to Manacor, famous for the subterranean Dragon Caves and fine imitation pearls. After Manacor the line turns north again, and we finally arrive after almost four hour's journey at Arta, 59 miles from Palma.

Fares are very cheap, but unless one travels First Class severe overcrowding must be endured. The main lines to Arta and La Puebla have two trains a day each way and the Felanitx and Santany branches three railcars. On the two main lines all trains are mixed, and on the two branches separate freight trains are run if required. Unfortunately none of the four lines quite reaches the sea, but, nevertheless, the Mallorcan Railways provide an admirable means of seeing this beautiful island; long may they continue to do so.

(Author's note:– I am indebted to Lawrence Marshall for permission to quote from this previously published account of the Mallorcan Railways under EFE control)

The Soller Railway Rule-book

As with all railways the daily workings of the FC de Soller were governed by a comprehensive set of regulations, and in the main these corresponded with those set out in the Law of 23rd November 1877, governing the workings of Spanish railways in general. However, the Soller company split their rule-book into seven sections, all printed separately, which could be given to the members of the various operating departments according to need. Apart from a set of General rules, there were booklets entitled Track Maintenance and Safety, Traffic Movement regulations, and those applying to Locomotive Crews, Train Crews, Stationmasters and Pointsmen. The rules were comprehensive and covered every aspect including the qualifications for recruits in the various departments, together with a list of the duties to be performed by each grade of employee. A representative selection is given below.

The minimum age for work on the footplate or as a member of the train crew (Conductors and Brakemen) was twenty years of age, but while Drivers and Firemen had to be "of a robust and healthy constitution" the former also had to be of good conduct, be able to read and write and have a notion of arithmetic, as well as being able to undertake running repairs to the locomotive. A Conductor had to be able to read, write and have a good knowledge of the four rules of arithmetic. In addition he had to have at least one year's service with the railway (or provide a suitable reference) and undergo a medical examination. He would need to have mastered the General Rule Book as well as the regulations for Traffic Movement, footplate and train crew regulations, and know the audible signals used on the line. In addition a Conductor would need to be able to send and receive telegrams. It was the practice to have more than one Conductor on a train, and in this case the oldest man was designated Jefe del Tren with control over the other Conductor(s) and Brakemen as well as the footplate crew – while the train was in motion. While stopped at stations responsibility passed to the local Stationmaster.

At either end of the line the Stationmaster at Palma or Soller had a long list to check before allowing a train to proceed. He had to ensure that the footplate men and train crew knew the full details and timings of their trip, that all staff were wearing the correct uniform, maintained in a clean and smart condition, and that the driver had the correct tools, lamps and signals (presumably detonators – the rule does not specify). The Conductors had to be checked to see that they too had the necessary safety equipment, copies of the Rule Books and the correct paperwork for any freight consignments being carried by the train. The Stationmaster also had to inspect the train himself, to see that the rolling stock was in good condition, that the buffer heights matched and that the vehicles were correctly coupled. When departure time arrived the Stationmaster would ring the station bell twice, which the Jefe del Tren would answer with two toots on his horn (somewhat similar to the shunters' horns once used in Britain, and on Mallorca used instead of a Guard's whistle). This musical start to each journey was the signal and acknowledgement of the passing of responsibility from one official to the other.

While the train was being inspected, the locomotive crew would have been coaling, watering and checking and oiling the engine, before bringing it over from the shed. Approaching the carriages the engine would be brought to a halt 5 metres in front of the train, before slowly being brought into contact for coupling up. After this had been accomplished the continuous brake was tested – the minimum air pressure required being 6kg. The engine had to be coupled to the train at least 10 minutes before the scheduled departure time, no doubt to allow time for the brake test to be completed. Extracts from the General Rules stated that the locomotive should always run at the head of the train, except when performing shunting duties in the vicinity of stations, and no more than two working locomotives should haul a train unless authorised by the Ministry of Public Works. Depending on the number of engines, an equivalent number of "non-passenger vehicles" (presumably brake vans) had to be marshalled between the locomotive(s) and the carriages. The provision of a tail end "non-passenger vehicle" was advised by the Regulations, but the company could omit this at its discretion. Possibly as an assistance to braking power, the Jefe del Tren's brake van was always to carry a load of 2,000kg. If its payload weighed below this amount, then ballast was to be added to bring it up to the required total.

Once the train had started its journey various rules governed any unexpected stops along the way. If help was needed the Jefe del Tren was to send to the nearest station, either by detaching the engine (assuming that it was not itself out of action) or by sending a relay of messengers on foot. One of the Brakemen would probably start by carrying the message, which would be passed on to any available platelayers or trackside workers for onward transmission. The message might be sent by different means in the same direction, but help was not to be sought from two directions simultaneously. If, under the instructions of the Jefe del Tren, the locomotive was permitted to leave the train between stations, or if the couplings broke leaving the train stranded, then the train's manual brakes had to be applied and a "stop signal" (three detonators) placed on the line 500 metres beyond the train to warn the returning locomotive. These latter rules also applied if the locomotive was in danger of running out of water and had to run ahead "light engine" to the next available water supply. Backing the train to the previous water tank was not allowed. In the event of an accident blocking the line a message to this effect had to be sent to the nearest station on either side of the train, with a copy to the Traffic Manager describing the nature of the incident, what help was needed and whether anyone had suffered injury.

Along the way, the level crossing keepers were often recruited from among the wives of other trackside employees. When not working at the barriers under their control they were authorised to attend to their household duties, but were forbidden to take their children with them when working alongside the railway.

Once a train had arrived safely at its destination the train crew were to place themselves at the disposal of the Jefe del Tren in order to unload any freight consignments and to assist the departing passengers. Only when these tasks were completed would the Jefe del Tren give the other staff permission to leave the station. Meanwhile, he had to complete the paperwork relating to his freight consignments and ticket returns, and write up the train report, before turning all this over to the Stationmaster. During this period the engine crew would have taken the locomotive back to the shed where a final check would be made, any faults being recorded in the Depot Register. At the end of the shift the Fireman had to drop the fire, and empty the ash from the smokebox, making sure to close the smokebox door afterwards to prevent damage caused by cold air cooling the boiler too rapidly.

Bibliography

P. Allen & R. Wheeler	Steam On The Sierra (Cleaver Hulme Press)
N. S. Cañellas	La Iarda Mallorquina (Conselleria de Treball y Transports, Palma)
N. S. Cañellas Serrano	El Ferrocarril a Mallorca; La Via del Progrés (Edicions Documenta Balear)
M. Kalla Bishop	Mediterranean Island Railways (David and Charles)
M. Maristany	Carrilets de España y Portugal (vol. 1)
Ramon Molina de Dios	Línéas Ferias Industriales de las Baleares
Ramon Molina de Dios et al.	Estudis d'Història Econòmic No. 16 (2000) "El Ferrocarril a Mallorca, 125 anys"
J. Morley and K. Plant	Minor Railways and Tramways in Eastern Spain
Bartolome Font Obrador	Miscelaneo Historica del Caserio del Arenal
Carlos Olmo Ribas	El Tren a Mallorca, 1875-2000 (AAFB 2000)
Jordi Biblioni Rotger	Palma: Història del Tramvia Elèctric
J. M. Valerio & E. de la Cruz	The Majorca and Soller Railways (Aldaba Ediciones)

Official Papers

FC de Mallorca	Annual Reports for 1877, 1880
FC de Mallorca	Freight Consignment Ledger, Llubi station (1939-41)
INECO	Plan Director De Transports de las Islas Baleares (1981)
TEIP	Annual Report for 1959
TEIP	Transformacion y Modernizacion de los Transportes Urbanos & Interurbanos de Palma de Mallorca, (1959)

Magazines and Journals

Associació d'Amics del Ferrocarril de Baleares (AAFB)	Es Furgó Correu, 3rd Trimestre 2002, No. 12
AAFB	Es Furgó Correu website, 26th February 2003
AVUI	28th September 1979; 8th October 1981
Carril	September 1966
Chemain de Fer Regionaux et Urbains	Number 148 (1985)
Continental Railway Journal	Autumn 1991
Diaro de Mallorca	6th April 1984, 2nd December 2001, 20th May 2002, 20th January 2003
Majorca Daily Bulletin	8th September 1999, 16th September 1999, 22nd September 2001, 9th November 2001, 2nd December 2001, 3rd January 2002, 14th February 2002, 10th September 2002
Modern Tramway	April 1985
Narrow Gauge Railway Society	The Narrow Gauge numbers 48, 104, 108
Railway Magazine	April 1936, November 1985
Sa Veu de Lluchmayor	Numbers 30, 32, 45, 46, 63
S' Union de S'Arenal	Number 10
Ultima Hora	3rd January 2003

Miscellaneous Sources

AAFB Website	Historical Section: Locomotives of the FC de Soller/Industrial Railways
ADL Tours	Ad Lib Newsletter – Issue 92 (April 2002)
G. E. Baddeley	The Continental Steam Tram (LRTA, 1982)
C. T. Bidwell	The Balearic Islands
Encyclopaedica Britannica	
Lindsay H. R. Fisher	A Layman's History of the Steam Railways of Mallorca (Ashbracken, 1982)
M. J. Fox	Last Steam Locomotives of Spain & Portugal (Ian Allen)
Industrial Railway Record	Number 89 (June 1981)
Industrial Railway Society	Industrial Locomotives of Spain and Portugal
Jane's World Railways	
F.S. de Soller	The Wonderful Soller Train
Carles Salmeron i Bosch	El Tren d'Olot (Generalitat de Catalunya)
K. P. Plant	Personal notebooks (1960)
Gordon West	Jogging Round Majorca (Black Swan, 1994)

A Note on the Drawings

These drawings have been prepared largely from photographic evidence, supplemented by certain known dimensions. They are therefore offered as 'general arrangement' drawings and should not be regarded as definitive in all details.

MAJORCA RAILWAYS NASMYTH WILSON 0-4-0T (REBUILT FORM)

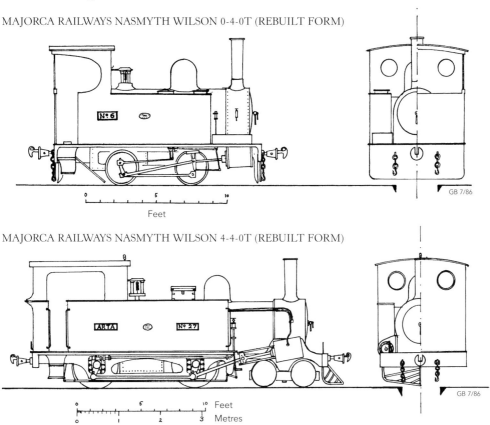

MAJORCA RAILWAYS NASMYTH WILSON 4-4-0T (REBUILT FORM)

MAJORCA RAILWAYS NASMYTH WILSON 4-6-0T

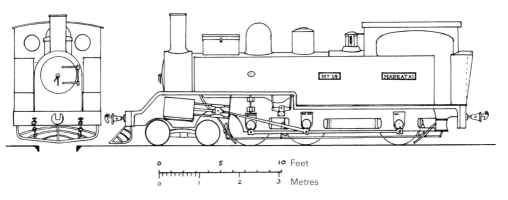

MAJORCA RAILWAYS MTM 2-6-0T LOCO

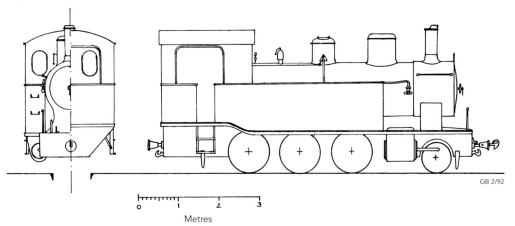

GB 2/92

0   1   2   3

Metres

MAJORCA RAILWAYS KRUPP 2-6-0T

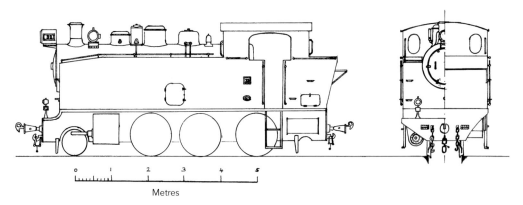

0   1   2   3   4   5

Metres

MAJORCA RAILWAYS BABCOCK & WILCOX 2-6-2T

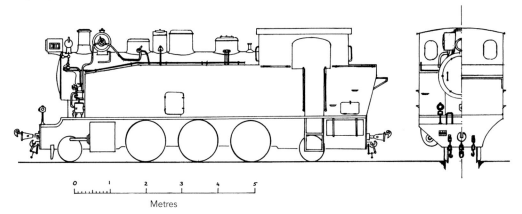

0   1   2   3   4   5

Metres

MAJORCA RAILWAYS (E.F.E. era) CREUSOT DIESEL LOCOMOTIVE

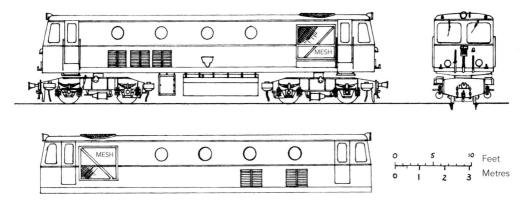

Drawn from photographs and dimensions taken from a similar locomotive on the Rio Tinto Railway

MAJORCA RAILWAYS (FEVE era) FERROSTAHL RAILCAR – 1958

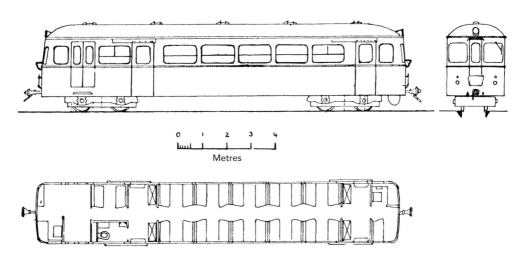

2-CAR DMU: MAN – 1984

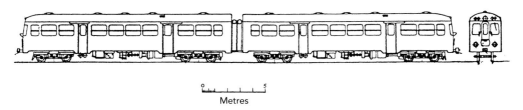

MAJORCA RAILWAYS MIXED CARRIAGE: Second/Third CLASS COMPARTMENTS

Source: Maker's drawing (Brown Marshall) dated 1873

As drawn 1873 **As running 1960**   **1873** **1960**

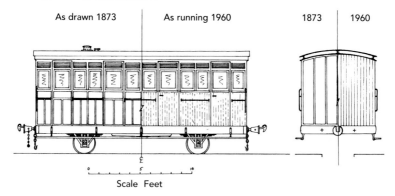

Scale Feet

MAJORCA RAILWAYS MIXED CARRIAGE: Second/Third CLASS WITH GUARD'S BOX AND SCREW
BRAKE   Builder: Brown Marshall. Drawn from maker's plans.

Notes

1873: Has Guards box, full panelling, door handles on
the right of the doors. Class divisions: Three Third
Class compartments, one Second Class.

1960: Guard's box removed. Matchboard body. Door
handles on the left. Class divisions: three Second
Class, one First Class.

1873   **c1960**

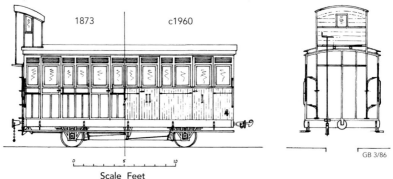

GB 3/86

Scale Feet

MAJORCA RAILWAYS MIXED CARRIAGE WITH Second/Third CLASS ACCOMMODATION PLUS
GUARD'S COMPARTMENT. Builder: Brown Marshall (1873) as running c.1960.

Notes: Original drawings show full panelling, although by 1960 matchboarding had been substituted. At first brake wheel
fitted in Guard's Compartment but vac. brake added later and latterly out of use without hoses.

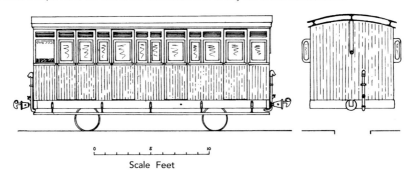

Scale Feet

MAJORCA RAILWAYS BRAKE VAN (originally supplied for the Santany)

Notes: It is not known whether this vehicle was a Brake Van with a Mail Compartment (as shown here with a post box at one end of the carriage) or a Brake /3rd. Another picture source shows two similar vehicles minus the post box and with an extra door (shown dotted).

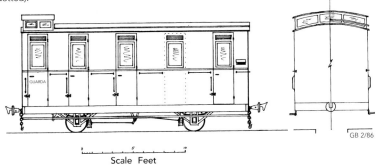

GB 2/86

Scale Feet

MAJORCA RAILWAYS BRAKE VAN (CLASS E)

Three examples rebuilt from redundant Santany line coaches.

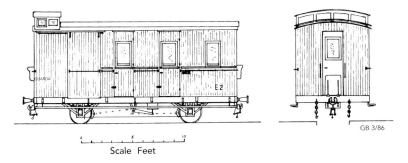

GB 3/86

Scale Feet

MAJORCA RAILWAYS HIGH-SIDED OPEN WAGON (Class A)

Source: (Lower) Brown Marshall plans dated Dec 1873. (Upper) photographs c.1960

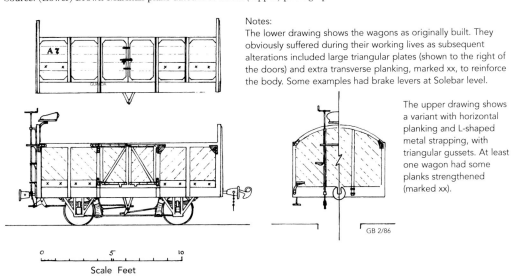

Notes:
The lower drawing shows the wagons as originally built. They obviously suffered during their working lives as subsequent alterations included large triangular plates (shown to the right of the doors) and extra transverse planking, marked xx, to reinforce the body. Some examples had brake levers at Solebar level.

The upper drawing shows a variant with horizontal planking and L-shaped metal strapping, with triangular gussets. At least one wagon had some planks strengthened (marked xx).

GB 2/86

Scale Feet

MAJORCA RAILWAYS DROPSIDE WAGON (Class B)

Source: Brown Marshall drawing

Notes: 1) The brakeman's seat probably did not last long in use.
   2) Some examples had conventional solebar brake levers.

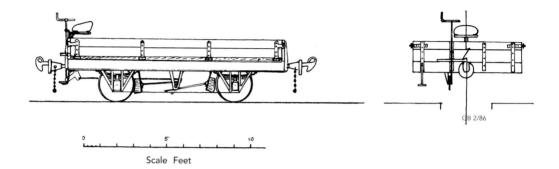

Scale Feet

MAJORCA RAILWAYS DROPSIDE OPEN WAGON (Class B)

Builder CAF Beasain c.1887 – c.1917. Drawn from measurements taken in 1984.

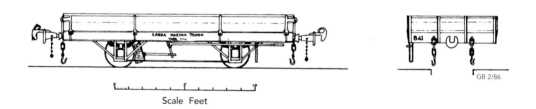

Scale Feet

AN ALTERNATIVE BRAKE ARRANGEMENT (? built 1889)

Drawn from photographs taken in 1984

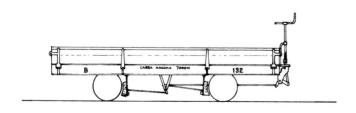
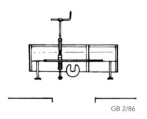

MAJORCA RAILWAYS LOW GOODS VAN (Class C)
Source: Maker's drawing (Brown Marshall)

Notes: 1) The drawing shows the roof-top brake as originally fitted. Later vans have conventional brakes at Solebar level.
2) Coupling hooks and safety claims were fitted at both ends some have been omitted for the sake of clarity.
3) Steps to the roof were fitted at one end only.

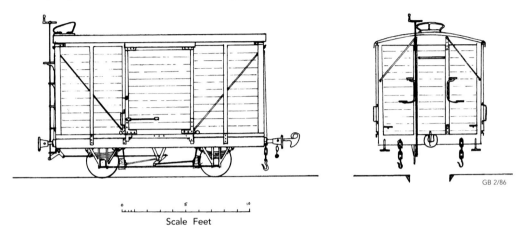

GB 2/86

Scale Feet

MAJORCA RAILWAYS HIGH-BODIED VENTILATED VAN (Class C)
Builder thought to be CAF Beasain. Drawings based on photographs incorporating some known dimensions

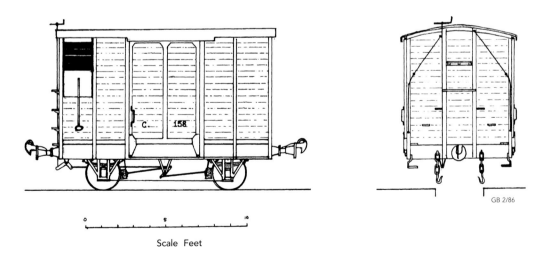

C. 158

GB 2/86

Scale Feet

MAJORCA RAILWAYS SERIES F – BRAKE VAN

Drawn from measurements taken in 1981

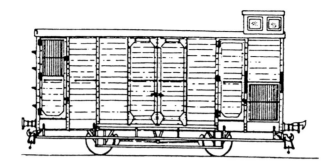

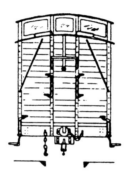

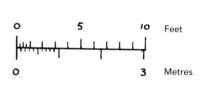

0   5   10   Feet

0   3   Metres

MAJORCA RAILWAYS FLAT TRUCK (Class P)

Possible builder CAF Beasain. Drawn from measurements taken in 1981

Notes: A shorter version on a Brown-Marshall chassis also existed.

Deck of wagon formed of 26 planks – random widths between 6" and 8"

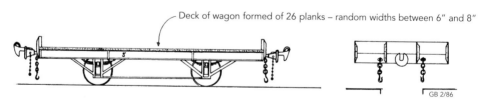

GB 2/86

Brake details probably similar to Besain-built open wagon.

MAJORCA RAILWAYS BOGIE FLAT WAGON (Class R)

Drawn from measurements taken in 1984

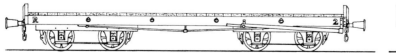

All Soller Drawings from measurements taken in 1984

SOLLER RAILWAY
MOTOR COACH No. 1

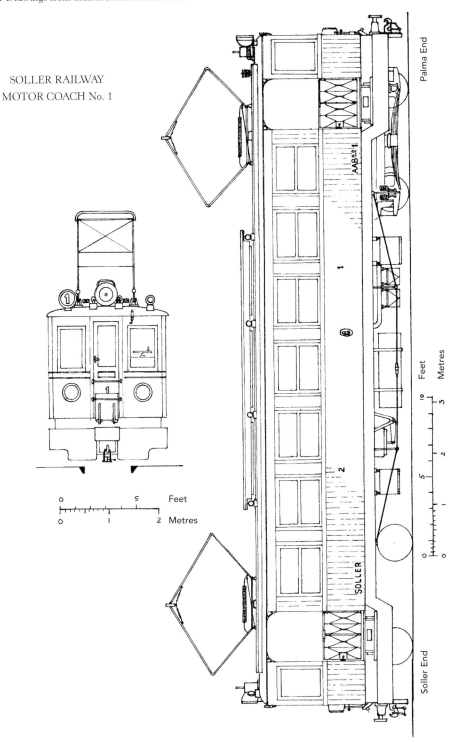

Palma End

Soller End

0 ┤┤┤┤┤┤┤ 5 Feet
0 ┤┤┤┤┤ 1 2 Metres

Feet Metres

SOLLER RAILWAY COACH No. 8

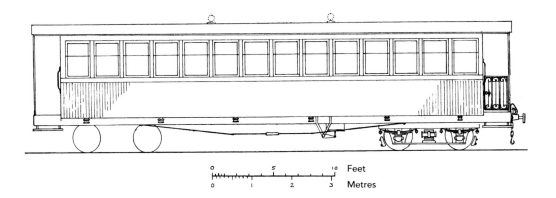

Feet

Metres

SOLLER RAILWAY BALCONY AND END DETAILS OF COACHES AND BRAKE VANS

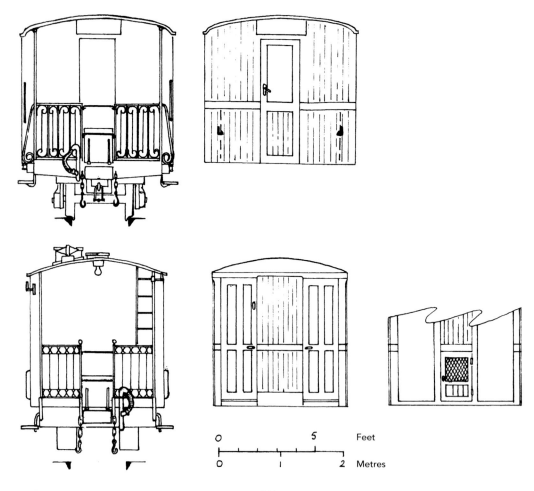

Feet

Metres

SOLLER RAILWAY BRAKE VAN No. F1

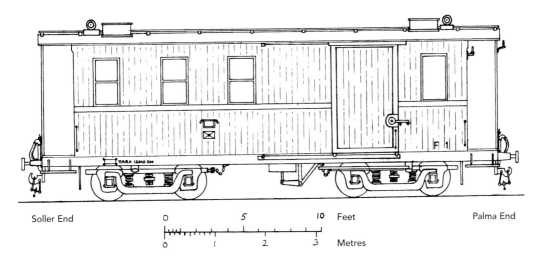

Soller End   Palma End

0   5   10   Feet

0   1   2   3   Metres

SOLLER RAILWAY BRAKE VAN DETAILS

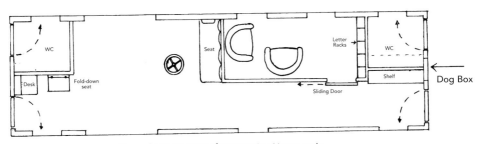

General arrangement of van interior. Not to scale

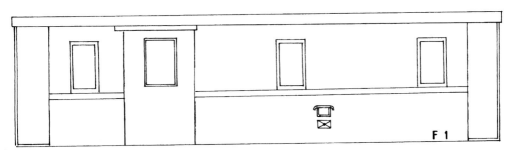

Van F1 has an extra window in the sliding door of the "off" side

SOLLER RAILWAY HIGH-SIDED WAGON

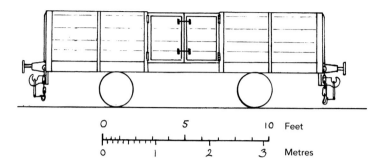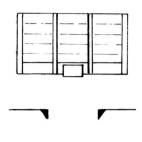

0   5   10   Feet

0   1   2   3   Metres

SOLLER RAILWAY DROPSIDE WAGON No. B1

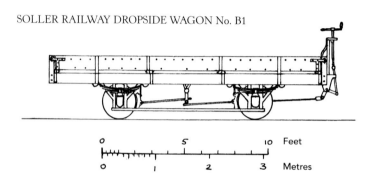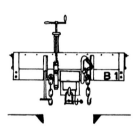

0   5   10   Feet

0   1   2   3   Metres

SOLLER RAILWAY LOW-SIDED WAGON No. B9

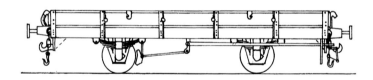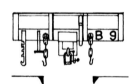

SOLLER RAILWAY GOODS VAN No.8

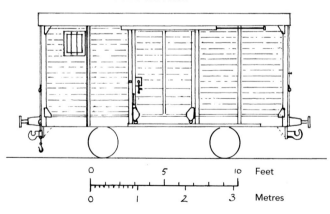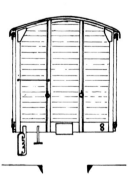

0   5   10   Feet

0   1   2   3   Metres